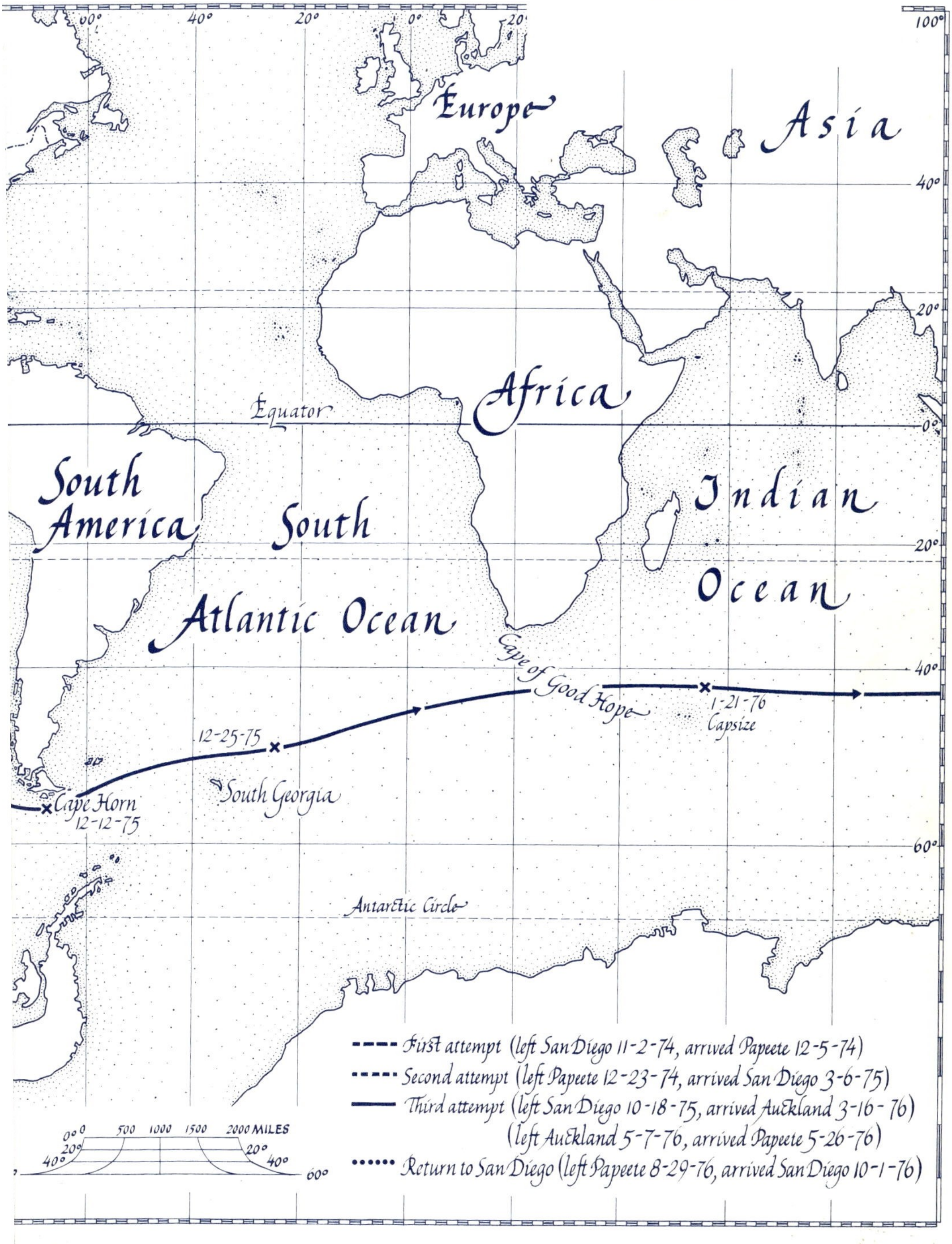
Europe
Asia
Africa
Equator
South America
South Atlantic Ocean
Indian Ocean
Cape of Good Hope
1-21-76 Capsize
12-25-75
South Georgia
Cape Horn 12-12-75
Antarctic Circle
First attempt (left San Diego 11-2-74, arrived Papeete 12-5-74)
Second attempt (left Papeete 12-23-74, arrived San Diego 3-6-75)
Third attempt (left San Diego 10-18-75, arrived Auckland 3-16-76)
(left Auckland 5-7-76, arrived Papeete 5-26-76)
Return to San Diego (left Papeete 8-29-76, arrived San Diego 10-1-76)
0 500 1000 1500 2000 MILES

Storm Passage

Webb Chiles

Storm Passage
∽ Alone Around Cape Horn

 Times BOOKS

Copyright © 1977 by Webb Chiles

All rights reserved, including the right to reproduce this book or portions thereof in any form. For information, address: Times Books, a Division of Quadrangle/The New York Times Book Company, Inc., Three Park Avenue, New York, N. Y. 10016. Manufactured in the United States of America. Published simultaneously in Canada by Fitzhenry & Whiteside, Ltd., Toronto.

Second printing, October 1977

Library of Congress Cataloging in Publication Data

Chiles, Webb.
   Storm passage.

   1. Egregious (Cutter) 2. Chiles, Webb.
3. Voyages around the world. I. Title.
G420.E35C48   1977   910'.41 [B]   77-79025
ISBN 0-8129-0703-5

To:
Suzanne ∼ Mary

Nor law, nor duty bade me fight,
Nor public men, nor cheering crowds,
A lonely impulse of delight
Drove to this tumult in the clouds.

——William Butler Yeats

Part One

• I •

DAY 1 • *November 2, 1974*

I was born for this moment and for all the days ahead. Egregious's yellow hull passed Point Loma and entered the open ocean at noon local time.

We are under only main and jib, heeled well over against a 16-knot wind from the south, blowing directly from where I want to go. I am leaving San Diego, California, aboard my 37′ cutter to sail alone around the world by way of Cape Horn. Countless times I have stood beside the sea and dreamed of the voyage; now at last it has begun.

I expect to live intensely; but I do not know as the land recedes behind me that for more than 310 days during the coming two years and for more than 38,000 miles, I will be alone at sea. I will find defeat, despair, fear, beauty, serenity, and peace. Although often I will doubt I will survive, ultimately I will fulfill my dream; become the first American to round Cape Horn alone, complete one of the longest solo passages of all time, and make the fastest solo circumnavigation ever in a monohull.

But before I do, I will be tested far beyond anything I have imagined by survival storms, three capsizes, hurricane-force winds off Cape Horn, sleet, snow, frostbite, a cyclone in the Tasman Sea, week-long calms, tropical heat, a leak which forces me to bail 12,000 pounds of water daily, near-shipwrecks at Tahiti and New Zealand, and the loss of the love of those I love. And for almost all of those miles and all of those days, the Egregious will be severely damaged. In my innocence, I sail on.

Usually there is northwesterly wind here. Even before I cleared San Diego Bay, I was wet; and now, an hour later, the wind has gone to the west and lightened to under 5 knots. I am being tossed on the leftover seas and will have to stop writing in a moment to retrim the sails. It is as if the wind were trying to warn me that I am to undergo an ordeal, that my voyage will not be an idyll. But I have—I hope—no illusions. I expect an ordeal, an ordeal of grandeur.

* * *

3:00 P.M. I'm still north of the Coronado Islands, three mountain peaks that rise from the sea 15 miles south of Point Loma. For the past hour and a half, I had the tiller. The seas, with some waves of 5 feet and light-to-nonexistent wind, were too much for the vane steering.

DAY 2 • *November 3*

WE had an entire year's weather yesterday. Headwinds, calms, then shortly after sunset the wind filled in from the northwest and blew 18-20 knots as it is supposed to. We were going 7½ knots in the right direction, and even though it lasted only for two hours, we may have made up for the slow start.

About 9:00 last evening, the wind decreased, and I saw lightning ahead and to the east. For the next hour, rain came down hard, so I went below and tried to sleep. About 11:30 I awoke and knew the rain had stopped. I went on deck to check our course and stepped into one of those moments that make sailing worthwhile. The sky had cleared of clouds, revealing a full moon and stars one never sees in cities. The midnight air was warmer than it had been earlier, and we were moving easily at 6 knots. I sat in the cockpit for an hour, grateful to be precisely there.

I do not, however, truly belong at sea yet. I move about the boat unnaturally, having consciously to think about each step and handhold. The muscles in my arms and shoulders are sore. I have to review the necessary corrections for a moon sight. And I am procrastinating about setting a larger headsail even though Egregious could carry it.

Returning to the sea always requires a transitionary day or two for me. I have never been physically seasick to the point of making use of the lee rail, but the first night offshore usually finds me with a less-than-vigorous appetite and unable to read without becoming more aware of the boat's motion than my book. I realize how alone I really am—which of course is what I've wanted and worked toward for twenty years—how dependent on so many little pieces of aluminum and steel and fiberglass. My mind fills itself with potential disasters. Imaginary ships loom out of the night. The compasses—all three of them—enter into a conspiracy; and instead of heading offshore, we are actually about to drive headlong onto a rocky Baja beach. Having been through all this before, I know that such notions are ridiculous, but still I go on deck to look around more often than is actually necessary.

DAY 3 • *November 4*

YESTERDAY was a beautiful day. Too bad I wasn't here to enjoy it. But the plain truth is that the bold, intrepid sailor was sick—really seasick—for the first time in his life. That was not one of the new experiences I came out here for.

Part of the problem was the noon sight. There was some huge error in my calculations, and I spent too long over the chart table trying to rectify it. All to no purpose other than to destroy my breakfast.

I should set the spinnaker, but am feeling too weak. Even though I know I should eat, so far I have only managed some wheat germ and water and a few dried apricots.

Just after dark last evening, when I was half asleep on my berth, a radio announcer from a San Diego station was exclaiming that I had left on a great adventure. I was beginning to believe that I might be the first man to sail supine around the world, when something flew past my face. I would be pleased to report that I said something witty, but such was not the case. I grabbed a flashlight and discovered a sparrow sitting on the rail of the port upper berth. We stared at one another as if to ask, "Well, do *you* know what *you're* doing here?" Apparently neither of us did, so I lay down again, which is becoming my universal response to all stimuli.

After a while, we both fluttered to the cockpit: I to check the compass and he to sit on the cockpit coaming. I offered him some wheat germ, but apparently he is not a devotee of health food. So I went below and lay down. An hour later, when I again went on deck, he was gone.

I am feeling much better this morning. My digestive tract has finally accepted that this is what life is going to be like for the next couple of hundred days. I was beginning to fear I would develop bedsores.

I should set the spinnaker, clean up the forepeak, where I dropped the jib and staysail without rebagging them, and clean myself—I have not washed or changed my clothes or shaved since leaving San Diego. Indeed I should. Perhaps later I even will; but for now I am going to sit here in the cockpit, finish drinking my tea, and enjoy my partially restored health.

MY noon position showed us to be 10 miles west of Guadalupe Island. As visibility is very good, and I have not yet gone completely blind, and I cannot see the faintest smudge on the horizon that could possibly be Guadalupe, this is somewhat disconcerting.

About 3:00 this afternoon I tried to take another sun sight, which was spoiled when I misread the stopwatch. I tried again, only to have the sun disappear behind the only dark cloud in the sky. That was more than a half hour ago. So much for finding out where I am today. Presently we are headed 165° at 6 knots. That is where I want to go, and there can't be anything ahead of me for hundreds of miles (to be remembered when I go aground tonight); the sun is still behind that cloud, probably making obscene gestures.

I had better get myself and my navigation sorted out one of these days. Ultimately it is of some importance. Although I suppose I could simply keep on sailing south until the rigging freezes over and then turn left.

DAY 4 • *November 5*

6:00 A.M. The sea is absolutely black, carved of obsidian. To the east the sun is half-visible between two layers of clouds above the horizon, and even as I write, is touching the rest of the sky with color: just a little rouge on a very old grey lady.

We are rolling along directly downwind, under main and genoa top at between 6½ and 8 knots. Although I slept very well last night, I did get up three or four times to check our course and speed and am certain we've averaged at least 6½ for the last twelve hours. I would guess the wind is going to increase with the daylight, so we may really get some miles in hand before the doldrums.

I have not yet explained what I am doing out here. I am sailing my 37' fiberglass cutter, Egregious, of a class known as an Ericson 37, around the world alone via Cape Horn. The word "egregious" is from the Latin. *E* meaning out of or away from and *gregis*, meaning herd. It has two antithetical definitions: one, now rare, suggests that someone or something away from the herd is of greater quality, distinguished by individuality; while a more modern meaning, consistent with the leveling of equalitarianism, expresses the belief that someone away from the herd is worse, flagrantly bad. So, distinguished or flagrantly bad, but in any event away from the herd.

"Egregious" is found in every dictionary I have seen, but most people seem to think I made it up myself. Once, when I was repainting the name on the hull, while docked at Harbor Island Marina, a woman watched over my shoulder for five minutes before she firmly informed me, "I suppose you know you've misspelled 'gregarious.'"

In the ten years since I bought my first boat—a 26' sloop—and taught myself how to sail on San Francisco Bay, I have come to believe less and less in the perfect boat. The most one can hope is to find a boat compatible with his own temperament. For myself, I do not like engines or gadgets, and I do like to sail fast. I have said that there is safety in speed at sea and that complicated machinery is unreliable. Perhaps those statements are true, but they really only reflect my bias toward simplicity.

Because of that bias, Egregious has no engine, no head—other than a bucket, no through hull fittings below the waterline, no lifelines or pulpits, and no electrical system. Only kerosene lamps illuminate her cabin, which is conventional in layout.

As one climbs down the companionway ladder from the cockpit, an L-shaped galley is to starboard and a navigator's station, with chart table, to port. Aft of these are two quarter-berths. Forward is the main cabin, with an upper and lower berth on each side—the upper berths used for stowage. Forward of the main cabin, a compartment designated as the head is to port, and a hanging locker for clothes to starboard. Beyond them is an open area used for stowage. And, in the very bow, a chain locker.

Egregious is cutter rigged; that is, she has only one mast and is designed to set a mainsail and two foresails. I have found, as have many other sailors, that with such a rig I can reduce sail more easily in heavy weather. But I would not want to argue that it is the best possible rig or Egregious the best possible boat for this voyage. I will know more 25,000 miles from now.

I feel strongly that if anyone chooses to go to sea in a small boat, he has no right to expect anyone else—especially the government—to save him if he gets in trouble. Having no electrical system, of course I have no radio transmitter and no way to call for help. One must, after all, have some principles about something.

I will consider my voyage a success if I complete the circumnavigation, but I also intend to try to make the voyage nonstop if everything holds together. Solo nonstop circumnavigations have been made three times: twice by Englishmen, once by a Japanese, Kenichi Horie. The fastest voyage was 276 days by Horie. My goal is 200 days. I believe this to be possible because I have a fast boat, I sail her aggressively (when I am not seasick), and I have kept her in racing trim. Leaving with supplies aboard to last a year, the Egregious sat right on her lines and displaced less, I believe, than the average boat of her class at the start of a distance race.

This was accomplished by the weight saved by not having an engine or fuel tanks (about 500 pounds) and by a saving of 900-1,000 pounds in crew weight. Not that I used to weigh that much, but a boat like this is required to have a crew of seven when racing. I estimate my supplies weigh 1,500 pounds: 500 pounds for food, 1,000 for 25 gallons of kerosene, and 85 gallons of water.

To make the passage in 200 days, I will have to average 5 knots from San Diego to Cape Horn, 6 knots from Cape Horn to the South Cape of New Zealand, 5 knots from New Zealand back to the equator, and 4 knots from the equator to San Diego. Perhaps that doesn't sound all that difficult; but then no one has ever done it.

Just as I wrote "San Diego," a particularly large wave foamed up on the starboard quarter and started to come aboard. Because I am sitting 6 inches from its projected point of entry, I took some interest in its plans. Almost in slow motion, it climbed the hull, but as it reached deck level and saw me, it changed its mind and receded in a shoal of bubbles.

What joy to be alive, sailing 7 knots in the right direction, and so unsavory that waves won't break on me. I am going below to find something to eat for breakfast.

I am a new man. Since this morning, I have cleared the forepeak, rebagged the cutter jib and staysail, retrimmed the spinnaker pole, which holds out the genoa topsail; shaved and washed myself; and taken some sun sights I finally believe in.

At noon we were 390 miles from San Diego.

DAY 5 • *November 6*

ALREADY, except for navigation purposes (that's a private joke), I have lost my sense of time. I had to look back at yesterday's heading to see what number day this is and what day of the week. In fact to number this "Day 5" is somewhat misleading, as it will only be four full sailing days at noon.

First thing this morning, I took rather extensive exercise on the foredeck. The wind went far enough to the northeast to lure me into believing I could get the boat from a run onto a reach. So I jibed the main and decided to remove the spinnaker pole from the topsail. A very simple procedure, it required only five round-trips from the cockpit to the foredeck. During which time Egregious happily imitated eight different amusement-park rides simultaneously, with a rumba step thrown in at odd intervals just to keep me guessing. At one point, I released the jib sheet from the cockpit and before I could run forward, the sail had gift-wrapped itself around the headstay.

In the fullness of time, I finally managed to unwrap it—if I hadn't, I wouldn't be writing this now—and then the wind promptly went back north. So I rejibed the main, reset the pole, and we are very much as we were before my exertions.

I seriously believe this voyage to be a heroic adventure, but it seems so far more like a Donald Duck cartoon. I have not tried to talk since I left San Diego, and am reluctant to do so for fear I will discover I sound like him, too.

Last night I fixed my first real meal for dinner. It was supposed to be chicken curry, but I decided that asking my stomach to accept curry powder would be an unforgivable infringement upon at best a delicate relationship. So call it a chicken casserole. Really it doesn't matter what you call it—even without the curry powder, my stomach didn't like it.

We are making good progress, but are stuck rolling dead downwind. Stuck because we are getting where I want to go at better than 6 knots and can't gain sufficient speed to compensate for the additional distance if I put the boat onto a reach. The rolling is quite unpleasant. I would be very grateful for a wind shift in almost any direction. Already I regret having said that. The wind will probably oblige me by coming from dead ahead.

For whatever reasons, and the rolling is certainly one, I have never had a more difficult transition to the sea. I have thought of and missed those I left behind more than I would have believed possible. I have been physically seasick, which I have never done before. Perhaps it has been a natural reaction to the more festive life I led ashore immediately before my departure, and perhaps it is just that I am coming actually to understand as never before the enormity of the undertaking I have chosen.

As I write, I am reminded by its repetitious sound of a problem which seriously concerns me. From the general area of the rudder head comes at intervals a rather deep, resonant moan. Assuming that no one is down there trying to learn to play the bassoon, and having already established that nothing I can do modifies it, I just hope everything holds together. Only 23,500 more miles.

A moment ago I noticed we were headed on a course of 135°. I would like 165°, but will apparently have to settle for 185°. In rejibing the main, I spontaneously made an obscene and biologically impossible assertion about the wind's parentage. I am pleased to report that I do not sound like Donald Duck. Yet.

I have mastered the lost art of washing myself in less than one cup of water. This requires one toothbruth, two pieces of soap—the one used for shaving is too bewhiskered for anything else—one towel, two washcloths—one for washing, one for rinsing—a razor, and a paper towel. This morning I successfully brushed my teeth, shaved, and bathed, and still had one-quarter cup of water left. I am saving it for an absolute orgy of cleanliness tomorrow.

TODAY is one of those on which all romantic notions of sailing are based. The wind is a bit cool, but steady at about 10 knots, the sky clear and blue, the ocean touched by an occasional whitecap. I think the spinnaker could be set, but we are doing almost 7 knots without it, and I am feeling rather lazy. If I can only survive preparing dinner, I will be a happy man.

NOW it is after sunset, and I am a happy man. I ate dinner in the cockpit at dusk. This evening, as on the past two, the waves are like the lives of men in Hobbes's state of nature; "nasty, brutish and short." Our speed varies from just over 6 to just under 8 knots, and our course from 150° to 220°, depending on which way we roll when a wave catches us. Egregious simply takes off too fast for the self-steering vane to hold course.

There is no parallel in life ashore for sleeping under these conditions. I have done relatively well the past two nights, which means that I sleep for up to an hour while the boat rolls routinely. Then suddenly the main partially backs or the genoa collapses, and she spins off 30° or 40° and picks up 2 knots of speed before being brought back on course by the vane. The sails refill with a crack, and I get up to determine if the mast is still standing. Since by then I am wide awake, I check the course, which is pointless because the compass always seems to read south; and the boat speed, which is unnecessary because I already know by the angle of heel and the sound of the water rushing by the hull how fast we are going to within a fraction of a knot.

Things are really creaking and grinding away on deck tonight. I'd better go up and observe nature in her splendor.

DAY 6 • *November 7*

LAST night, not long after I went to sleep at about 10:00, the wind veered to the northeast. Presumably the trade winds at last. I got up and jibed the main for what I fervently hope will be the last time for a long time, and we took off at 8 knots on a broad reach.

This required a change of accommodations for me. That is, I moved my pillow and sleeping bag to the starboard transom berth, rather than the port one on which I had been making my home. This is a distance of about 2 feet, but there are an entirely different set of squeaks and groans to starboard. It is like moving into a new neighborhood.

I found myself thinking this morning of my preparations for this voyage and how for more than the past year I have closely followed a plan and a schedule, despite all obstacles and vicissitudes, expected and unexpected, including significant changes in my relationships with Mary and Lynn.

Back in 1973, even before this boat was built, I set November 4, 1974, as my departure date. I took delivery of the cutter, outfitted it, paid for it, and provisioned it exactly as I had planned. I did not want any last-minute crises, and there were none.

The weather patterns of the world provide compelling reasons for leaving San Diego on such a voyage as this in early November. The tropical-storm season is over off the coast of Mexico; I will be at Cape Horn about Christmas and through the Southern Ocean during its summer, when the weather, though unpleasant, is as good as it ever is; and back in San Diego before the tropical-storm season next year. I had specifically chosen November 4 because it was a Monday, and I had thought a year ago that it would be good to spend a last weekend with Lynn, who was then my wife. A few months ago, however, I realized that I would not be good company for anyone that weekend, particularly if the weather was fair, and decided to leave Saturday morning. A bit later, because a number of people expressed a desire to see my departure, I committed myself to setting sail at 11:00 A.M., weather permitting.

That Saturday morning, precisely at 11:00, Mary cast off the bow, I let go the stern line, and I left. It was a perfect departure; a perfect ending to a year in which I accomplished exactly what I wanted.

But my preparations really began much, much earlier than 1973. When I was eleven or twelve years old, I decided someday to sail around the world alone. There was no specific influence that led to that act of will, no relative who sailed, no motion picture or book I sought to emulate.

I lived with my mother and stepfather in Kirkwood, Missouri, a suburb of St. Louis, where I was born on November 11, 1941, far from any ocean. I had never been aboard a sailboat, had never that I remember actually even seen one. Children often dream such dreams, I am told. But I was not like other children, as I am not like other men. And one of the ways in which I am not is that I kept that dream—or it kept me—for twenty years.

Some people who have known me relatively well have seen my desire to sail around the world alone as an obsession. They have been partially right, but the obsession has been with greatness, with the heroic, of which the voyage is one possible exemplification.

Even before I was consumed by the idea of a solo circumnavigation and long before NASA was in existence and the "space race" in the public mind—before 1950, when I was still in elementary school—I can remember praying that when I grew into adulthood I would become the first man to stand on the moon. Not long thereafter, that dream was quashed when I had to start wearing eyeglasses, and I mention it only because I have always wanted to live on the edge of human experience, have always considered myself capable of great acts, have always aspired to the heroic.

* * *

I have been deeply involved with three women during my adult life and, partially because of my obsession, the course of none of those relationships has been smooth or simple. To and through them I moved ever toward the voyage, which was never forgotten, never forsaken for even one of those seven thousand days which elapsed between my first childish fantasy and the real departure six days ago. At various times I could have come out here and been fleeing from unhappiness. I am grateful that is not the case.

THE last two hours have been incredible.

I am writing, as usual, sitting in the cockpit in mid-afternoon. What is not usual is that we are rushing along at 8 to 10 knots, wing and wing, under main and genoa top held out by the spinnaker pole, slashing off waves, our own bow wave climbing inexorably toward the deck. Sitting 4 feet behind me, the aft-starboard mooring cleat clenched firmly in one claw and one wary yellow eye firmly fixed in my direction, is a white bird, identical in size and shape to the black-crowned night herons in San Diego, who has decided to come along for the ride. The sky is light blue, spotted irregularly with clouds; the sun is shining brightly. It is quite warm. And the boat speed just reached 11! I have never sailed so fast before in my life.

Earlier, I was prevented from getting my noon sight by an apocalyptic line of black clouds which appeared in the northeast and quickly covered the eastern half of the sky. I prepared for rain, but there was only a slight sprinkle. Not even enough to clean the deck.

The squalless squall passed quickly. I got a fairly good sun sight at 12:30, calculated we made over 160 miles in the last twenty-four hours and have a good chance at a 1,000 mile first week, when suddenly we took off.

The strangest aspect of the afternoon has been that the wind does not seem all that strong or the seas very high. I would estimate that right now it is blowing 25 or perhaps 30 knots, and the waves are generally not more than 5 feet.

Regularly we surprise a school of flying fish, bearing down on whom we must appear to be the vengeance of God incarnate, and they take flight above the waves.

Just then we again went over 10 knots. I can hardly believe the tremendous power of that surge in speed. At about 9½, there is a qualitative change in the sound of the bow wave, almost as though we pass through a barrier, shake ourselves free of the water momentarily, and take flight after the fish.

I had seen the white bird sitting on the stern earlier and took a couple of photographs of it. But when I returned from putting the camera away, he was gone. I must have been sitting here for more than an hour, watching the compass, knotmeter, sails, and waves, when I turned to look over my right shoulder and found myself eye to eye with my passenger. He is still there and seems somewhat less concerned about my presence than he was; because he has turned his back on me and is staring astern too, apparently making his own estimate of the waves.

This is truly glorious, and it is not even compromised by my earlier discovery that I have a leak at the gland where the rudder passes through the hull. It is not a bad leak, although frustrating on a boat from which I eliminated all possible through hull fittings below the waterline. So what happens—the one fitting that cannot be eliminated, leaks.

Egregious is a pleasure to sail. If she holds together, I believe we really will complete the voyage in under 200 days.

DAY 7 • *November 8*

THIS morning I am sitting on the port cockpit seat, eating my breakfast of grapefruit, biscuits, and coffee; and my friend, the white heron, is sitting to starboard within my arm's reach. That is a reach he has accurately concluded I am not going to make, and he seems content there, his claws wrapped about a coil of the jib sheet. For herons, this boat does not have a nonskid deck, and he slips every time he stands on the fiberglass.

There was only a thin sliver of moon last night, and the sky was cloudy and dark. Yet each time I came on deck, I could distinguish his white form hunched near the self-steering vane. He has, however, repaid my hospitality in a most inconsiderate manner. Perhaps he is aware of the price fertilizer brings in the United States, for he has made an extraordinary start at turning my beautiful cutter into a guano island.

In all other respects he is a most acceptable companion, and I fear probably an ill one. I do not have anything to feed him. He hardly seems the type for wheat germ. I can only wish him well and hope he recovers enough strength to fend for himself.

Much of last night I lay awake listening to and thinking about the rudder. Even when I made the first light reference to it, I sensed the potential for serious trouble in that seemingly innocent sound. By yesterday afternoon and evening, it had become decidedly more ominous, and I seriously considered whether I ought to return to San Diego to have it repaired and then start again. Psychologically, that is unacceptable to me, and at best would prevent my restarting until early December.

I have, however, done just about all I can and all to no avail. The rudder shaft is definitely rubbing against something somewhere. My concern is that it will break when we are in the Southern Ocean. I can grossly steer by trimming the sails, but would not like to have to try in 30-foot waves.

My mind was taken away from the rudder by my passenger's skulking toward the companionway hatch. When I realized his intention was to go below, I waved this notebook at him and he backed off. Most assuredly, these tourist-class passengers must be prevented from using the first-class accommodations.

In the time it took me to write the above paragraph, he made two more forays toward the cabin and defecated once on the cockpit seat in spite and/or frustration. I think he is beginning to understand the word "no," but like a recalcitrant child, won't accept it. I have been too kind. A little fear of authority is a good thing.

I have rung for the cabin boy to come and sluice down the deck, but regret I must report that this ship is run by nepotism. The cabin boy bears a striking resemblance to the captain.

The cockpit is waist-deep in wheat germ, oil, and heron droppings, and I have a squeaky rudder with more than 23,000 miles of the roughest sailing in the world to go, but I am having a good time.

* * *

THIS afternoon I cleared enough of the debris in the lazarette—mostly spare line and buckets—to climb in and check the rudder shaft where it passes through the hull. There is no externally visible evidence of whatever is causing the problem, and I lubricated everything reachable, without any noticeable change in the frequency and timbre of the grinding sound.

In mid-afternoon, I saw a school of porpoises ahead to starboard, and almost simultaneously they must have seen me; for they were diving and leaping all around the boat, and then as quickly gone.

I was reminded of a grey morning in February a few years ago, when I was sailing alone at dawn off the south side of Catalina Island. Everything—the sky, the sea, the island cliffs—was grey, and I was barely ghosting along, when a single dolphin came and swam slowly alongside for almost an hour. I felt closer to him then than to any other living being on earth.

MY friend and confidant—the white heron of alimentary-tract fame—finally successfully circumvented all defenses and flapped into the cabin. By the time I caught up with him, he was standing on the chart table, one foot on La Paz, the other on Acapulco. At a wave of my hand, he obediently flew back to the cockpit, probably less in fear than because he had seen what he needed of the chart.

He immediately began to preen himself and, except for some tufts of down stuck to his beak, which made him look like some very distinguished gentleman who has taken great care of his appearance, dressed in style, and then gone out leaving a dab of shaving cream under one ear, quickly turned himself into quite a presentable bird. Then, with an imperious glance, as if to show that he was through slumming and about to return to the very important business of the real world, he took flight. I watched him head north, working hard against the wind, until he was lost among the whitecapped waves.

Apparently he thought he was working rather hard, too, because in about five minutes, he came back on a long glide from the east and skidded to a landing on the cockpit coaming, looking rather harried. I thought it best not to say anything and continued reading.

He preened himself some more, thought matters over carefully, and left one last farewell offering on my clean deck before taking off again; this time to the east and for good. In all ways. I wish him well and hope he enjoys Acapulco or wherever, but I fear our interests and habits are too divergent for us ever to have become permanent shipmates.

DAY 8 • *November 9*

LAST evening at dusk, I decided for some reason I cannot explain that the wind was going to shift to the northeast during the night. I took the spinnaker pole down from the genoa, not wanting to have to handle it later in the dark. This act of confidence led to the long-desired result. At about midnight, I checked the compass in the cabin and saw we were heading rather desultorily on a course of 180°-200°, went on deck, jibed the genoa, readjusted the vane, and we started sailing precisely as I wished at 6 knots on a heading of about 150°.

Unless there is a significant change in its status, this will be the last I write about the rudder. At perhaps 2:00 A.M. it began sounding more tortured than usual, so I again went on deck and decided to steer for a while. The night was warm and dark, marked only by the last crescent moon, which I mistakenly thought to be a ship when it first appeared through some low clouds. I wanted to get the feel of the helm and determine if I could reduce the noise, but it was such a good sail that I stayed out for well over an hour.

The helm felt normal, and under my hand, the grinding was substantially reduced. The obvious solution is that I steer for the next six months. Because I am somehow as yet unwilling to do that, I will try to stop dwelling on the constant sound and, as I said, stop writing about it.

This morning is the most perfect weather thus far. The wind continues from the northeast. It may even be the putative northeast trades. An albatross circles the boat, hunting fish disturbed by our passage. I would estimate the air temperature to be in the high 70s. I deliberately did not bring along a thermometer because I don't want to know how cold it really is in the Roaring Forties.

I have determined to get myself clean this morning. Because that may take several hours, I'd better get started.

12:30 P.M. Position 116°48′West, 17°26′North. The first week at sea has just ended. Almost certainly we have sailed more than 1,000 miles, but because of the curve of our course, we are only 950 miles from San Diego. We have averaged 5.5 knots, for which I am certainly pleased. Whether we will make the equator on time—say another twelve days—still depends, as it always has, on how we get through the doldrums.

At the moment I am sitting almost naked in the cockpit, and life does not seem quite so arduous as it did a few days ago. In fact, except for the problem I am not to write about anymore, everything would be perfect; and perfection, strangely enough, is one of those qualities I have come out here to seek.

The first week was more difficult physically and mentally than I anticipated. And what then ought I to expect from the real dangers that lie ahead? Hopefully that now I am ready to meet them.

The routine into which I have settled surprises me in that I sleep more and eat less than I planned. Sunset is early, and darkness complete by 6:00 or 7:00 P.M.. Usually by 8:00 I am asleep. It is true that I get up every hour or so throughout the night, but often that is no more than a momentary interruption. By 6:00 in the morning I am wide awake. I feel rested and have taken no naps during the day as yet.

Thus far I have done almost no reading, although I have about two hundred of my favorite books along. I believe I will begin reading regularly soon, but am faced with an embarrassment of riches and can't decide where to begin. Dickens, Balzac, Hemingway, Isak Dinesen. A Greek play. Or Mark Twain or Joseph Conrad or Kazantzakis. Or any of a hundred others.

Already there have occurred moments and experiences that I would very much regret having missed. The great roaring ride two afternoons ago; the beautiful tranquil hour I steered through the warm darkness last night; the day the heron spent aboard; the flying fish we startle into flight almost every minute;

the powerful, assertive flight of the albatross, hunting those very fish. And this is only the beginning.

5:00 P.M. We are sailing between two parallel lines of huge grey clouds about 10 miles apart. Directly above us a narrow strip of sky remains blue. I feel as though I am standing between two doors, waiting for them to slam.

I've grabbed a quick supper of soup and have placed a few buckets about the cockpit to catch rain, if any falls, and have closed the companionway hatch for the first time since I left port. I've considered changing down to a smaller jib, but we can run off downwind and still carry this one for a long time. Probably it will all pass over, but for the moment the world seems inimical.

8:00 P.M. The sea and sky are a painting by Albert Ryder: the sea completely black, the waves completely indistinguishable, except for the phosphorescence which illuminates the cutter's passage across its surface in an eerie green light. Unexpectedly and irregularly, a wave crests, and the ocean seems to open up to reveal a flash of that same green light shining up from deep within the sea; as though a woman opened a window and as quickly shut it when she saw me too near, as though I were sailing through a city blacked out by its inhabitants so that I would not suspect its existence. The windows open in front of me and close; then to starboard, then ahead again, then behind, and I can almost hear the frantic whispers: "He's gone. I'll just peek. Yes." "No, he's right there! Draw the curtain! Quickly! Quickly!"

I call down to them. "Don't worry. I'm sorry to disturb you. I won't harm you. I don't even want to be your friend. Just to sail on and leave you and be left in peace."

Still the windows open and close.

There is no moon, yet the horizon is distinct in every direction; the layer of clouds just above the surface of the sea thin enough to let starlight lighten them not to a shade of grey, but rather a ghostly pallor. And the sky overhead is not as black as the sea below, but is broken into phantasmagorial shapes by the same unknowable light. Unknowable because there is no moon, starlight is not really enough, and yet . . . and yet there can be no other out here a thousand miles from land and man.

As I stand on the companionway steps, my head and shoulders above deck, the bow seems always to be pointing downward; as though we sail down the face of a gradually rising wave, miles down a gigantic crest, sailing not upon—but into—the sea.

DAY 9 • *November 10*

A night sky by Ryder and a dawn by Turner. Followed by 28½ drops of rain. This has all been some peculiar cosmic prank; a marshalling of majestic forces, following which the gods all got drunk, forgot their intentions, and went home to sleep it off.

Last night certainly saw our slowest overall progress. Assuming I can get a latitude sight at noon, I would not be surprised to discover we have had only a 100-mile day.

AN hour ago, Egregious's speed dropped to less than 5 knots: long enough for me to set the spinnaker, which has brought us back up to 5½.

Setting a spinnaker alone on this size boat is not really as difficult as one might imagine; it requires only forethought, nerve, and lack of good sense. If you square off the pole, cleat the sheets and guys, and hoist on the halyard as though your life depends on it—which it does—and are blessed with dumb luck, all will be well. Getting it back down—particularly after the wind has increased to 20 knots even before you return to the cockpit—is the tricky part. But there are days when no other sail will get you where you want to go. And the pride one takes in being able to handle it alone is—I say immodestly but accurately—deserved.

To give some idea of size, the spinnaker measures about 1,300 square feet, and the next largest sail—the genoa topsail—555 square feet. With genoa top, genoa staysail, and main, I have over 1,000 square feet set: 555, 225, and 247 square feet respectively. With the spinnaker and main alone, over 1,550.

The biggest problem with setting a spinnaker is that I am unwilling to leave it up at night. I had hoped the winds would be constant enough to permit that. But such good, trustworthy winds, if extant anywhere, have yet to make an appearance.

For the moment, though I am going onto the foredeck to gaze up at the yellow and white arc overhead. It may be my last chance for quite some time.

4:30 P.M. Only a few hours later, yet too long. I sat on the deck, leaning back against the mast, enraptured by the sail above me, the sea, sailing, being alive, being here. After a while, I came below for a drink of water and decided that I should check the bilge. I lifted the hatch and—it is impossible to exaggerate my fall from bliss—was overwhelmed by despair. Instead of the gallon or two of water I expected, the bilge was full—was overflowing—with water only an inch beneath the cabin sole. The trickle from the rudder had become a torrent.

It is, I think, now fixed. I hove to, dove into the lazarette, and tightened the bolts around the collar where the rudder passes through the hull; that seems to have stopped the leak.

No man should ever be dependent on any machine as a sailor is on his boat, or as I am for my happiness on this voyage. In that oily water—oily from the lubricants I have copiously and futilely applied to the rudder—I saw possibly the end of my dream, but I am resolved to go on south. I never expected to have problems so soon. I am still 15° north of the equator.

DAY 10 • *November 11*

TODAY is my thirty-third birthday. I have never liked holidays very much because they require me to celebrate as a conditioned social response, and I prefer to be festive spontaneously.

The only gift I really wanted, I was afraid to open. That, of course, is a dry bilge. Finally, after taking a sun sight and eating breakfast, I gathered my courage and my flashlight, crawled aft, and was rewarded for being the essentially good person I am by an absence of water running down the rudder shaft.

* * *

Last night, the gods delivered the rain that had been proposed for the preceding evening. This time there was no prelude, no great cloud masses rushing about; just a low overcast to the east at sunset, followed an hour later by a standard tropical downpour; that is, for thirty minutes I was unable to determine where the sky ended and the ocean began.

Our progress was most erratic. Practically every time I awoke, a major change of course and sail trim was required. At various times I found us headed due east and at others due west, which is not the most efficient way to average south. More than usual, I am looking forward to the noon sight with curiosity and wonder. The sextant has become a magic box which enables me, after a few calculations, to place marks on a piece of paper. It is something of a sacred ritual and may bear no logical relationship to reality.

However, it makes me feel secure, so I am going to continue.

I have noticed this morning a most peculiar odor—very much like overcooked broccoli. I just realized it is me. Perhaps I'd better use an extra quarter-cup of water for my bath.

TODAY is spinnaker weather, much more so than any day so far; yet I have decided not to set it, preferring to write a preface to this voyage I had intended to write earlier.

We are near 13°North latitude, sailing gently—too gently—south at 4 knots. The wind is 6 knots out of the east, and although most of the sky is clear blue, clouds are forming, which I hope will bring more wind. I wouldn't even object to more rain. The doldrums should lie about 100 miles ahead, yet we are obviously already beyond the north-northeast wind pattern which has carried us so well thus far. We are also beyond the flying fish and sea birds. In every direction low swells are unbroken by any trace of life. The direct sunlight is too warm, but where I am sitting is within the shadow of the genoa and quite comfortable. Egregious's bow wave gurgles softly. For the moment, I am grateful for the respite and want to take advantage of it to relate what I expect this journal to be about, to whom I write it, and what I claim for myself.

Quite simply, this is about the voyage which has been my life. I hope it will be about happiness, joy, and success. That, however, is not completely in my control, and it may be about despair and failure because I will faithfully record whatever happens.

I write to several possible audiences. I write to myself. I write to those I love and to my personal friends. I write to an unknown boy who lives in a crowded city far from the sea. I write to those who love solitude and sailing and the sea. And I write perhaps most of all to a being who may exist only in my perhaps-too-vivid imagination.

One night more than a year ago, a few months after Egregious had been built, I sat looking up at the stars from her deck. In the southern sky was the constellation we know as Scorpio, with its brightest star, Antares. I had been wondering how many other planets have oceans and beings who love to sail upon them; and as I gazed toward Antares, I became convinced that at that moment someone on the third planet of Antares was preparing to sail across its seas, just as I was ours, and that he was thinking of me, as I of him, and that across space we both knew and understood. So I write this also to my friend on Antares.

A fanciful, childish thought? But I don't wish to grow any older.

I claim for myself that I am an artist and an original and an anachronism at age thirty-three. A sailor is an artist whose medium is the wind; a writer an artist whose medium is words. I am both of those. A voluptuary is an artist whose medium is flesh. I have been such. And I may in the course of this voyage become an ascetic; an artist whose medium is spirit.

I believe in greatness, the heroic, the epic, pride, honor, and my dreams. And I believe the hardest people in the world are not cynics, but those romantics who will not compromise; who insist that their dreams become reality. I am an adamantine romantic.

DAY 11 • *November 12*

TODAY is a gift. Yesterday was a gift. To whoever is responsible—I am grateful.

Salt spray splashes over the port bow. An occasional wave dashes across the deck near the mast. We dance from crest to crest at 7 knots. Our noon position shows us at 10°30′North of the equator. We are, of course, in the dreaded doldrums.

The doldrums are not the place of literally no wind I had at one time imagined them to be, but simply that area—usually about 300 miles wide—between the two great circular hemispheric wind systems, in which periods of calm alternate with wind that may come and as quickly go from any and every direction. The location of the doldrums is not constant, although they are always north of the equator, and according to the November pilot chart usually between 11°-5°North this month.

I did not actually expect to sail blithely up to the 11° parallel and come to a screeching halt, but I did not expect to be sailing here at 7 knots either. Quite probably my pleasure is premature, and just over the horizon I will find the barricades. At present, though, it is a hot, humid, overcast, uncomfortable, beautiful day. That a grown man should be so happy just because the wind is blowing is absurd.

FOR the first time since that first hour out of San Diego Bay, we are sailing to windward. I am writing this immediately before sunset, which will be about 5:30 at this latitude. I had intended to write earlier, but have been sitting mesmerized as we fly south. Two hours ago, I looked up from the book I was reading and noticed we were off course. Because once it is trimmed, the vane keeps the boat on a given heading to the wind, I tightened up on the main and genoa sheets and reset the vane until we were again heading south. I resumed reading, but in a few minutes was distracted by something peculiar about Egregious's motion. I checked our heading again and then I realized that the wind was blowing from 5° forward of the beam and that the ocean swells were coming from the southeast rather than the northeast. We were rising to meet them rather than sliding down them, as we have done for the past thousand miles.

This is a lovely sailing vessel. She leans a bit away from the wind, steadies and runs evenly, effortlessly up the swells, down into the troughs, on and on, without faltering. Our speed has not dropped below 6 knots for the past twenty-four hours and the wind is only moderate. I believe that in last year's race from Los Angeles to Tahiti, almost all the boats sailed through the doldrums without a problem. I am almost afraid to write the words, but is it possible we will do the same?

DAY 12 • *November 13*

THE sea and sky through which we have been sailing these last two days are a vast machine for manufacturing clouds. At times I can almost see the sun draw moisture from the sea into the air to initiate the process. Clouds of every shape and state of development are here simultaneously, as though strewn about a workshop; and they change so rapidly that at one instant a giant cumulonimbus billows upward to the east, and when I look again a short while later, it has gone or been transformed.

Usually at least a third of the horizon is covered by a low, inchoate grey mass which seems to be the primordial source of life itself. I can easily imagine the stroke of lightning which broke through that mass, fusing atoms there and in the grey sea below, creating life where none had been before, and millions of years later bringing me home.

The process is continuous. Often the low clouds, newborn, with vague wet shapes and smudged edges, the nimbostratus and stratus, obscure those higher; but at other times, such as now, I can see beyond them to the whiter, firmer cumulus and altocumulus, and then to a third level of the wispy formations of the higher atmosphere. All levels are moving independently, drifting away to fulfill their destiny, and perhaps to return in time, as I have, to be formed anew.

AHEAD, a line squall is coming toward us. To the southwest, rain is clearly defined in one limited area, and the remaining clouds are white and serene. To the east, the sky is dappled, clear blue, white, light grey, dark grey. Black and very low, almost touching the ocean's surface, is a great damp cloud with four arms exploding upward. Directly overhead, the lowest strata of clouds drift majestically to the northwest, while above them, the intermediate layer rushes southeast.

I do not have to look behind us to know that there the sky and sea are one and indivisible. We just sailed out of that deluge which caught me in the cockpit retrimming the vane steering. Everything was uniformly grey, but as I was about to climb into the cabin, a white form rose from the sea and flew off. We had startled a bird, but at the moment it seemed as though a piece of wave had come to life before my eyes, as though life were still being formed here. Never before have I been in a place so dominated by the sense of birth, where everything is in the process of becoming.

THE albatrosses I have seen are, I believe, Laysan albatross, of which the bird guide says "seldom follows ships." They do, however, often come and hunt in the cutter's wake. Birds that trail after large ships are seeking garbage. One has only to glance at these to know they are far too honorable for that.

Until today I had only seen them singly. But this afternoon two stayed within close range for an hour and flew together with elegance and grace, swooping and gliding, rising with synchronized strokes of their powerful wings, then swooping almost to touch the waves. Then they separated; each soaring off, circling away from the other, up over the swells, down into the troughs, then back once more side by side. First one would lead, then the other; until at last they landed a dozen yards off our beam and sat close together, seemingly as pleased with their performance as I was to witness this ballet of the albatross.

DAY 13 • *November 14*

DURING the night, we were becalmed. I awoke several times, but there was nothing to be done. Although the speed indicator registered zero, we maintained steerage way, and I had a good night's rest.

This morning I took the tiller and managed at last to find an almost imperceptible breath of wind which moved us more or less south at a knot or two. Now, at 10:00 A.M., we are roaring along at 3 whole knots, and I am more pleased with those 3 knots than I have been with 7 or 8 in the past. This was to be expected, and we are so far ahead of even my most optimistic schedule that it does not bother me. But to paraphrase Villon, where are the squalls of yesterday?

AN hour later. We are becalmed. The sea is glassy—not a sight or sensation of wind anywhere—but there are swells enough to toss us back and forth, collapsing the sails side to side. We point generally southwest, but that is of no importance because we are going southwest no more than northeast. The eastern half of the sky is overcast, and I look hopefully but vainly for some tentative movement in the clouds which might mean wind. The sun is very high overhead and hot even through the clouds. I glance to my left at the leaden water and see the bubbles formed by our rocking sit there. Just sit there. Often several minutes pass before they drift the 3 or 4 feet necessary to remove them from my view; but more often they burst before completing that tremendous trek, as though the mere contemplation of it were too much for them. A single dark shearwater glides about the swells on scimitar wings. I cannot see how he can glide with no breath of air. Perhaps he flies when hidden in the troughs and creates his own apparent wind. I envy him.

I am ambivalent about the amount of respect to which man, the species, and I as an individual, are entitled; and have often thought that we are much less *Homo sapiens*—knowing man—than *Homo insipiens*—foolish man. At times I am very impressed, but at other times . . . well, for myself today has been one of those other times.

I was very surprised to learn that our day's run for the twenty-four hours ending this noon was 220 miles . . . due west. I shall always remember it as the Day of the Great Leap Sideways.

I have not recorded this startling news until I found the error, which was simply a matter of marking off a line on the chart in one direction when I should have marked it in the opposite. What is even more distressing is that in reexamining my worksheets, I discovered I made the same elementary error not only yesterday, but the day before as well.

To people living ashore, my insouciance about knowing where I am might seem inappropriate, but normally it does not matter all that much at sea. If I am able to draw a circle with a 10-mile diameter and know I am somewhere inside, that is good enough. But 220 miles *is* somewhat excessive. In fact, it is unforgivable.

We are sailing south again at 4 knots. After taking half a dozen sights at various times today, I think I now know fairly accurately where we are. The captain has informed the navigator that his shore leave has been canceled indefinitely and that he is an incredible dunce.

DAY 14 • *November 15*

THE last twenty-four hours have been the most inconstant so far. We have sailed through so many squalls that I cannot number them. The boat responds identically to each. Heading due south, we are turned 20° east and start racing along at 7 knots as the squall approaches. Inside the squall itself, the wind backs and we go south again. But after about ten minutes we are left behind, now heading due west at 2 knots in sloppy seas and too little wind for the vane to bring the boat back on course.

At noon today we were 5½°—or 330 miles—north of the equator. If the southeast trades are where they should be but probably aren't, we will reach them tonight.

DAY 15 • *November 16*

WE ran into a squall last night and haven't come out yet. I do not know where this wind is coming from, and already it has lasted much longer—over twenty hours and 150 miles with no sign of lessening—than I expected.

During the night, we started to pound into the waves, so I let us run off on a close reach to the southwest in the hope that the wind would drop or back or that something would happen. What happened was that the wind increased.

Today is a day only for essentials. No breakfast, no sun sights, no nothing, except to reduce sail and tighten the shrouds. Even with a reefed main and cutter jib—less than 330 square feet—we are moving at better than 7 knots, though not pounding so much.

The waves are particularly sharp and jagged. And often so close together that Egregious is struck by two almost simultaneously.

Two flying fish and a small squid were washed into the cockpit during the night. Fried flying fish for breakfast is one of the standard pleasures of tropical sailing, I am told. But in this heat and humidity, nothing less than the threat of instant dismemberment could have made me eat these. I swiftly reconsigned them to the deep.

During most of the night, Egregious made an interesting—though not entertaining—assortment of grinding, rasping, crackling, popping, ripping noises, much as though the ends of a broken bone were being ground together. There has been no damage; this music is to be endured.

Frankly, I am surprised to have been able to write this much today. I am not seasick, but the motion is such that I can hardly keep the pen from skidding all over the paper. Perhaps there is some basis for hoping I can get a pan to stay on the stove long enough to heat some soup.

I have been sitting on my berth this afternoon listening to tapes of music by Mozart and Vivaldi. Ironically, one of the concerti on the Vivaldi tape—No. 5 in E-flat Major—is labeled "La Tempesta di Mare," which my computerlike mind assumes means "storm at sea." There is reassurance in hearing the beauty and order men have created out of chaos at a time when chaos is so near, when I feel each lurch of the boat in my soul and continually wonder how the hull stays intact and the mast upright. Vivaldi's notes run on gracefully against the brute counterpoint of the real storm at sea. I doubt if anyone has ever felt the contrast more acutely.

EVERY movement I make today is calculated. I literally pull myself from my berth and find a handhold before each successive step. I am six feet tall and usually weigh 150 pounds. I have never been fat nor out of good physical condition, yet in these two weeks at sea my body has been honed down and is harder than ever before. I could almost wish for some excess flesh; my hips are beginning to be covered with bruises from being flung against countertops and cabinet edges.

DAY 16 • *November 17*

THE sea is not as rough as it has been, and we are not being tossed into the air quite so often. There is still enough wind, though, for us to be going south at 7 knots under reefed main and jib, and still too much water coming over the deck to read or write in the cockpit.

We are obviously beyond the doldrums, which were not at all what I had expected, and hardly dull. If today is an example of what the southeast trades are going to be like, the next 2,000 miles are going to be wet and fast.

Egregious has behaved beautifully, and I believe we are going to reach the equator soon. One reason we are sailing to windward so well is that I have followed racing practice and kept weight out of the ends of the boat. This reduces the pendulum-like pitching motion that successive waves can impart to a hull and thereby greatly retard its progress. But beyond that, Egregious just steadies down to business and seems to want to go fast.

A week ago I did something I said I would never do: I stopped shaving. It took more time than the rest of my daily ablutions combined and, if I missed a day, was remarkably painful. I also chopped my hair off short several days ago. My appearance is bearable only because I don't look in a mirror. I did once and found the combination of cropped head and skid-row beard so frightening, I swore to abstain from mirrors for a week. A month might be more appropriate.

THE equator by midnight! I just worked two noon sights and we are 1°North. If this wind holds for ten more hours, we will cross the equator fifteen and one-half sailing days from San Diego.

* * *

THERE is such a lot of wind out there and it has been blowing for so long that I began to wonder if perhaps it belongs here, and I consulted the pilot chart, which I read as a kind of science fiction. It states quite confidently that the wind in this vicinity blows from the southeast at Force 4, which is 11-16 knots. But because I am not accustomed to a Force 4 wind driving water constantly across the deck or speeding us along at 7 knots under reefed sails, I am beginning to think something unusual is happening here.

DAY 17 • *November 18*

I am a block of salt, without even the compensation of having seen Sodom and Gomorrah. To go on deck is to be inundated, but I do so from time to time to see if the wind is still there and to look at the waves in disbelief—as one might at an elephant which appeared suddenly in his backyard.

More violent than merely the force of the wind, which I would estimate at 30 knots, is the size and shape of the waves: short, jagged, and often coming from two different directions at once. Every movement on deck or in the cabin must be planned and calculated, and even then I have a fair number of scars to show for my feeble efforts at ambulation.

The one desirable consequence is that we are going very fast. We crossed the equator last night about midnight. This is better than a 6-knot average from San Diego, considering sailing distance, and three and one-half days faster than I had planned for this leg. The boat has sailed well through this heavy weather, never being slowed much by the waves; just running over, through, and sometimes under them. But for the groans from the rudder, I could almost enjoy my discomfort in the knowledge that we are so far ahead of schedule.

I have disengaged the vane and have the boat steering with the tiller tied down. This works well when we are going to windward, and I think it wise to reduce wear on the vane whenever possible.

In sailing south I am chasing the sun. Since we left San Diego, I have covered 34° of latitude, while it has crossed 5. I will catch it in the next week or so, but would really like to pass Cape Horn and head back north before the solstice on December 22.

Crossing the equator has made me realize—as nothing before—the tremendous length of this voyage. I have sailed more than 2,000 miles, and it is nothing. Sailors can circumnavigate in the trade winds without making any single passage much longer than that; yet I am now to sail 20,000 miles in the Southern Hemisphere and then back to windward the 2,000 miles I have already come. My mind cannot fully comprehend the magnitude of such a distance, so I will continue to attack it piece by piece. Cape Horn is about two times farther than I have come. So it will be Cape Horn by Christmas. Or better yet: turn north before the sun does.

FOR a single hour this morning, the wind blew as it normally should in these latitudes and seemed to say to me: "See how pleasant the voyage could be if I blew this way. You would sail almost as fast. You would be dry and warm. You would not be bruised. Your discomfort is gaining you nothing that could not come easily, if I choose to blow like this. But I don't. I only wanted you to see."

DAY 18 • *November 19*

WHEN I went to the chart table to work the morning sight yesterday, I had one of the pleasures unique to long voyages: I found I had sailed off the old chart.

The new one covers the mid-Pacific, and while showing no land directly south of me, has scattered to the west—but close enough so that I cannot help but notice them—the fabled islands of the South Pacific: the Marquesas, the Tuamotus, the Societies. They sit on the white paper with the smug confidence of aged sirens whose practiced allures have successfully snared sailors for centuries. I, too, sense their attractions. I look to the western horizon and know that if I turned off the wind, these insidious waves would be behind me rather than on the bow; that I could run comfortably down the trades and in a week or two be at anchor in some idyllic cove, reading at my leisure, eating without engaging in gymnastics, making love again. It all sounds pleasant, but not for now. For now, the more austere charms of Cape Horn.

The British Admiralty sailing directions for this route to Cape Horn say: "After entering the Southeast Trades, stand to the south to the latitude of the westerlies, and then proceed directly to Cape Horn." Stand to the south. A noble phrase. So we stand to the south. Romantic islands must wait. I long for grandeur.

NOT until a few months before I left on this voyage did I read *Walden* through completely. While I admire many of his fine words, I was shocked to discover that as a recluse Thoreau was a fraud. I had some notion of him living in the woods all alone for two years. Nothing could have been more inaccurate. There were people all over the place—walking out from town to chat, cutting the ice on Walden Pond, neighbors visiting. Compared to my idea of solitude—total, complete, uncompromising solitude and silence—the man was running a wayside inn.

THIS was to have been a joyful entry because I was certain we had made exceptional progress these last days and I merely wanted to wait until after the noon sight before writing about it.

I took special care at noon and took several sights. They verified that we were 4°50′ South. This means 6° of latitude, or 360 miles in two days. No wonder the ride has been so rough. We have been ripping through the water. And then, at 11:00 this morning, the ocean and the wind both changed. The sky became blue and the wind dropped a few knots. The short, rough seas of the past have been replaced by larger swells, up and down which we ride more easily. I was ebullient—until I routinely checked the bilge. Again it is full, but this time not from the rudder. Water seems to be oozing from somewhere amidships. If that is in fact the source, there is a crack in the hull. Tomorrow I will stop and go over the side to see what I can find.

It is iniquitous. I cannot express my disappointment. I cannot write more.

DAY 19 • *November 20*

AFTER I last wrote, I went to finish rereading Isak Dinesen's *Out of Africa*. The first words I saw were "Gods and men, we are all deluded thus!"

Disaster has multiplied itself. At about 11:00 last night both of the bolts holding the mast in place at deck level broke. I hove to and have made some repairs which are at least momentarily adequate.

We lost twelve hours but are again heading toward Cape Horn at 7 knots. I no longer think of a nonstop voyage.

I am too exhausted to write more.

DAY 20 • *November 21*

9:30 A.M. I spent last night lying sleepless in my berth, listening to the mast and the rudder and the water splashing in the bilge, with the unanswerable question continually forming in my mind: Should I put in to port? I desperately do not want to. I belong out here. I do not want to see people. I do not want to give up my dream. And besides, there is no where convenient to go. The Marquesas, which I so proudly disdained a few days ago, are closest but would avail me nothing for they have no repair facilities. I could go on to Tahiti, where there are boatyards, and the bolts I need could be sent by air from California. But it is in the wrong direction. Right now I would settle merely to get past Cape Horn during this austral summer. All the west coast of South America or back to San Diego is more than 2,000 miles to windward and therefore completely out of the question. Despite my best if meager efforts, the mast will never stand up to hard beating. I almost believe that if we can get far enough south for the wind to be behind us, conditions will be easier. Imagine thinking of the Roaring Forties as a place of refuge.

What distresses me most is that all this has happened so early in the voyage and without our meeting weather conditions of any great severity. I have sailed in worse weather than this many times before. Even knowing its futility, I ask myself time and again: Why me?

THE first of the bolts holding the mast broke with a hard, clear crack at about 10:15 night before last. I was asleep, but of course immediately awoke and rushed on deck, thinking that some part of the rigging had let go. When a careful examination revealed nothing amiss, I discounted the sound as having been just another of the peculiar noises sailors often hear at sea and went back to bed.

I had almost fallen asleep when I was startled by a repetition of the same metallic crack. This time I did not have to move from my berth to find the trouble. The mast was jolting to and fro inside the cabin, banging against the deck. I lit a lamp and saw the two broken half-inch stainless steel bolts.

Immediately I climbed into the cockpit, disengaged the steering vane, and brought the bow through the wind and hove to. Then I returned to the cabin to survey the damage in detail. I had no time for any emotional reaction. My only thought was of how I could effect repairs quickly and turn back south.

Reaching inside the cabin from beside the mast across the full beam of the vessel are aluminum supports 5/8 inch thick. Each support terminates with a flange about one inch from the mast, through which are drilled holes for the bolts, which pass directly through the mast to hold it steady. The whole assembly is an essential structural member which provides rigidity to the hull at one of the points where it is most likely to flex. With the bolts broken, the mast is free to move several inches fore and aft and side to side. It is restricted only by the size of the deck opening.

In the limited light of the kerosene lamp, I could do little; so my first attempt at jury-rigging a repair was delayed until dawn yesterday morning. My basic approach to all problems has been to try to eliminate them before they begin, but I do have an assortment of tools, spare parts, and repair materials on board. I decided to saw wooden wedges and drive them around the mast at deck level. This took several hours, because despite being hove to, we are still thrown about considerably by the 10-foot waves and 40-knot wind, which is increasing in force.

The first three wedges I cut were splintered by the mast almost as quickly as I drove them into place, so I tried sawing some from a harder piece of scrap wood. The second batch held somewhat better.

All this can be told so quickly, yet absorbed all my strength and energy. Many of the wedges turned out to be of an unusable size, and more than a few were blown overboard before I could drive them home. During the last hour I had to stop to rest five minutes for every five minutes I worked. Lack of sleep, using muscles that have not been used for weeks, and skipping breakfast all caught up with me.

Finally, about 11:00 in the morning, I decided I had done as much as I could and turned us south again.

Within only a few hours, several of the wedges were pulverized and had to be replaced. I have also lashed the mast inside the cabin to the aluminum flanges, which seems to have helped some even though the line stretches and has to be retightened often.

We have now been sailing again for almost a full day. The mast is still moving about, and the bilge is filling faster. I do not really have much confidence in my puny repairs, but can't think of anything else I can do here at sea. My determination to complete this voyage is as great as ever.

I am going to continue south as long as I can.

2:30 P.M. It is all over. I am wormwood. I am ashes ground beneath the feet of gods in which I do not believe or revere and who therefore are free to destroy me as they will. My cries of "Why me?" are louder and more anguished. What difference would it have made if my dream had come true? What harm would it have done anyone if I had been allowed to continue?

I had planned to write that I thought I had found the source of the leak. Forward of the galley sink is a steel support, perpendicular to the center line of the boat, which is fiberglassed to the keel and to which is bolted the bulkhead separating the galley from the berths in the main cabin. I unscrewed the liner beneath the sink and saw that water seems to be seeping in there. The hull is heavily reinforced at that point, so I believe—or perhaps merely hope—the leak cannot be more than a hairline fracture.

I had again begun to think of rounding Cape Horn, which is only three or four weeks away. I had decided I could endure the grinding rudder; I could live with the leak, which now fills the bilge more than twice daily; I could live with the wandering mast and even thought it might stay up.

All that is academic now. As I write, we are hove to at 10°South, 122°West. An hour ago I was sitting on the port cockpit seat, watching the largest seas of this voyage and perhaps the largest I have ever seen, rush toward us, and admiring the way Egregious sped through them, when something about the rigging caught my eye. The port lower shroud—the one to windward—was peculiarly slack. I followed it upward and saw that one of the tangs securing it to the mast is broken. Fortunately—a strange word to use when I feel anything but fortunate—it is a two-part tang, and the lower part remains in place; so the shroud has not fallen completely away. I do not know how long it has been that way, but there can no longer be any question of our driving on for more than another thousand miles to windward and then facing the Horn. Before I could heave to, I saw the shroud being snapped taut by the flexing of the mast. The pull on the remaining tang is an off-center twist, which will inevitably break it, too.

All options open to me seem undesirable. I must simply decide which is the least undesirable.

4:30 P.M. I am sailing toward Tahiti. Since I last wrote, we have experienced the heaviest wind and the hardest rain yet. It lasted only about ten minutes, and I saw it in time to get the boat closed up. This was the first wind so strong as to overpower the vane completely, round us up, and really lay us on our ear. Webb's corollary to Murphy's Law—if anything can go wrong, it will—states that at sea it will go wrong at night and then be followed by the heaviest weather you have had during that particular voyage.

I decided on Tahiti because it is the closest place to leeward—although some 1,800 miles away—where I can get Egregious hauled and have parts sent by air from the United States. Hopefully I can get everything back together enough to try for the Horn again before the season is too late.

I have tried to love this boat. She is beautiful; I thought she was well constructed; and she certainly sails fast. If she had held together, the record would unquestionably have been ours. But it is difficult to love something which seems intent on destroying you. She has now broken on me four times: rudder, leak, mast, shroud. I said I was too dependent on her, and I was. She is a bitch.

DUSK. Sad to sail toward the setting sun when it ought to be—as it has been for so many days—on the starboard beam. Hard to turn away from Cape Horn, when Cape Horn has been my dream for so many years; when I had so hoped this would be the year in which I fulfilled that dream; when I have been turned away really beyond her outermost line of defense. To be philosophical, to say that others have faced far greater disappointments and far greater losses, to remember Ecclesiastes: "I have returned and saw under the sun, the race is not to the swift nor the battle to the strong . . . but time and chance happeneth to them all," does not hide the profound disappointment I feel. I know that I am still alive and that I will be able to continue sometime. Still, this is a bitter day. Perhaps the worst of my life.

. II .

DAY 21 • *November 22*

I have thought seriously this morning of heading for Valparaiso instead of Tahiti. I reread the Sailing Directions, the pilot charts, and recalculated the distances. The problem with Tahiti is that it is in the wrong direction: 4,000 miles out of my way—2,000 there and 2,000 back. But I know ultimately that the problem with Valparaiso—that it is to windward—is greater. Is in fact insuperable. There is no chance at all we could get there without being dismasted.

Since turning off downwind, the leak has diminished to less than a gallon in the past twenty-four hours, even though the east wind is blowing hard enough to drive us at 7 knots with only the reefed main set, 180 square feet of sail. I lowered the jib because in these wild, rolling waves, it was constantly collapsing and then snapping full; shaking not only the mast, but the entire boat.

I had never considered having to put in at Tahiti and have no detailed chart of the area, as I do have of Capetown and parts of Australia, which I had considered to be likely ports in case of damage. Without any chart other than the general one of this third of the Pacific Ocean, I intend to steer clear of the Tuamotus, sailing north of them until I can turn directly south toward Papeete. If, as I hope, we can arrive there in two or three weeks, and if I can make the necessary repairs quickly, I will start for the Horn again this year. If not, I don't know what I will do with myself until next fall, when I can try again.

There is more than enough to think about just in getting to Tahiti with the mast upright. I must try to limit my thoughts only to that problem for now.

DUSK. I am very sad. Not depressed. Only sad. I never thought I would be stopped before Cape Horn. Afterward, quite possibly. But never before. And yet my grief must not be allowed to feed upon itself.

I shook the reef out of the mainsail at midday, when our speed occasionally dropped as low as 5 knots, and we have made a steady 6 ever since. It seems we are not to be given any peace. The wind is increasing, and our speed is returning to 7 knots. I cannot afford to drive the boat hard and better put the reef back in while there is still some daylight.

DAY 22 • *November 23*

IN a few hours, I will have been at sea three weeks. Three weeks. I am beginning to suffer from echolalia. It seems so long and yet so short a time. I am not the same man I was three weeks ago.

I continue to consider ways I could sail south, but know that such ideas are only the children of desperation.

My decision yesterday evening to rereef the main was sound. The night became rough, with rain pounding down and pouring into the cabin from around the mast. The waves have increased in size time and again. Often they combine in 20-foot-high two-part improvisations, and we surf down a sloping crest; only to have the second crest break and cover the deck. Our speed has not dropped below 8 knots since midnight.

The water coming into the cabin around the mast is going to be a constant problem until we get to port. In hammering in the wedges around the mast, I had to cut into the mast boot—the canvas collar which seals the mast-deck opening—and it cannot be resealed while we are underway. Water penetrates everywhere amidships.

I did not sleep well last night and find myself making more mental errors today than before. I will have to watch myself and try to get some rest during the day.

I particularly regret—just then a maverick wave hit us broadside and flooded through the open companionway hatch—that this delay will mean I will not see those I love again for much longer than I had planned.

2:00 P.M. That after the damage we could sail only downwind toward Tahiti is more obvious with each passing hour of this storm. Small cracks have appeared in the deck around the port side of the mast, and the remaining half-tang on the lower shroud looks paper thin.

I tried to sleep this morning and did fairly well until about 11:00, when the motion was as rough as if we were driving hard to windward, even though these waves are coming from behind us. I checked the compass and then looked outside. The sea was a moonscape. Whitecaps were everywhere. I think it has abated somewhat, but we need more moderate weather if we are going to make Tahiti in one piece—not this scene from Conrad's *Typhoon*.

Despite the seas, I have managed to get several sun sights today which give us a noon position of 10°16′ South and about

138°West. We still have a very long way to go. It is as though someone had gotten into trouble in New York while on his way to Europe, and for some reason had to go all the way back to Denver for repairs.

EVENING. Both Egregious and I are relatively cleaner than we have been since the beginning of the series of events which culminated in our turning toward Tahiti. Not clean, but at least cleaner.

My will to continue the voyage has failed for never as much as a full minute—seconds perhaps—but a continuous minute, no. It is not enough that I do my best. That was not my bargain with myself. That was not what I told myself I would do. I believe I will succeed. I so believed I would make the voyage nonstop, I made certain before I left San Diego that I had correct change for the telephone calls I would want to make upon my return. Right now my concern is not that I will fail, but that the circumnavigation will become a prolonged ordeal which will take years to complete.

I refuse to consider myself particularly lucky or unlucky. In almost every other respect I consider myself exceptional, but in the matter of luck I am average. To take consolation by thinking I am unlucky could be self-defeating.

My life during the year before I left San Diego would have seemed idyllic to many; at times it seemed so even to me. I had a secure job which provided me with more money than I needed, an impressive yacht, perfect health, and the love of beautiful women. I was happy, and yet I thought often that it would be tragic if that year were to be the best of my life. By my standards, then, my life would be a success only when I completed this voyage. That I could be delayed was not in my control. But that I would ever quit short of absolute victory was unthinkable. There was no room in my thoughts for rationalizing failure. There is none now.

This boat has cost years of my life. Another would cost more, and I told many people, half in jest, that I feared losing Egregious while I survived more than I feared that I would be killed. That is still true now when the possibility of losing the boat is increasingly real. If the mast comes down, I expect I can jury-rig something with the spinnaker pole that will get us to land; but I have serious doubts about being able to maneuver well enough to keep her off the reefs which surround all of these islands and have already destroyed thousands of well-found vessels.

THIS afternoon, I looked in my copy of *Radio Navigation Aids for the Pacific and Indian Oceans* to learn about the beacon at Papeete. Because there is an airfield, I knew there must be one. The index did indeed list it. I turned to the proper page to check its range and frequency and found that page is missing. As far as I can determine, that is the only page missing. I can give you particulars of radio beacons from Kenya to Alaska, from India to Chile; but not the one at Papeete. Is someone up there—or down there—telling me something?

DAY 23 • *November 24*

ODD how only a few hours in which nothing particular happened can make such a vast difference in my mood. I was feeling so much better late yesterday afternoon; now, at 7:40 Sunday morning, I am very depressed.

The wind was not especially bad last night. There was no rain. Only one wave broke over us, and it did not even get the cabin wet. We are making 6 knots in the right direction. I know matters could be much worse. But, for the moment, reason does not reach my despair.

Even if the mast stays up and no more damage occurs, we have a minimum of ten days before we reach Tahiti. That is a long time in which to brood, a long time during which my thoughts are trapped in a closed cycle that runs: I will have to deal with the bureaucrats in Tahiti, and the delays in the boatyard, and perhaps wait for parts from the United States, and it will be the rainy season there—the rainiest month of the year—and perhaps I will wreck the boat trying to get through the pass, where 7-knot speed is recommended by the Sailing Directions because of the currents and if the wind is light or from the wrong direction, I may not be able to do 7 knots, and the cost of living is reputedly among the highest in the world. And if I get everything fixed and start again and sustain damage again before I get to the Horn. If I get killed or lose the boat or get dismasted. If little bits of metal keep breaking. Today is November 24, and in less than a month I would have been around the Horn if everything had held together. I feel as though the Pacific is a prison in which I am trapped. I feel as though I have struggled for twenty years for nothing, that I have always deluded myself that I am an exceptional man. I am thirty-three. By that age men have conquered empires, written masterpieces. I have done nothing but scribble away on my worthless autobiography. An autobiography of failure. The only arts I have mastered are those of suffering and self-pity. That I so wanted this to be a good time in my life, that I fear I will always fail at that which is most important to me, or spend years trying to accomplish what others have done more easily. Living not on the edge of human experience, but failing in its backwash. This dream of mine—this great glorious chimerical dream—has cost too much.

I try to step aside and view myself objectively. I try to tell myself that I must fight against this mood, and for a few moments—sometimes even a few hours—I succeed. Yet always it returns and often with increased strength, feeding upon itself; for there is nothing else for me to think about while we roll on to Tahiti, still more than 1,400 miles distant. I try hard to suspend thought about the future, but I am not by nature passive enough to live in suspended animation for two weeks.

I had thought I might exorcise my pain by writing, but I do not know if I have not made it worse instead. I hope that your voyage is going better for you, my friend near Antares, than mine is here. I am going to force myself to read and occupy my mind with something else.

AFTERNOON. The wind is more what trade winds should be. If I were going this way by choice and in a healthy boat, I would think what a grand sail it is.

Not having to be concerned any longer with rationing my supply of fresh water, I washed myself completely this morning.

My face and body were so impregnated with salt that I had to rinse four times.

I have rigged a number of lines to the port side of the mast in a probably futile effort to prevent it falling if the lower shroud does give way. The running backstay, of course, is set up taut on that side; and I have also run the jib halyard, the spinnaker pole topping lift, and the boom vang, from the mast to deck fittings. Unfortunately, all except the boom vang, which I attached to the track for the spinnaker pole, lead from far above the point where I expect the mast most likely to buckle. Nevertheless, they do no harm and provide me with the illusion of having taken some precautionary measures. The port side of the mast is now ensnared in the monstrous web of a berserk spider.

WHENEVER the weather moderates even slightly, the desire returns to change course to the south and force a conclusion. It would be wonderful if I could get around the Horn. It would, in fact, be more than wonderful. It would be impossible. And I know that the only conclusion I can force is a dismasting.

Now that I am heading toward land, I think more often of those I left in San Diego. I regret the misspent anguish I am causing them.

There is no point in writing more. I began only because my mood was better.

I sit in the evening darkness, which has become one of the unexpected joys of being alone, pleased to look back at the sea, pleased to know that I carve great arcs through the waves, ephemeral curves that endure only in my mind; a wake that fades even as it appears, leaving no trace of my passage. I feel as though I both do and do not exist; as though I am here and not here simultaneously.

The nights are dominated by sounds; in the past almost always by sounds of the sea, but tonight the wind is less than it has been since that afternoon so very long ago—was it really only eight or nine days?—when we were becalmed. We continue at 6 knots under mainsail alone, but our speed drops occasionally to $5^{1}/_{4}$, and tomorrow I may raise the jib. And because the wind is less, the sounds of the boat are not lost against the constantly rushing water outside the hull. I could wish *Egregious* were as quiet as I, but most definitely she is not. With each roll to starboard, the galley bulkhead—the one bolted to the support beneath which I suspect the leak—squeaks and strains and whines. The mast emits a variety of noises, most frequently different knocks and taps, as though two people were outside a closed door; one rapping patiently at intervals, the other pounding impatiently for attention. From aft comes the lugubrious bassoon solo of the rudder, often one quick note followed by a prolonged, tormented groan. Rigging jangles against the mast and thumps on the deck. Bottles and jars rattle in the galley. There is a clicking sound and one of glass shattering, which I cannot account for. And very often there are human voices.

Not only since I've had to turn away from Cape Horn, but since the beginning of the voyage, I have been amazed by the quite-human voices floating around the cabin. I know they are merely the creations of wind and sea, but they are often deceptively real, with a wide variety of tones and accents. Some are women, some men, and usually they do not belong to anyone I know; although the morning before I noticed the broken tang, I distinctly heard Mary call my name in fear.

Most of Egregious's sounds now are cries of distress. I am sorry for you, boat; I am sorry I called you a bitch; and I will heal you when I can. Perhaps someday I will even think of you as my friend. But you do seem to protest too much for having done too little, and to fill the night too constantly with your whimpers. I had expected this voyage would be a struggle of you and me against the wind and the sea, but it has become me against the wind and sea and you.

DAY 24 • *November 25*

NOT until today have I been bored. The day itself is lovely. The trades are becoming more normal, and we sail at 5 to 6 knots, still under main alone. Again this morning I had to convince myself that turning south would be hopelessly bad seamanship.

There is very little to do now. Navigate, keep alive, read. The sun is too intense for me to spend much time on deck, so I remain in the cabin and strive to concentrate on something other than myself. Just before I started writing this entry, I finished reading *Shadows on the Grass*, Isak Dinesen's sequel to *Out of Africa*; and for as long as it lasted, I was able to lose myself in her eloquent descriptions of Kenya. Too bad it was so short.

I have sailed far beyond the sunset. In San Diego it is 6:15 in the evening and already dark an hour. But here the sun is still many degrees above the horizon. It is Monday evening; Mary will be home from work. She is thousands of miles north and east of me, lost in the darkness of another hemisphere. Yet I see her clearly.

WITHOUT books I would be lost—more truly, I believe at times—than if I could not sail. Now it is 10:00, and as soon as I finish writing, I will go to bed. This evening I read Euripedes' *Helen* and found consolation in comparing my problems with the seven years Menelaus was sea-driven after the fall of Troy; even if I have sailed farther in these last days than he did in all those years. One might scoff that Euripedes' characters are only myths. Yes, and so am I.

DAY 25 • *November 26*

THIS morning I jibed the main, so the wind is now on the starboard quarter. We have 900 more miles to go west before we can turn south for the last 300. We are sailing north of the Tuamotus and south of the Marquesas. Also west of the sun and east of the moon—an old Polynesian chant. By sailing directly toward Tahiti through the Tuamotus I could save one or two days, but because they are all low-lying atolls, surrounded by unpredictable currents, they are also known as the Dangerous Archipelago, and two extra days are not worth the risk. When the mast falls a day out of Papeete, I may reconsider that opinion.

THERE are worse things than being bored, and one of them is sprawling in a dinghy while the stern of your boat rises 5 feet above you and then falls 6 in a sincere effort to impale you on the broken end of the self-steering vane; and another is to hammer your thumb rather than the chisel you are using to try to remove the broken self-steering vane coupling; and another is ever to have made a vow to yourself which you can never break and which involves the sea.

The ever-humorous gods awoke early today and looked down and saw that I had begun to accept my present plight, so they broke the coupling which links the servo-rudder to the self-steering vane.

In the early afternoon, I was below, napping secure in the false belief that nothing too bad ever happens in the daytime, when I felt the mainsail jibe. "Felt" is the accurate word, for the entire hull shook. I assumed that perhaps one of the tiller lines had broken again, but found instead when I went on deck that the servo-rudder was surfing gaily along behind us.

Fool that I am, I was not at the time more than slightly irritated. I have had this vane for three years, and little has gone wrong with it. I knew I had a spare coupling and a spare servo-rudder on board. It would be a simple matter of heaving to and replacing the broken part. A delay of half an hour, at most.

I will not relate all the disgusting details, but the essential fact is that I am not able to remove the broken coupling from the vane shaft. Not by pulling on it from the dinghy in the water; nor by hanging over the transom and hammering at it from above; not by curses, imprecations, tears, pleas, or promises of extravagant offerings to the gods. And if I can't remove it, I can't replace it. And if I can't replace it, the vane is useless.

I am not entirely certain why this does not bother me more than it does. One reason may be that I actually have accepted my present situation and realize that whether I am able to continue to the Horn this year is no longer—if ever it was—in my control. And another is that I know how to get the boat to steer by sheeting a headsail to the windward side of the tiller, balancing it to leeward with shock cord. But probably the main reason I am not more troubled by this latest breakage is that I am numb. Or dumb.

As I write, the storm jib set as a staysail is steering satisfactorily, but because this system will work only on a reach, Tahiti is farther away this evening than it was this morning. Not literally, but in terms of the distance we will have to sail; zigzagging downwind from broad reach to broad reach.

DAY 26 • *November 27*

WHEN it rains in these latitudes, it rains very hard; and harder inside Egregious, I think, than out. There is only a small space toward the end of each berth in the main cabin which stays relatively dry. I am sitting in one such island of dryness now, watching raindrops run down the mast and fall from the overhead. I feel like an orchid.

A substantial amount of this water falls onto the packages in which I have my provisions. Most of my food is canned, and I packed it in plastic bags; two weeks of food to a bag, and then put two of those bags together into a larger bag and then another over that. All sealed. But there has been such a lot of water that I will be surprised if some of it has not found its way inside. I will probably have to open everything for Customs in Tahiti, so I will live with the suspense until then.

According to the *Sailing Directions*, December is the wettest month of the year in Tahiti, with rain falling an average of 17 out of 31 days and totaling more than 15 inches for the month. Somewhere aboard I have Somerset Maugham's short stories. Perhaps I should reread "Rain."

WE made 120 miles yesterday, but mostly to the northwest. Our noon latitude today was 12°01'South; yesterday it was 13°.

THE sea is extraordinarily grand. Blue-black with white breakers. Small puffs of cloud to the east and north, building into great masses to the south and west. As usual, as sunset nears, the wind blows harder than it has during the day. We are slicing through the waves at 7 to 8 knots. Taken in themselves, these past hours could be counted among the reasons I came on this voyage. Yet I cannot enjoy them. My fears for the mast increase proportionately with the increasing speed. Nothing matters aboard a crippled boat except making port, and every pleasure is lost in worry. I am at home out here. I am at the height of my powers and strength. I could sail on for years if need be. But all I can do is try to get us to safety before something else breaks.

From within the cabin I sense each increase in wind. A few knots, the spare halyards vibrate. Another knot, the storm jib sheet snaps through the blocks leading to the tiller. I rest my bare foot against the mast and feel it flex with the gusts and wonder if each will be the one that will carry it away. Suddenly the storm jib collapses, blanketed by the mainsail, instantly we heel to port instead of starboard. Will the shock cords bring the tiller back in time, or will we jibe? Every atom of my body tenses as I hear the mainsheet go slack and know the boom is rising . . . then, in the fullness of time, at last it falls back without swinging over. A squeak comes regularly from the rigging. I stand and look up through the hatch at the mast. The lower shroud tang looks all right, or at least no worse than it has. So does everything else. But then nothing up there will break slowly. One instant it will be intact, and the next, the mast will be gone. We do 7 knots, 8. Under the storm jib and mainsail. Perhaps 350 square feet of sail. On a broad reach. I consider reefing the main, but to do so we would have to come up into the wind; and that would be harder on the mast than to continue running under this vast spread of canvas. Not once since we entered the Southern Hemisphere have I had even the designated sail area of 613 square feet on Egregious. With the cutter jib and main, there were about 540. With that jib and a reef in the main, about 90 feet less. And since we turned west, only the main, until I raised the storm jib for steering. So we rush on at 8 knots, and I cannot relax until we slow again to 6. An ordeal it has been, but not of grandeur.

DAY 27 • *November 28*

TODAY is Thanksgiving Day. Despite the rain, which has visited us five times during the last few hours and is transforming the cabin into a research center for mold growth, I am thankful. Thankful that the mast is still up. Thankful to have begun this voyage and to be here, despite our problems, rather than still waiting ashore.

I have just spent three hours raising, lowering, and restitching the mainsail.

At 1:00 P.M. I noticed what appeared to be a hole about a third of the way down from the head of the sail. So I lowered it, found a few spots that needed chaffing patches, and sewed them on. But I could find no hole. So I raised the sail—and raising and lowering the main under these conditions where I am unable to keep the bow into the wind, is a matter of minutes not seconds—got it almost all the way up, when I saw the hole again. So I wrestled the sail back down and examined inch by inch the area where the hole had seemed to be. Finally I discovered that the stitching was worn in a seam and resewed it. I started to raise the sail again, got it halfway up, and found a broken grommet. So down again, more repair work, and then—finally—I raised the sail for what I hope will be the last time until after it has been furled in Papeete Harbor.

I said that I would not write more about the rudder unless there was some substantial change in its performance. Such a change has come, and naturally it is not for the better.

The rudder is making much more noise and the fitting which connects the tiller to the rudder shaft has somehow become bent. The threads on the 3/8-inch bolts joining the two are wearing away. I have spares, but not an infinite supply.

We have sailed almost 4,000 miles. I am beginning to feel that Egregious is wearing out on me too quickly. That all the work has been for nothing. Perhaps this is merely a passing mood; but for the first time, I almost do not care what happens after we get to Tahiti, or whether we get another chance at the Horn this year.

Tahiti is southwest. Our course—the best we can steer without coming too close to the Tuamotus—more or less northwest.

I am a fraud. A posing, posturing fool. The great individualist, the lone hero in a decadent age.

I have claimed to be solely responsible for this voyage. But that is not true. I have exploited everyone who has loved me. Without any of them, I would not be here now. I have used them all. And to what purpose?

I have always been convinced of my genius, my greatness, my originality. But they are only words. I sought freedom. And so I am free to sail endlessly back and forth across the empty sea and read books I could more easily have read on land. I thought I would make the sea my home as no man ever has. Nonsense. I would become the greatest solo sailor the world has known. Foolishness. I came to sea to find solitude and grandeur and victory. Instead I have myriad petty breakage and despair and defeat.

My vision of myself has formed my life. I have benefited by it, and now I suffer from it. Through a process of self-deception for twenty years, I am become a victim of my grandiloquent dreams.

I have no intention of quitting. But that is as much because I can think of nothing else to do with my life as because my "indomitable will" is unshaken.

In the years while I was working to acquire the boat and money for this voyage, I wrote a story about a man who wanted to sail around the world alone in the expectation that he would find great themes to write about at sea. He did not, however, and merely had to endure an uneventful voyage around the world. "Merely to endure" I wrote then, having no idea how great an achievement merely enduring is.

I do not believe in an underlying principle of justice in the universe. But if there is such a principle, whatever suffering I face I deserve.

Obviously these slow days are grinding me down in a manner rough weather never could. Almost certainly in an hour or a day or a week or sometime, I will be more cheerful. Yet what I have said today is true and those who have loved me have treated me better than I have treated them.

A properly spectacular tropical sunset is being enacted. Low puffs of lavender clouds, broken by gold and pale rose swaths of sunlight. To the east, the full moon is a swollen sphere just above the horizon. We sail at 5 knots, and the air is so warm that I am comfortable wearing only shorts.

After writing this afternoon, I decided to try to do something constructive. Egregious's motion has become comparatively mild, so I hung over the stern and tried to cut away the frozen coupling with a hacksaw. My efforts were not particularly useful in breaking the immortal embrace between coupling and vane, but they did succeed in raising my spirits.

There are places in which to be alone and there are places to be with someone. The tropics are gregarious. Their pleasures to be shared. A romantic night alone is a contradiction in terms. Yet it is probably just as well that I am alone. If a woman were here, I might turn my foul moods upon her. Yes, better by far that I remain a solitary tinker's helper in the tropics.

DAY 28 • *November 29*

I dream more at sea than on land, or remember my dreams more clearly. Perhaps that is because I sleep less soundly and awaken so often. Last night I dreamed I was talking to a friend about the voyage before I left. I was telling him how the preceding night I dreamed Egregious had been damaged south of the equator and I had to sail 1,800 miles to Tahiti for repairs. We both laughed. And then I woke up. For a moment, dream and reality were confused, and I thought I was still on land and the damage to the boat was only in the dream. But then a slatting sail made me realize it actually had happened. For that brief moment of confusion, I was truly happy again.

ONE consequence of being alone at sea is that I take very personally what I know are actually impersonal conditions. Storms seem to be directed solely at me. Accidents are the specific punishment of the gods. A moment ago an incident occurred which illustrates what I mean.

Several days ago I realized that in a foredoomed effort to keep wearing dry clothes, I could go through every article of apparel I have on board within almost any twenty-four hours of foul weather. So, rather than have a cabin full of soggy pants and shirts, I have tried to wear one set of clothing in the cabin and change into the least wet of what I have already worn before going on deck. Generally this has worked fairly well, and one of my special pleasures has come whenever I change into a clean set of "cabin clothes."

This evening I made such a change and then poured myself a glass of port, which I sipped while standing on the companionway steps, gazing astern at a beautiful full moon, shining on small, regular waves. No water has come aboard all day; none has even threatened to. But I had been standing there for less than five minutes, when suddenly in the corner of my eye, I saw a swell looming up from the south, at right angles to all the other waves and to the wind of the past weeks. Before I could duck back into the cabin, it flooded over my fresh clothes, my drink, me. I know that was simply a freak chance event, but it did little to reduce my nascent paranoia.

DAY 30 • *December 1*

YESTERDAY'S entry was too depressing. I tore it up.

Today Tahiti is about 500 miles away—more or less the same sailing distance as San Francisco to San Diego. At the moment, we are sailing at only 3 knots through very sloppy seas. Make that 2 knots.

I had to stop writing because of a minor problem: the tiller fell off. As I noted a few days ago, the tiller-head fitting has become bent and wears away the bolts connecting it to the rudder. The bolts are not expensive, but they are being devoured at a rate which causes me to have serious doubts whether they will last to Tahiti. I have only two more spares.

I just sighted some terns, which I assume live on the Tuamotus, scattered about 100 miles south of our course. They are the first birds I have seen since we turned west.

DAY 31 • *December 2*

LAST night was the easiest in a long time and permitted me the luxury of an almost-uninterrupted sleep. I am a new man.

THE day has become hot and muggy. Rain is falling, but not hard enough for me to use as a shower.
    We are 360 miles from Tahiti and sailing toward Matahiva, the westernmost of the Tuamotus. Navigation is becoming more critical. I have seen no land since the Coronado Islands were lost in the twilight a month ago. Naturally I am concerned, particularly in these waters and with this northwest wind; the very wind which makes for the most unpredictable currents.

WITHOUT telling anyone, I believed before I left San Diego that we could complete the circumnavigation not only in less than 200 days, but in less than six months. I wrote six monthly positions on a slip of paper and put it in the chart table, intending to check our progress on the second day of each month. Today's position was to have been 116°West, 32°South. I am not even especially saddened by the certain knowledge we would have been well past that had everything held together. All that matters now is to get on with preparing for a second attempt to round the Horn this year.

I have just had a most startling experience. It was a few minutes after 9:00 P.M. when I finished reading a chapter of Solzhenitsyn's *Gulag Archipelago* and decided to go to bed. Before doing so, as is my custom, I stepped to the main hatch to look about. For thirty days I have seen nothing other than the ocean and the night sky. But tonight, less than a mile to the north, were the running lights of a large ship.
    I watched those lights in disbelief—until I was certain we were on divergent courses. The ship is heading in the same direction we are and has already disappeared over the horizon. No longer to have the ocean to myself is a tremendous shock. The world is closing in. I will even go so far as to do what I said I never would again and make a prediction: Papeete by Christmas.

DAY 32 • *December 3*

8:00 A.M. We are sailing south!

I expect to be near the westernmost of the Tuamotus—Rangiroa, Tikahau or Matahiva, at sunset. If I can see them, we will sail on through; but if I cannot, I will have to go farther west and stay awake most of the night. These next forty-eight hours are crucial.

1:00 P.M. Unfortunately my noon sights reveal that we made only 90 miles during the past day, so there seems little likelihood any of the islands will be in view before nightfall. We are sailing directly for the channel between Tikahau and Matahiva, which is 14 miles wide, but I doubt I will risk sailing through it.

EVEN while I find consolation in comparing my problems with the perhaps-imaginary trials of the ancient Greeks and the all-too-real ones of Isak Dinesen and of the Russian people as related by Solzhenitsyn, I am aware that such comparisons create for me almost as great a problem as they resolve. Particularly the comparison to the epic sufferings depicted in the *Gulag Archipelago*. The problem is, of course, what does anything I do matter when compared to such suffering?

It has been said that we do not live in a heroic age, but that is not true. During my lifetime, epics have been enacted time and again. But they have always been epics of evil and the only men of heroic scale have been monsters.

Precisely against such men and such an age, I affirm my belief in the importance of my private dream; in the value of any dream to which an individual devotes his life and which harms no one else. My dream of simple pleasure has become only a more complex pain. I will live with that pain. I will try to keep it in perspective. But I will not lose it or myself in the statistics of mass horror or in the trivial concerns of the sybaritic shadows that in this age pass as men.

TONIGHT is different from other nights. The sea and the sky look as they have for weeks. But tonight for the first time in over 4,500 miles we are going to close with the land. Somehow I can sense emanations from those atolls barely rising above the sea 30 miles ahead.

As I write by the last rays of the setting sun, itself already hidden by the clouds to the west, two birds fly across the bow, heading for their nests on those islands. Fly home, my friends. I wish I knew the way as confidently as you.

I have taken every precaution. Checked the sextant and the chronometer. Gone over every calculation at least twice. I believe I know our location within 5 miles, but there is only one real proof. I will not sleep well tonight.

DAY 33 • *December 4*

THE wind and weather continue to be perfect. I awoke to blue sky and sea and wind from the southeast at 8 knots.

The Tuamotus appeared to me identical to the Marquesas. This is somewhat surprising because the Marquesas are high islands, mountaintops jutting 3,000 and 4,000 feet above the sea; while the Tuamotus rarely rise 50 feet above sea level. However it is less surprising when I admit I did not see the slightest trace of either group.

Just after I stopped writing last night, I jibed Egregious and set a course due west. By 7:30, after the sun had set, I was very glad I had done so. The night sky was almost completely cloud-covered, and visibility extremely limited. I doubt I could have seen Mount Everest a mile away, much less Matahiva and company.

At midnight I decided that if my navigation was even remotely accurate, we could safely turn toward Tahiti. As I went on deck to make the course change, the gibbous moon appeared from behind the clouds, so I stayed out for more than an hour, enjoying the sail.

Several times after I returned to a fitful sleep in the cabin, Egregious would take one wave slightly different than she had taken others, and instantly I would be wide awake, thinking we had gone aground.

This morning we are either south of Matahiva or we are very,

very lost. Tahiti should be 175 miles directly ahead, deep water all the way, and no obstacle other than the tiny Tetiaroa atoll 30 miles north of Papeete. We will probably arrive there sometime tomorrow afternoon, hopefully in time to enter the harbor before dark.

LIFE is worth living only because some moments are so good that they make the rest tolerable. Despite my disappointments, there have been many such moments on this voyage; another just occurred.

It is 5:00 P.M. An hour ago, I had finished eating what masquerades as my dinner—I have stopped reading Hemingway here at sea because his characters are always eating food which makes my limited fare that much less palatable—and was sitting in the cockpit, watching the clouds drift by.

Today has been lovely. Less sultry than the past several. Blue sky. Small puffs of white cloud. Sparkling blue sea. Reliable trade winds. When suddenly the cutter was surrounded by porpoises. They leaped and dove about us, then slowed to our 5-knot pace and swam along side for fifteen minutes, their grey bodies clearly visible below the surface of the sea. Finally they had enough of dawdling along and sped off. As they left, I spoke my first words—other than curses—in a month. "Good-bye. Live well." And one of them leaped as if in acknowledgment.

MY silence and solitude have become very important to me. I will regret relinquishing them and my hard-won adaption to the austere rhythms of the sea.

DAY 34 • *December 5*

LITERALLY I tremble. At 10:55 A.M. I saw the definite outline of a mountain peak ahead off the port bow, precisely where it should be.

I spent all morning in the cockpit, not daring to leave for a single moment, constantly searching the horizon for Tahiti, which rises to over 7,000 feet and may be visible for 60 miles, or for Tetiaroa, which should have been within 10 miles of our position. I kept reassuring myself that my navigation could be trusted. And then there it was.

I cannot determine how far off we are or when we will get in. We may have one more night at sea. But, after these thousands of miles, land is in sight. The land which I have despised is a most welcome vision.

A black night. Water like ink. From alongside the hull to the stars overhead is one continuous ebony sphere.

I am at anchor in Papeete Harbor. It is 8:30 P.M. here and 10:30 in San Diego. Too late to telephone there, too late to learn anything about what facilities are available for repairs here.

The sail in was spectacular. The pleasure that began with the first sight of land increased throughout the afternoon. As I closed with the coast, more and more detail became apparent and I realized I was heading toward Venus Point about 3 miles east of Papeete. I continued on until I was only a few hundred yards from where the waves were breaking on the reef, then turned parallel to the coast.

By then it was almost 4:00 P.M. I gave myself another thirty minutes to find the pass into the harbor before I would have to head offshore for the night. Land is a very mixed blessing, and I most definitely did not want to stay so close to the island that I might become becalmed. Finally, as the thirty minutes were up, I saw a power boat coming toward us from the general direction of Moorea, Tahiti's exotic sister island 7 miles away. As I watched, it cut across our bow and disappeared into what I knew must be the pass.

I came about. Another power boat was going in. I trimmed the sails—still just storm jib and main. Our speed was a knot less than the 7 recommended by the *Sailing Directions*, which I told myself always tend to be overly pessimistic. Six would be enough. Six would have to be enough. I headed in.

Waves were breaking ahead beside the two buoys which mark the pass. Then the buoys and the breakers were abeam, and before I even had time to start to worry, we were safely through.

I trimmed sail again, coming harder on the wind, and the harbor opened out before me to the east, a mile long and a half mile wide.

Flying our yellow "Q" flag—the internationally recognized signal requesting clearance—from the starboard shroud, we sailed slowly to and fro between the commercial docks to the north and the pleasure craft anchored in front of the main part of the town along the south shore. And when by 5:30 no one had come out, I sailed over to the yachts. A man called from one of them that I could anchor in any vacant space and clear customs in the morning. So much for my worries about the local authorities. At least until tomorrow.

However there was still a problem in maneuvering Egregious into the required position, which is perpendicular to the prevailing wind. I sailed back into the center of the harbor, before committing us to an approach that under sail had to be right the first time. Like the rest of the world nowadays, Papeete is arranged for the convenience of power boaters, not sailors. The meek are inheriting the sea, if not the earth.

Both anchors were ready to be set, and I decided to sail slowly under storm jib alone, drop the small anchor from the stern, take lines ashore in the dinghy, and then turn Egregious around and set the big anchor at my leisure.

That essentially is what I did, except that two young men from an English ketch came out in their dinghy and took the lines ashore for me. I appreciated their help, even if it was offered in self-preservation as they saw me bearing down on them; but frankly did a good job myself in sailing into a difficult spot. Enough of my pride.

It is very odd to be here, to talk to people again, to see through the main hatch the leafy upper branches of a tree a few yards away. I suppose I am in shock; but for the moment, I cannot assimilate all this. I cannot quite believe it is real, that I am no longer at sea.

AFTER I got the boat cleaned up, sails stowed, lines coiled, I rowed out into the harbor and drifted in the night. I looked back at Egregious. She is a lovely sight, and I hope her troubles are over. I sat quietly, reluctant to return near the land. Automobile traffic on the street along the shore. A dog barks. Some girls sing as they walk by.

I row slowly back to the boat and wander restlessly. As I pass the compass, I automatically check the heading, but then realize there is no need. It is 11:00 P.M. At sea I would have already slept a couple of hours, have already awakened to check the course and wind and speed a couple of times. But now there is no need. No need to go on deck to balance the steering, no need to scan the horizon for land or ships. No. I am safe. Safe. I, who was to have been rushing toward Cape Horn, am safe in a secure harbor. Perhaps tomorrow I will understand.

• III •

SUNDAY • *December 15*

PARADISE. Paradise imposed.

I am writing this in Egregious's cabin on the afternoon of my tenth day in port. Time flows differently here than at sea. There I was aware of time to the precise second, but the division into days of the week was irrelevant. Here I am less aware of the exact time, but very much a prisoner of hours and days, of shopkeepers and airline schedules.

If one of the truer signs of intelligence is to know its own limitations, then I must admit that I am not entitled to an opinion of Tahiti. I have not seen Tahiti—only Papeete, and not even really Papeete, except for a limited perspective: green mountains rising above a dirty boatyard in the foreground; beautiful Moorea beyond the surf breaking on the reef seen through the windows of the post office, where I repeatedly wait for hours to telephone the United States for spare parts; exotic flowers blooming outside another window, this one in customs, where I wait while eighteen forms are completed so that I can import those parts. Never have I been so aware of a natural setting so destroyed by an encrustation of bureaucracy and commerce.

Only once, for a brief and fleeting moment, do I experience that natural beauty directly.

Yesterday morning I went by the post office and got a telegram which said that the parts would arrive tomorrow. There is nothing more I can do until I get them, so I walked to the central marketplace, a huge open shed with a corrugated roof beneath which produce is sold, and climbed aboard *Le Truck*.

There are three things I especially like about Tahiti: the long loaves of hard French bread, which are cheap—I eat an entire loaf every day; the water, which is good and free; and *le truck*. *Le truck* is a generic term for what are open buses, really only a roof, sidewalls, and benches built of plywood on a flatbed truck. They are the chief means of native transport—I have always been the only non-Tahitian whenever I have ridden on one—and bump along, horn tooting, in a manner reminiscent of San Francisco's cable cars, on their irregular schedules between varying destinations. They will stop for you anywhere along their route and cost little. I paid the equivalent of about 50 cents for a 15-mile ride down the west coast of the island to the village of Paea.

Obviously price is noted prominently about the things I like here. That is because Tahiti is perhaps the most outrageously expensive place on earth. It is totally beyond my experience or even my imagination. And, even as one stands there, mouth agape with astonishment, it becomes yet more expensive. I changed money on Friday, December 6, at the rate of 81 francs to the dollar and made arrangements the next day to have the boat hauled out of the water at a local yard the following Tuesday, at a cost of $200, more than four times what I begrudgingly paid for the same service two months ago in San Diego. But when I went to exchange more money to pay the yard bill, the dollar had fallen to only 78.5 francs, and the cost of the haul-out was therefore that much higher.

My unfortunate experience is that everything is 50 per cent to 400 per cent more expensive than in California. A telegram costs almost $1.00 per word. A small, undistinguished ice cream cone 60 cents. A half pound of butter $1.00. A dozen eggs $2.00. And meat is so expensive that I would have had to finance a steak for seven years. With a balloon payment at the end.

Some part of the exorbitant prices can be justified by shipping costs and a limited local market—the island has only 80,000 inhabitants and about an equal number of tourists each year—but I do not think those facts account for the entire difference. This is, I believe, simply an economy gone mad. My advice to anyone coming to Tahiti would be to avoid Papeete, eat the bread, drink the water, and bring more money than he ever considered bringing in his wildest dreams—make that nightmares.

Enough about prices. Although obviously a topic near and dear to my heart. I was talking about *le truck*.

The native driver could not believe I had no particular destination in mind when I boarded his vehicle, and I think my peculiar behavior disturbed him. It was something of a reversal of cultural roles: the natives all on purposeful, hurried trips; I indifferent to time or destination. Finally everyone had gotten off but me, and he pulled to a stop in front of an isolated general store, which was as far as he traveled south before returning to Papeete.

I climbed out, paid my fare, and walked on down the road. As I did so, he and his ten-year-old son, who rode along as a junior conductor, watched me in bewilderment.

Tahiti is an island of high mountains bordered by a narrow coastal plain, along which everyone lives. The only road follows the coast, so there is not the least chance of becoming lost.

I walked a mile along the road, stretching muscles that had not been much used during the month at sea. Past a church, a few old houses built of wood. Past palm groves, in which chickens pecked among fallen coconuts. Past exuberant tangles of lush green foliage. There was little traffic. Perhaps one car or truck every minute or so, and between their passage, complete quiet except for the waves breaking on the reef offshore.

The road curved to the west and descended a small hill. I could see along the coast before me to a point of land another mile ahead, on which palm trees clustered. I paused for a moment in which time was lost and a hundred years vanished and I had the island to myself. That point of land was as it had been then. With the mountains behind and the ocean before, it was the idyll I imagine Tahiti to have been.

I started walking faster, but the sky quickly became grey with clouds flowing down from the mountains; in a few minutes, hard rain was falling. I sought refuge under a tree growing along the shore and waited, gazing down the coast at the point and the palm trees, often obscured by rain. I kept relatively dry where I stood. Several of *les trucks* slowed as they passed, and finally I accepted that the rain had settled in for the afternoon and climbed aboard one and rode back up the coast to Papeete.

For the moments I stood there, though, I sensed something about Tahiti I would like to explore and experience more fully; something that life along the waterfront of Papeete, with its restaurants and curio shops, had made me doubt still existed. I will always wonder what I would have thought and felt had I been able to reach that point of land.

I am not lonely, although I do miss specific people, and obviously do not mind being alone. But as *le truck* bounced north, I thought how good it would be to have a woman I loved with me and for us to have brought a picnic lunch and climbed into the hills on a fine day, to have removed our clothes and been naked there beneath the sky, as I so often have been at sea, and to have made love simply and innocently as children.

Yet I am not simple or innocent or a child, and have no real wish to be. But that was the thought at the time.

I am sure Tahiti ought not be judged by Papeete any more than Mexico should be judged by Tijuana. I mention them together because surprisingly I have often been reminded of Tijuana as I walk through Papeete.

Tijuana is perhaps ten times larger and does not have Papeete's spectacular physical setting. But there is now about Papeete the same congestion, the same flimsy stalls purveying garish travesties of "native art," and too much of the same rough, shoddy concrete construction. I have never been so foolish as to believe in "the good old days" or any concept of the "noble savage," but there can be no question that Tahiti was a more desirable place to visit—and I suspect in which to live—fifty or even ten years ago than it is today.

The initial adjustment to life near shore was as traumatic in its way as was adapting to the sea. There were simply too many stimuli. Too many people, too many sights, too many sounds and too much activity; and my first full day in port found me more exhausted than I ever was at sea and concluded with one of the worst headaches I can ever remember. All with my accomplishing absolutely nothing productive.

My first impression was that the town was run by half-arrogant, half-diffident, and completely incompetent clerks. Gradually I have revised that opinion and now believe that what I thought was an unwillingness to be helpful is due to training. Most people here are like children who have been taught to do a job one way, and within the limits of their familiar routine, are efficient and courteous. But if something must be done other than by rote, they are lost. That is probably true of most people everywhere, but somehow seems more pronounced here. Time and again I have encountered this, but one incident will serve to illustrate them all.

The airport is 3 miles west of the central business district, where I went to the office of Air France to inquire about the cost of shipping supplies by air from Los Angeles. The girl behind the counter told me that air freight is handled at the airport. She made no effort to use the telephone on the desk immediately in front of her, until I asked if she would call for me and find out about the costs. I do not think she was being deliberately obtuse. It was just that to her air freight was something handled at the airport; she would never have thought of telephoning them if I hadn't suggested it, although once I did, she quickly found what I needed to know.

MY greatest problem since I have been here has been with the telephone. After looking forward to talking to Mary for so many days and miles, I did not learn until it was too late to place a call that first Friday, that one can telephone to the United States only from the post office and only between the hours of 8:30 and 11:30 Monday through Friday morning. Ultimately, I sat there all Monday and most of Tuesday before I was able finally to speak to Mary, who then arranged with Egregious's builder to ship the parts I expect to receive tomorrow. But those interminable hours were not wasted. Or at least they were not, if knowledge of the exact number of tiles in the floor of the Papeete post office ever becomes essential.

WHEN I arrived, my repair list included six items recorded in order of descending importance: lower shroud tang, mast bolts, crack in hull, rudder, mast boot, self-steering vane. Today the list is only half as long, and if the parts actually do arrive tomorrow, I have hopes of being back at sea Wednesday.

Most of what I have accomplished so far was done during my $200 haul-out. The boatyard is located across the harbor from the anchorage and is nothing more than a shed behind which have been laid railroad tracks, a turntable similar to those used to turn locomotives in a roundhouse, and a single set of tracks sloping down into the water in immediate proximity to a coral head. To my shame, I must admit being so intimidated by that bit of coral that I had Egregious towed around to the yard. Afterwards, I could see how I could have sailed in, had it been absolutely necessary. I partially salvaged my self-esteem by leaving the yard under sail.

I am always anxious when I have a boat hauled from the water. What was graceful at sea becomes a cumbersome monster when removed from its natural element; and the scene which unfolded before my startled eyes as the yard crew went into operation did nothing to allay those fears.

First two ancient men stripped to swimming suits, donned face masks and dove down to clear the slipway tracks. For several minutes their progress could be followed only by a steady eruption of tin cans, chips of coral, rotten lines, and rusty nails.

As soon as they assured the boss that the tracks were clear, two other workers gave the cradle in which Egregious would be pulled out a casual push; and it careened down and splashed into the harbor, almost amputating one of the diver's legs. This resulted in an outpouring of verbal abuse, the nature of which I could well imagine, in a language which sounded like Chinese to me, but which I was informed was Tahitian by a Frenchman who had come over to watch the show.

I stood on the shore feeling increasingly forlorn as I watched

Egregious being pulled by more and more men toward the waiting cradle. Seemingly an endless parade of workers appeared from obscure corners of the yard in which they had been hidden, stripped down and joined those already in the water. A cacophony of French and Tahitian, of hammering as wedges were driven to hold the boat on the cradle, of cries and curses and commands and excuses, filled the air. Somewhat more than a dozen men—it was impossible to count them all at any one instant—pulled, held, tied, hammered, dove, and looked worried. Looked worried? Why, oh why, I asked myself, do they look worried? Perhaps I should not bother to have the boat hauled out after all.

The crew boss, who was the son of the yard owner and who spoke English somewhat better than I speak French, emerged from the water, screamed something I did not understand but which resulted in four men running off toward the shed at the far end of the yard and all the rest falling into complete silence. He then wrapped himself in a towel and ambled slowly over to me.

The problem, he explained, was that Egregious with her short keel might fall over as the cradle was pulled up the slipway. They were accustomed to the full keels of older craft and had little experience hauling modern hulls similar to mine.

Wonderful, I thought, and was about to tell him to forget the whole thing, when he continued to say that he thought they could brace it with a jack he had sent the men to fetch. I do not know why, but I said nothing—possibly I could not have spoken—and merely nodded my head in what he interpreted as my consent that they should proceed.

I do not know what kind of jack I expected, but I do know I was quite unprepared for the rusting contraption of gears and tubes which the four men worried across the yard and down into the water.

Its arrival was greeted by a resumption of the chaotic activity of moments before, which continued for about ten minutes during which the image of Egregious lying on her side, hull split wide open, half in half out of the water, was etched in ever greater detail in my mind. Finally everything was ready—or at least as ready as ever it was going to be.

The owner's son climbed onto the cradle, looked over at me and gave, I thought, an almost imperceptible shrug of his shoulders. Then, when I remained motionless—frozen is more accurate—he yelled to the winch operator. Slowly the cable connected to the cradle came taut. Another yell and it stopped. The next pull would move the boat. In a minute it came. The cradle swayed, the hull lurched forward, then back, then trembled like a frightened animal. But slowly the whole contraption continued up the incline from the water. I had just felt the first sense of relief when suddenly it stopped. The winch still pulled, but the cradle was stuck; and before the command could reach the winch operator, the cable was drawn so taut that it began to sing. A ghastly high-pitched whine. I knew that if whatever was holding the cradle gave way at that moment, everything was lost. Boat and cradle would have catapulted yards forward and toppled over.

After two eternities, the winch operator responded to the frantic cries from those in the water, and the cable went slack. Not so slack as I, but slack enough. The cries which now arose made all that had been uttered before seem to have been the most enchanting of lullabies. They continued until the two old men who had been the first in the water sheepishly made their way forward and dove down to clear the rails of an offending scrap of metal, which in all fairness may have fallen there in the commotion after their initial efforts.

I am extraordinarily grateful to report that the rest of the haul-out proceeded without incident and that, after the entire process with all attendant orchestration and choreography was reversed two days later, the boat was back in the water without the slightest scratch. I will never be happy about the cost, but I must admit they earned their pay.

I kept Egregious out of the water for only two days, not because everything had been repaired that quickly, but because I had done everything I could do, which unfortunately is not at all the same thing.

During those two days, I established that there is no crack in the hull. Although I still find it difficult to believe, all that water must have come over the deck and in through the main hatch, which was often left open because the days were warm despite the wind; or around the lazarette hatch, or the mast, after I cut into the boot to drive the wedges.

After a titanic struggle, I also managed to batter the broken coupling from the wind vane and replace it with a new one, so I now again have a usable self-steering device.

The rudder, however, is only slightly improved. The yard workers were not able to be of much help, again because they are more familiar with traditional cruising designs; so I repaired some damage to the fiberglass and disassembled and reassembled the fittings where the shaft passes through the deck and through the hull. On none of these was there any sign of unusual wear, but the rudder continues to grind, though perhaps not quite so much. I wish it were better, but am not so concerned that I will not go on with it as it is.

I have also generally cleaned the boat—it took over two hours one morning merely to remove the rust stains from the galley, and dried and aired everything which had gotten wet, which was practically everything on board, although my food supplies did remain dry in their plastic bags.

The mainsail has also received a fair amount of my attention. Due to some confusion between the boat's builder and the sailmaker, I have had problems with that sail for as long as I've had the boat. The forward edge of a mainsail—the luff—is attached to a mast either by a boltrope which runs in a groove in the mast or by slides which ride on a track screwed onto the mast. My first efforts to set the main after Egregious's launching came to an abrupt halt when I discovered that her mast has a groove but the sail had slides.

As a compromise, the sailmaker suggested that I use slugs, which could be shackled to the sail as were the slides, but which would ride inside the groove. In the usual moderate winds around San Diego, they presented no problem; but at sea, during this voyage, the shackles repeatedly jammed when I tried to raise or lower the sail, making what should be with a crew or an unbroken self-steering vane a relatively simple task, for me a series of erratic sprints between mast and tiller and back again. To avoid such exercise in the future, I have removed all the shackles and tied the slugs with strong synthetic twine. The lashings may chafe, but I prefer having to replace them to the prospect of one day not being able to reef the mainsail.

Other than that problem and a few worn seams, which I mended last Sunday afternoon, the sails have taken the first 5,000 miles beautifully. If only everything else had held together so well.

PAPEETE'S main street, Boulevard Pomare, named after a Tahitian king whose chief distinction was that he so enjoyed Benedictine that his tombstone is shaped like a bottle of that liqueur, runs along shore off Egregious's stern. Last Sunday, while I sat sewing away in the cockpit, I viewed a parade of Tahitian life.

I particularly enjoyed seeing the native women, many of them matrons in their best floral-print Sunday dresses and great floppy hats, riding to church on the backs of motor scooters. They would climb down, brush themselves off, and then turn to greet their neighbors as graciously as Methodists anywhere.

Then in mid-afternoon, a Russian cruise ship steamed into the harbor and disembarked several hundred young Communists. Some stereotypes are valid and I would have recognized the girls as being Russian even if I had not read the name and port on the ship. They wore tight sweaters and long skirts that did not sufficiently cover sinewy legs. They stepped right out of 1946 and marched grimly by, to return in an hour carrying flowers, seashell necklaces, wooden Tiki statuettes, and even a potted palm tree. I could imagine its fronds poking forlornly through the snow of a Moscow winter.

A Russian cruise ship in Tahiti. Behold the revolution.

THERE are about twenty visiting yachts in the harbor, as many from England, France, Australia and New Zealand as from the United States. The people on other boats have been very helpful to me, giving me the tow over to the boatyard, inviting me to dinner, lending me some tools I do not have, and I have found that most of them like it here. Particularly those who have come in from the Tuamotus or the Marquesas, where they have been out of touch with the world. They enjoy many of the very characteristics of Tahitian life I dislike. To them Papeete is civilization again; to me it is merely an inconvenient town.

I am the only one here to have sailed a long distance nonstop alone, although not the only solo sailor in port. Restudying my course, I have determined that I sailed over 4,800 miles in thirty-two days four and one-half hours. Even with reduced sail the last 1,800 miles, we averaged six knots for the entire journey.

I have reread what I wrote during the first day of the voyage. So I had no illusions? This was to be an ordeal of grandeur? I am proud of those words; they have a good sound; perhaps someday they will even become true. But thus far the ordeal has been not of grandeur, but of frustration.

I am beyond caring about records, beyond setting schedules, beyond making plans. All I can do is make what further repairs are possible when the parts arrive and sail on as far as the cutter will carry me.

Time and chance and Cape Horn: I am still coming at you.

MONDAY • *December 16*

ALWAYS the noble phrase followed by the petty delay. Yesterday "Time and chance and Cape Horn: I am still coming at you"; this morning a visit to the airport the conclusion of which I cannot yet believe.

I could barely sleep last night because of the prospect that I would get the parts today and soon have Egregious ready for sea. Every hour or so I awoke and looked at my watch. I was far more excited than the night before I left San Diego.

Finally, at 5:30 A.M., I got up, made some coffee, and prepared the papers I need to clear port; for although I said I hoped to leave by Wednesday, I thought to myself that it was unlikely but not impossible that I might be able to leave this afternoon. At 7:30 I went ashore, flagged down *le truck*, and was at the airport before 8:00.

Papeete has a beautiful modern airport. The terminal building is clean, well lighted, and compares favorably with any I have seen. It has only one disadvantage: no planes land there. Well, hardly any. Consequently, whenever I have been there, it has been deserted. This morning was no exception.

My shipment was to have come in on a Pan American flight which arrived yesterday. I walked across the polished floor toward the Pan Am counter. Naturally, there was no one at the counter. There was also no one at the counters of Air France, Qantas, Air New Zealand, Hertz, or Avis. There was no one in the coffee shop. There was no one at a booth marked "Information." There was no one at the baggage dock. There was no one at the taxi stand. Unwittingly, I had found the quietest spot within 5 miles of downtown Papeete.

Finally I spied an elderly Tahitian woman who was pushing some imaginary speck of dust about with a broom. How can there be anything to clean up when no one is ever around? Perhaps one shift brings trash with them from home to scatter so the next shift will have something to do.

The lady in question greeted my cries of "Pan Am. Pan Am" by pointing with her broom in the general direction of the deserted counter. I could not remember enough French to ask if they had an office, so I stood there stupidly repeating *"Où est Pan Am?"* until she finally again shook the broom, this time vaguely in the direction of an open door at the far end of the building. At least I thought she did; perhaps she was merely trying to dislodge whatever she thought she was sweeping. A good piece of dust is not to be wasted at the very beginning of a long day.

I trudged across the terminal and went through the door, then along a sidewalk and into a building, in which I was surprised to find a door marked Pan American Air Freight. I was not surprised to find that it was locked.

A light was on inside, so I knocked. Nothing. I knocked louder. Still nothing. I rattled the handle. And at this a man came to a door farther down the hall and said they were not open; but if I wanted Pan Am, I should go to the counter in the main terminal. I was so grateful to see another living being that I almost ran over and embraced him.

"But there is no one there either."

"Then try their other office. All the way through the terminal and then upstairs."

I thanked him and retraced my steps. Along the sidewalk. Into the terminal. As I passed the woman, still lovingly caressing the floor with her broom, I thought I saw the least trace of a smile. Out the door. Up an unmarked stairway. Along a corridor to a door on which was printed in exceedingly small letters, Pan American. I felt as though I were intruding as I knocked, and even more so when a voice which sounded unaccustomed to being disturbed, cried for me to come in.

I identified myself, signed two receipts, was given a fistful of invoices, and told I could get the package at the customs office in the freight depot, which was located . . .

I know. I know.

This time, when I passed the old woman, who was still the only occupant of the main terminal building, she could no longer restrain herself and broke into a huge grin. I did, too.

The remainder of what had been a fine morning was wasted in wresting the package from the customs officials, who were no worse than any other examples of their species. How happy I was at long last when I had the package in my arms and was riding *le truck* back to the boat.

And then how unhappy I was when a few minutes ago I opened that package and found that somehow someone somewhere neglected to include the mast bolts in it. They are listed on the packing slip. They are listed on all the invoices. They are listed on customs documents filed away and even now starting to collect dust in Los Angeles and Washington, D.C. and Papeete and Paris. But they are not here. Incredible. Absolutely incredible.

TUESDAY • *December 17*

I am a Tahitian until at least Friday. The next flight on which the bolts can be sent leaves Los Angeles Thursday and is due here Friday morning. I replaced the broken tang and the mast boot this morning, so if the bolts actually are on that plane, I ought to be able to clear port Friday afternoon.

WEDNESDAY • *December 18*

I am spending my enforced leisure pretending to be a tourist and am seeing enough of the island to want to visit here again during a different season and under different circumstances. I have not changed my opinion of Papeete, but other parts of Tahiti, seen via *le truck*, look inviting. Nothing, however, is more intriguing than Moorea. I have considered sailing over and staying until Friday, but am reluctant to sail even those few miles without the mast bolts. After coming so far without them, perhaps a few more miles should not bother me; but they do.

THURSDAY • *December 19*

I have not formally been introduced to my favorite Tahitian character and know him only as one knows any true artist—by his works. He is a rooster who resides—and no doubt presides—somewhere nearby ashore. Unwilling to accept normal constraints, he does not crow merely at dawn, but lets go anytime the mood strikes him. Thus he crowed a minute ago in the middle of the afternoon, and I have awakened to his call at 3:00 A.M. It is not especially obtrusive, but somehow conveys a tone of rebelliousness. I truly admire him. Obviously he is a bird of character and independent thought.

I have sailed for thousands of miles, spent a month alone at sea, been tossed and driven by wind and wave, soaked with spray, seasick and sick at heart, experienced moments of great beauty and a perhaps even more intense sorrow, finally to come to anchor here in a tropical paradise, in the fabled South Seas of Gauguin, Stevenson, Maugham, of Captain Cook and Captain Bligh, finally to come to rest directly offshore from a neon sign with five black letters in five plastic squares; the first two lime green, the next one white, the last two red. And what poetic Polynesian evocation do these letters spell? Follow them with me: black P against green; black I against green; black Z against white—have you understood Tahiti's intimate call to me?—black

Z against red—surely now you know—black A against red. There it is. Sit with me in the cockpit in the morning as Moorea emerges from the mist; then we turn toward shore and there among the palm trees. PIZZA. The word that will always mean Polynesia to me.

FRIDAY • *December 20*

MANY people have observed Egregious's problems and commented that the boat simply does not want to go on south, that the delays are omens for me to linger and enjoy these islands. Some have said that they could understand when I was trying to set a record, but not now that I have had to stop.

I have not tried to explain that my commitment is not to a record, but to an arbitrary childhood dream; which even I do not believe has any importance beyond that created by my devotion and sacrifice. And I have not said that I do not believe in omens. It is just as well, because I am almost beginning to think they are right.

All day today I waited in vain for the arrival of the flight from Los Angeles, which was held on the ground there for twelve hours by fog. Eventually it arrived at 5:10 P.M. Customs closed for the weekend at 5:00 P.M. I may still be coming toward Cape Horn, but today's progress has not been perceptible.

FOR the first time in several weeks, I approve of my appearance. Ever since I chopped off my hair and let my beard grow, I have not liked the way I looked. My beard was every possible color: black, red, brown, blond, grey, and white, all mixed together in a curly mass—or mess—with no one hue predominant. I told myself that I would soon return to sea and that, although I did not like it, I should leave it alone. However, this evening, when the probability that I would not get the bolts today became a certainty, I felt an overwhelming need to do something; to take some positive act toward some useful end. So I shaved off my beard. Perhaps the God of Harbors will accept that hair as a sacrifice and now release me.

I left a moustache, and although the hair on top of my head is not a respectable length even now, six weeks after I cut it, I am again the handsome fellow I used to be.

SATURDAY • *December 21*

EXACTLY a month ago, to the very hour, I stopped sailing south. When I consider that in that month I have sailed here and made Egregious ready to return to sea as soon as the cursed bolts arrive, I think I have achieved a great deal, more than reasonably could have been expected, despite what have seemed endless delays.

Yet there is no room for satisfaction within me when I remember that tomorrow the sun slows its southern march, pauses for a few hours, then starts back north. Two or three days more than a month ago, I was certain I would be past Cape Horn by now.

SUNDAY • *December 22*

THERE has been some rainfall—usually in the afternoons or at night—every day since I have been here, but nothing like this. It began at midnight and has literally rained buckets, several of which are in the cockpit, normally used as wastebaskets or for washing clothes, and all are full to overflowing. The dinghy has several inches of water in it. And all this has happened without the rain seeming, except for brief periods, to be very heavy. But it is and has been steady and inexorable.

I do not mind the rain except that it has made what I am again telling myself is my last full day in port pass slowly. If the weather had been decent, I intended to raise the heavier of my two anchors as an act of faith and make some final adjustments to the rigging.

Both of those tasks can wait, though, without endangering my chances of being at sea tomorrow. What is of more concern to me is that with this rain there is no wind. Perhaps that is why I keep thinking it has ended. The fat drops fall straight down and make no noise upon the deck. Surely they will stop by tomorrow, and surely there will be some wind then. Every day I sit here is another day I will be later at the Horn and increases the likelihood I will be caught somewhere in the Southern Ocean by the oncoming austral winter in a few months.

I have sat today inside the cabin, as remote from the land as if I were back at sea, reading Ludwig's biography of Napoleon, who at my age was made First Counsel of France for life. When I was a child, I used to read the biographies of great men to learn how they became great; only to find that the biographers quickly passed over the process by which the great man elevated himself—or was elevated—from obscurity. Now I know that what is called genius stems only from an inexplicable innate belief in oneself, which in turn creates a perseverance in one's efforts that is unfailing. One cannot help but to continue to believe in oneself, so one cannot help but persevere and endure. Once I took those virtues lightly, but they are everything. Everything but luck.

EVENING. I sit inside the rolling cabin and read about Napoleon's invasion of Russia and look at my reflection in the mirror and wonder what tomorrow and the coming days will bring.

The cabin rolls because the wind I had sought is now blowing hard enough from the northwest so that waves are breaking heavily; not just upon the reef, but across the pass as well. The swell surges right into the harbor, and we are tossed as though in a heavy sea. These conditions are a new variation I had not contemplated on the ubiquitous theme of keeping Webb in Papeete.

The rain has never stopped, but it did slow sufficiently an hour ago so that I could go on deck to rearrange a few twisted lines and bail out the dinghy. The harbor is a deep brown, as muddy as the Missouri River in flood stage. Chips of wood, leaves, broken branches of greenery float everywhere.

I do not know why I look at myself so often in the mirror tonight. Perhaps it is a natural curiosity at seeing myself again. I have no regrets about the beard, even though the contrast between the white pallor of my chin and cheeks and my tanned forehead is startling.

That white chin is firm, strong, and cleft, and is in my opinion my best feature. The jaw line is also sharp and determined. The mouth is full, the lips thick, providing an impression of excessive and unrestrained sensuality, not compromised by the partially obscuring moustache.

My cheeks are more hollow than I remember them; taut as is all my flesh after these last weeks. My nose is quite peculiar. In profile it is straight and proportionate to the rest of my face, but seen directly on, it seems not completely formed; as though whoever had been molding it had been interrupted before he had time to finish.

My eyes are small and very deep-set. They are green with flecks of brown and gold. I am extremely nearsighted and wear glasses with a plain black frame. No one has ever claimed to have seen my soul through my eyes, and I have often said that because I cannot see out through them, there is no reason why anyone else should be able to see in.

I have a high forehead. My hair is curlier than I wish, mostly brown in color, although with streaks of blond and some grey and red. Usually it grows down over my ears, which are unremarkable, although I seem to remember that when I was younger they stuck out.

There is a mole to the left of my nose and another above my right eyebrow.

THE rain has stopped momentarily, but the northwest wind continues. Egregious bobs and sways. Someone neglects to put the bolts in a package two weeks ago; fog in Los Angeles last Thursday night; customs office closed yesterday and today. Is the litany to continue: waves breaking across Papeete pass tomorrow; Christmas holidays the days after? Am I to exhaust my life waiting? Have not twenty years been enough? I have the whole world to sail around. Will I ever get back to sea?

DAY 35 • *December 23*

WE are swinging slowly around our anchor 30 yards from the shore. I got the bolts this morning and installed them before noon.

We have officially cleared port and can leave anytime the wind decides to blow. We have been sitting here like this for three hours. The mainsail is raised but hangs lifeless. A light rain is falling, and within twenty minutes the sun will set.

A strange incident occurred an hour ago. While I was eating a can of cold ravioli for dinner, a man rowed out from the shore and asked if I wanted to sell the boat. I laughed and said, "Not today."

The strong winds . . .

. IV .

DAY 36 • *December 24*

AT the very moment I wrote "winds," I realized something was wrong. I dropped this journal and hurried on deck. A breeze had come out of the south, blowing down off the mountains inland. Because we were drifting directly over the anchor, with the rode taut, it was enough to break us free from the bottom. For the second time that day, Egregious was attempting to climb ashore. I did not know then that there would be a third. Quickly I raised the anchor and hoisted the jib. The fates had decided that, for better or worse, we were returning to sea this night.

Before recording the subsequent events, I want first to resume my interrupted account of what happened earlier yesterday.

Obviously I was very pleased to discover when I reached the airport in the morning that the bolts had arrived. But when I got back to Egregious, I was somewhat less pleased to find that they were ⅛-inch larger diameter than the first ones. Thirty minutes work with the file enabled me to fit them through the mast, at which time I was very displeased to discover they were also ⅜-inch shorter than their predecessors. So short in fact, that the nut on the upper bolt is held by only a single turn on the threads. Probably it will fall off, and I will spend the next six months replacing it; but to tighten it further now will bend the flange and crack the weld at the side support.

As soon as the bolts were more or less in place, I gathered together my documents and headed for the port captain's office. It was only 10:00 A.M. and I was confident I could clear before noon. That is, I was confident until I was greeted at his office by a notice stating he would not be in until 2:00 that afternoon.

I stopped to pay a last visit to one of my two Tahitian homes away from home—the post office—mailed my letters to San Diego, and then returned to Egregious to make preparations so I could set sail as soon as the paperwork was taken care of.

During the night the rain had stopped, and during the morning there had been very little wind; so I raised the big anchor, leaving us to swing on the small one, which I thought all too accurately would come up quickly. Although I had no reason to think I would be using it again, I am usually cautious when near land and left the heavy anchor in the cockpit, with the rode neatly coiled so it would run out freely.

An hour later I was in the cabin, finishing my lunch, when we were hit by a gust of wind followed by heavy rain. I looked out and everything seemed to be satisfactory, so I fell asleep for a brief nap.

When I awoke after thirty minutes, the wind was still blowing. I glanced routinely through the companionway hatch and was startled that the view of the shore had changed so dramatically. We were within a few yards of dragging broadside onto the rocks.

Rain beat down but I did not bother with foul-weather gear. Over the side with the 45-pound anchor and into the dinghy. Rowing hard against the chop out into the harbor, grateful to see the rope feed out behind me without a snarl. I dropped the anchor 200 feet from shore and flew back to Egregious, where I ran the rode to a winch and pulled the bow away from danger. Ten minutes later, the wind died.

When I was confident we would stay in place, I went ashore and arrived at the port captain's office punctually at 2:00 P.M. He arrived punctually at 3:45.

Sailing a boat without an engine is like working on a high trapeze without a net: there is no room for error. Yet I made a mistake last night that almost wrecked Egregious. I have slept so little and am even now half-asleep. Events of only a few hours ago seem distant, as though they occurred in a dream. But I know they were real.

We rode the land breeze slowly down the harbor toward the red and green lights on the buoys marking the pass through the reef. Darkness had fallen, and I was tranquil as I watched the picturesque lights of the town slip by. At last I was on my way again.

But as the white line of surf breaking on the reef came closer, our boat speed slowed. We were sailing at the edge of the land breeze. There was a moment a few hundred yards from the reef when I knew I should turn back, re-anchor, and wait for better wind. Our speed was not more than 3 knots—far less than the 7 recommended for traversing the pass, far less than the 6 which had enabled us to enter safely. But a few days earlier I had seen two other boats sail through in very light winds, and my desire to resume the voyage was too strong. If they could do it, I could. We sailed on.

The flashing lights of the buoys came closer, and our speed continued to decrease. Then, just as we reached the pass, the wind vanished. I try to turn back, knowing that the apparent wind would be greater if we were headed toward it. But it is too late. Egregious will not respond to the helm.

Waves break only yards to either side of us. A low swell from the north shakes us. The sails slat uselessly. We are stalled directly in the middle of the pass. The wind must return. It must. The buoy to starboard is farther away than it was a moment ago. We are drifting helplessly down onto the reef to the west.

I am terrified. Not for myself, but for Egregious. The bow falls farther and farther toward the breaking waves. In only a minute we will hit, and already I can imagine the hull grinding and splintering. The dream is to come to an inglorious end here. Egregious a total loss. And I have no one to blame but myself. Not for my pride in having no engine—even now I do not regret that—but for my foolish impatience and for allowing fate in the form of a dragging anchor to have dictated our departure.

Blindly, in agony, I cry out to the night sky: "Let me return to sea. Please, please let me return to sea." I do not know to whom or what I direct my words. We continue to drift sideways toward the reef.

Nothing I do makes any difference. We are so close that an anchor will not keep us off. My only hope is that we will somehow bounce across the coral without breaking up, even though I know that is impossible. Within a few seconds, her keel will strike; then she will be thrown over onto her side, lifted and smashed again and again until she is destroyed. I will live, even if badly cut by the coral. The shore is not far away. But I do not care. My last thought before I expect us to be caught by the breakers is that I should have sold the boat to the man who rowed out to us an hour ago.

We are there. The bow is to the line of white foam. Simultaneously, I feel the faintest breath of wind. Egregious responds to the tiller, but it may be too late. I try not to oversteer, careful not to diminish our almost-imperceptible headway. The waves clutch at the bow, unwilling to let what had seemed a certain victim escape. Slowly, painfully slowly, we ghost away from imminent danger, back to the center of the pass, then off to the northeast.

My relief and gratitude are immense, but not long-lived. A hundred yards away, we are again becalmed and start to drift down onto the other reef.

For the next hour, I fight for every inch of offing, use every breath of wind and every lesson learned in ten years' gliding engineless through the calms of Southern California, as I watch the night sky become increasingly dark to the north. Obviously a storm is coming, and if I can stay off the reefs until it reaches us, we will be saved. It is the longest hour that I have ever spent at sea.

I cannot leave the tiller for a second; not long enough to set the self-steering, not long enough to put on foul-weather gear. So when the storm hits in a frenzy of wind and cold rain, I can only sit shivering at the tiller, thankful that my physical discomfort is my greatest concern.

WHAT I thought would be a squall of relatively brief duration has increased into a gale and continues unabated. It has driven us almost 100 miles east of Tahiti and exposed all the minor problems which must be attended to whenever sailors return to sea.

They will have to wait. I have spent most of today trying without noticeable success to catch up on my sleep between regular trips on deck to reduce sail. At the moment, we are making 7 knots downwind under only the reefed mainsail. I have already completely soaked three sets of clothing. A new free-style record for twenty-four hours.

I am very glad to be at sea this Christmas Eve.

DAY 37 • *December 25*

THERE seems to be a regulation that I spend holidays repairing the mainsail: first Thanksgiving; now Christmas. The sun is shining and the storm is blowing itself out, but there is still enough wind so that we sailed at 5 knots under bare poles while I worked away this morning with needle and thread.

At dawn the fitting broke which holds one of the blocks through which the line passes from the self-steering vane to the tiller. The violence of the resulting accidental jibe left a 4-foot tear in the mainsail and broke the upper batten. Replacing the shackles along the luff with ties in Papeete proved invaluable. If the sail had not come down smoothly, the damage would have been much worse.

I am not entirely satisfied with the patch I put on, but after sewing for five hours, I declared a holiday.

We have lost a winch handle and the top slat of the three which served to close the companionway. I saw them being carried overboard by a wave which broke on deck while I was wrestling with the mainsail, but had enough trouble preventing myself from being swept away and could not reach them in time. I have two more winch handles and have fitted a half-inch-thick piece of plexiglas I had cut to cover the companionway in heavy weather. Business as usual.

DAY 38 • *December 26*

THE weather changed quickly, and today has been fine. Blue sky and sea. A south wind which enables us to sail east-southeast, directly toward Cape Horn. And good sun sights, which place us 300 miles southeast of Papeete.

Having at last caught up on my sleep, I finally have Egregious ready for sea again. The ground tackle has been stowed. Miscellaneous lines coiled. The self-steering vane adjusted for optimum performance. And all my wet clothing hangs from the boom, drying nicely.

I picked up a most unwelcome stowaway in Tahiti. He makes his presence known by ugly septic bites I find on my legs each morning. There are fourteen on my right leg alone. I am writing this while sitting in the cockpit because the cabin is filled with insect-killer. I fervently hope he has perished.

THE backing wind has caused me to turn south as I had expected. The course change was somewhat more complicated than usual. But I disengaged the vane and bravely put the tiller over and we smoothly came about, sailing under jib, main, two pairs of Levis, two shirts, and a towel. We are now heading directly for the Roaring Forties, some 1,000 miles ahead, where we will be able to turn east for the Horn, with all canvas and clothes flying. If the wind lightens, I may add another pair of pants and a washcloth as a skysail.

ALREADY the new bolts are enlarging the holes through which they pass through the mast. When we left Tahiti, the holes were snug but now they are about ¼-inch larger than the bolts. The mast is also off center to port, which I have partially corrected by sawing blocks of wood to act as spacers between the side flanges and the mast wall.

DAY 39 • *December 27*

THE island of Raivavae is a mountainous grey silhouette off the port bow. Late yesterday afternoon I calculated that if the wind remained steady, we would pass near the island between 8:00 and 10:00 this morning. At dawn it was clearly visible on the horizon and is abeam now at 9:45 A.M.

Ever since I entered this part of the Pacific a month ago and knew that the Marquesas and Tuamotus were within a few days' sail, I have felt as though all these island groups were a snare designed to keep me from the open sea. Now at last I am escaping from that trap. Should I be forced to the southeast, there are other islands in the way, but directly south there is no land until Antarctica. I am free.

YESTERDAY should become a world holiday. Parades and pageants should be presented; young girls should sing songs of joy and young boys recite the great deeds they will perform when they become men. The cause for such celebration: during the twenty-four hours of December 26, 1974, nothing broke aboard the cutter Egregious.

However, on December 27, I am again the foil of the gods, the prankster gods, the fun-loving gods of bibulous humor, the schoolboy gods who delight in tying tin cans to cats' tails and tormenting me with breakage. I am a vain man made vainly vaneless.

At 1:30 this afternoon, Egregious came up into the wind and quietly hove to. Which would have been fine if I had wanted to heave to. But I didn't. The breakaway coupling I installed in Tahiti is well named and has, for reasons of its own, broken away. It is designed to break if the servo-rudder should hit something such as a partially submerged log, but I am certain we hit nothing.

Because this happened while we were sailing on the wind in the full light of midday, I began to think the gods were becoming sloppy with their jests. It took only a minute for me to tie the tiller a bit to windward and have the boat steering itself south again.

Two hours later, however, I regained my confidence in the maliciousness of the powers that be. They had only been setting me up the first time. At 3:30 the wind died and we jibed. I had to go on deck and rebalance everything. In heavy rain.

THE sun and I passed one another today, heading, alas, in opposite directions. Although it seems to be directly overhead, the sun is now actually north of me. I wonder when I will be beneath it again.

THE late afternoon is delightful. The clouds have burned away and the cutter is sailing easily south. I sit in the cockpit, enjoying the sail and the open ocean spreading before me like an empty canvas. With the regained illusion that we are making progress, I have fully enjoyed these last two days.

EVENING. Raivavae is lost in the haze to the north. As I sailed closer to it, a tern flew out to welcome me. The island became green with foliage, and I could smell the unfamiliar odor of land.

Because it is so isolated and unknown, Raivavae appeals to my imagination much more than did Tahiti. The *Sailing Directions* claim that about 800 people live there, but I saw no sign of man. I wonder if those who do live there, literally at one of the ends of the earth, appreciate their remote home, or do they long for the bright lights of Papeete or Chicago. I wonder what the view is like from the highest mountaintop and whether the wooded islets inside the reef are as peaceful as they seem.

Almost certainly I was seen from the island. Few boats pass this way, so I imagine that many Raivavaens are speculating this evening on who I am, where I came from, and where I am going. They are all good questions. I often speculate about them myself.

DAY 40 • *December 28*

THIS morning I noticed my patch on the mainsail coming loose, so I lowered the sail and restitched it. When I set it again, I put in a reef and then replaced the jib with the storm jib. We are now sailing more comfortably south at 7 knots against a 30-knot southeast wind.

There has been no sun today, so I am only guessing, but I believe we made about 140 miles yesterday and ought to be nearing the supposed end of the southeast gales, euphemistically known as the southeast trades. I do hope so.

DAY 41 • *December 29*

WHEN more than a month ago I wrote that I had been turned away from Cape Horn beyond even its outermost line of defense, I was wrong. Any wind that blows as hard as the southeast trades have done almost constantly ever since we crossed the equator are a formidable defense indeed.

We have sailed 2,000 hard miles hard on hard wind. It has been and continues to be hard on the hull, hard on the rig, and hard on my nerves. A few days of moderate weather before we get to the Forties would be most appreciated.

A few hours ago I realized it is Sunday afternoon, so I decided to go for a Sunday-afternoon sail. Because we continue to have about 25-30 knots of wind and sharp five foot seas, every third or fourth of which breaks across the deck, I put on full foul-weather gear before I took the tiller away from the fifty-cent scrap of line which has been the self-steering device since the $1,000 vane broke.

Within a minute, my head and face were drenched; but after accepting that as inevitable, I continued to steer, letting the bow fall off a few degrees, constantly shifting my attention from the sails to the telltale on the masthead to the telltale on the luff of the storm jib, to the waves coming at our port bow, losing myself in the experience as we danced across the sea.

My sense of well-being is immense. I truly love sailing and am grateful for these last few hours.

DAY 42 • *December 30*

EACH day is cooler than the one before as we sail farther and farther south in search of the west winds which will carry us east around the globe. Even today, with the sun shining, I need long pants and a heavy wool shirt to be comfortable.

We will have been at sea a week at 8:00 P.M. tonight and will have made about 900 miles, not much less than we made the first week out of San Diego. This has been almost all to windward. Egregious has fully met all my hopes about her ability to sail fast. Now, if only she would hold together.

TODAY is the finest of the voyage so far. I do not know exactly why I feel that because it has not been exceptional in any specific way. We are sailing smoothly and well. Nothing serious has gone wrong. The sun is shining. Air temperature neither too warm nor too cold.

I have spent the day cleaning the boat and myself, navigating, balancing the sails for self-steering, reading. In working the noon sight, I had to turn the chart. That portion now visible is completely void of land, which may be the source of my contentment. I have a sense of space and openness and solitude in this Southern Ocean that I have not known before. I love the idea of the empty seas before me. Sail on, Egregious, sail on.

THE terror I was experiencing exactly a week ago in Papeete is as real now as then. I can still see the breakers so close, just beyond the green light flashing on the buoy a boat's length away, still feel the overwhelming helplessness as we wallow in the swells. How good to be safely at sea. The land is the enemy in so many ways.

DAY 43 • *December 31*

FROM being a Southern California sailor who tends to add more and more sail, I have reverted during this voyage to my San Francisco days and now take more and more off. We are sailing hard on the wind under mainsail alone at 6 knots. With the jib up we gain another ½ knot, but the pounding into these waves becomes intolerable. One of these days we will reach the westerlies. Or so I keep telling myself.

ONCE again it is impossible to keep clothes dry. A moment ago, I heard something scraping on deck. I walked inside the cabin to the forward hatch and saw that the shackle had come undone on the tack of the storm jib. Simply by opening the hatch, I could reach out and tighten it. I did so and two waves broke over me before I could get my arms and shoulders back inside.

For the past two hours, the wind has been increasing steadily, so I have been frequently on deck to tie the tiller ever a little more to windward. I was just out and don't think I am going to bother trying to get a noon sight. It is not worth exposing the sextant to a certain saltwater bath. I feel as though I have been battling this head wind all my life and it really has only been for the past two months. "Stand to the south" is easier to say than to do.

I am drinking a New Year's toast to the women I left behind. After Tahiti, I have reason to wonder if any of them care for me as much as when I left San Diego; but for 1975, I wish only that they be happy and that I successfully complete this voyage.

You are all invited to the New Year's Eve dance in the main

ballroom. The captain is retiring to his quarters rather early, so please keep the revelry to within reasonable bounds.

DAY 44 • *January 1*

LAST night, after drinking myself into a stupor on half a glass of brandy, I slept the blind sleep of the intoxicated and had the best rest since leaving Papeete.

Then, quite considerately, about half an hour after I awoke this morning, the wind backed to the northeast, allowing us to reach south at 7 knots.

And as if all this were not enough, I also saw my first wandering albatross. A great white bird, perhaps half again as large as the albatross I saw north of the equator, he soared above the waves in our vicinity for more than an hour.

I have finished rereading Dana's *Two Years Before the Mast,* which concludes with his return voyage from San Diego to Boston in 1836 as a seaman aboard the *Alert.*

We made the equator four and one-half days faster than they did, but after that they sailed on south in what are described as normal trade winds, while I ended up in Tahiti. I have been feeling these past weeks as though Egregious and I have been hard used, which is true, but after reading how the *Alert,* making a midwinter passage of the Horn, was delayed for weeks by ice and easterly gales before she finally rounded the Cape, I realize that everyone who comes to sea is hard used sooner or later.

EGREGIOUS sails south quietly, except for squeaks from where the bolts continue to grind ever larger holes in the mast. I do not write about that more because there is nothing more I can do about it, although I realize the ultimate consequences of that grinding may be very serious. I sit on my berth and put aside the biography of the Duke of Wellington I have been reading and lean back and close my eyes and listen to the water gurgle past the hull, the splash of the bow wave. I breathe deeply and am filled with peace. I have earned these moments. Nothing artificial need be done to make the challenge of the voyage greater. My hands are cracked and nicked with cuts. My back is blue with bruises where the storm jib sheet flailed me like a medieval penitent the day before yesterday when Egregious came too far up into the wind while I was struggling with the mainsail. Salt encrusts my hair and face. My bare feet are always wet and cold. Soon the sun will set and I will heat a cup of tea and drink in its warmth. Tomorrow or the next day, the struggle will be rejoined. Again the wind and waves will test me, but for now I have earned this peace and I welcome it.

DAY 45 • *January 2*

THIS far south, the sky is light by 4:00 A.M. and does not darken fully until after 9:00 in the evening. Early-morning clouds burn away, and the days are cool and crisp.

I had a ridiculous time working my morning sun sight. I made mistakes in addition, read the sextant wrong, and found that when I changed the battery in the chronometer yesterday, I reset it precisely one hour slow. All this after having another exceptionally good night's sleep.

INCREASINGLY, Egregious becomes the cell of a monk who has taken a vow of silence and poverty. I have vowed to myself not to speak, which one would perhaps not have thought necessary. But at moments of sudden distress, such as unexpectedly being doused by a wave, a curse comes automatically to my lips.

SINCE I left Raivavae behind, I have been happier than any time since the voyage began. My life is reduced to the essentials for which I have longed. I keep alive. I sail. I read books by or about genius. I write. That is all. There is only beauty and greatness here. An exquisite balance of the physical and mental. I am alive as never before. May it last throughout the coming months.

THE barometer is at 30.40, more than half an inch higher than normal for this area 38° south of the equator. In mid-afternoon the wind dropped, and I raised the jib in addition to the main and storm jib, which were already set; and our speed increased from 5½ to 7 knots. This is the first time we have been under three sails since the second day out of San Diego, and now that the vane is broken, these three will be all I will use for the remainder of the voyage. In fact, we go so well under this combination, that the bigger sails may face permanent retirement.

Imagine having such weather here on the edge of the Roaring Forties.

DAY 46 • *January 3*

IN very light air, the bow wave as heard from inside the cabin is the gentle babbling of a brook flowing over smooth stones. As the wind and the boat's speed increase, it becomes a rushing stream, then a torrent; and finally, when hull speed is reached and exceeded as on the day when we sailed 9-11 knots, a roaring cascade, a violent thundering rapids through which the bow races.

Today, at 39°South, it is the most gentle of brooks.

TORTURED self-questioning is a disease of the land, a contagious disease to which in the past even I have been susceptible. However, here at sea, the question trails far behind the fact. I did not seek any reasons why I want to be silent; an answer simply came to me this morning while I was sitting in the cockpit, drinking my coffee and watching us sail. The sea and the boat are one. Between them exists a perfect harmony, broken only when the wind becomes overpowering. I, too, can become part of that grand harmony, but only by modifying myself to belong to it. Therefore, I—as vain a man as has ever lived—must discipline myself to merge with those elements of beauty which belong here.

* * *

ALONE at sea I am very close to the primitive source of religion: I am clearly in the power of inhuman natural forces. That fact is equally true for those who live in cities, but usually much less obvious. It is very easy—indeed, almost impossible—not to anthropomorphize those forces and, without believing or disbelieving in any gods or goddesses, I have accepted them as a useful fiction. As I wrote earlier, so much of what happens to one alone at sea seems to be directed personally at the solo sailor. My thoughts have turned toward some power other than myself both in times of stress and in times of comfort. I would like to be able to express my gratitude for the fine sailing of these last days, just as I cried aloud for help in Papeete Pass. The fallacy is the same in both instances. The forces are as blind when they seem kind as when they seem spiteful. And it has become very important to me that I accept them as such.

I believe that I am an articulate man, but this is not an experience to be articulated. No nouns, no verbs suffice. There is the sea, but it is unremarkable just now. There is the wind, light and backing toward the north. There is the sky, covered by a layer of low, fuzzy clouds. There is the cutter sailing smoothly southeast. Nothing is exceptional other than the overwhelming sense of peace, which has increased day by day and is now absolute. I have never been so calm and content. I am always hungry, yet that only renders my senses more acute. A sailor is always aware of the wind, it is the great fact of his life, the medium of his art; but now I feel the wind more sensitively than ever before in my life. It touches my face, blows over my skin, enters my body, more essential than blood.

I have always psychologically and for the past several years physically lived on the edge of the human herd. All I have wanted from society is that it be well enough structured so that I can find its edge and live there. Yet, even on the edge, I was a part of herd life; and only now have the days at sea cleansed me. Somehow I always knew this peace was to be found here, and my disappointment in November was partially due to the realization that I was being turned back toward the land before I had experienced it. That this feeling will not last does not matter. That soon I will again be hard used by the wind and sea does not matter. As I naïvely—yet accurately—began this log: I was born for this. More then than I knew, I was born for this.

There is nothing ugly out here but me; and at this moment when I want for nothing, when I am no longer striving, when I am not in a process of becoming but of being, when I am whole, complete, one, transcendent, I am also transcended and do not exist, except as an essential part of the beauty around me. How incredible that this should happen here as I enter the Forties. How incredible that it should happen anywhere.

THE sea is steel-blue and the sky light grey. On the western horizon, a single pale yellow band lingers behind the already-set sun. Although it is dusk, there is a sense of dawn, of expectancy, of anticipation. I can easily believe that the world looked like this the first day after creation.

WHILE I drank my evening tea, I listened to my favorite Beethoven sonata—the Sonata in C—particularly the second movement whose gentle theme mingled with the sounds of the cutter slipping through the sea. Then Bach's Brandenburg Concertos. Bach and Beethoven belong here more than in any concert hall.

The peace is intact and enhanced and continues.

DAY 47 • *January 4*

I awoke this morning in the Forties and to an increasing northwest wind.

A storm is coming. The barometer has fallen precipitously from its unseasonable high of two days ago. Whitecaps are becoming prevalent. So prevalent, in fact, that this afternoon we almost sailed into two separate pods of whales before I saw them. Each pod consisted of about nine members, some of which were calves, all swimming slowly northward.

California grey whales pass very close to San Diego on their southerly migration to their breeding grounds each winter, and I have often sailed within a boat length of them without concern.

Somehow I feel differently on the open sea and gave those today all the room possible.

DAY 48 • *January 5*

EXCEPT for a few minutes in which I grabbed breakfast, I have been on deck making sail changes in a cold rain ever since I woke up this morning.

At midnight, Egregious was sailing at 8 knots amidst gale-force wind and waves. I pulled myself from my berth and saw we were still on the correct course, so I went back to bed. I woke several more times during the night; but again, although we continued to tear through the water and I feared an accidental jibe, it did not come and I returned to an uneasy sleep.

When I donned my foul-weather gear and went on deck at 7:00 this morning, I found that the storm had already made a good start at reducing what had been an orderly sailing vessel to chaos. The jib, which I lowered last evening and lashed to deck fittings, had blown free and was dangling over the side; the mainsail outhaul slide had broken, allowing the foot of the sail to lift and rip along the boltrope; and a line securing one of the blocks through which the storm jib sheet runs to the tiller was badly frayed.

Stowing the jib in the forepeak and replacing the frayed line were the work of only a few minutes, but the mainsail, as always, was uncooperative. I ended up putting the second reef in the sail rather than the first, because I lowered it about 5 inches too far for the first, and the wind was so strong that I could not hoist it back. It took more than an hour merely to accomplish what I did.

The two highlights of that exercise were a wave which broke completely over Egregious and me while I was working near the mast. There was a moment, which I will not soon forget, when I looked around and could not see the boat beneath the white water. It was as though I were standing on the boiling surface of the sea itself. And then, ten minutes later, while I was hanging onto the boom, trying to feed a reef line through a fairlead, an accidental jibe suddenly slammed the boom over and almost launched me into the water. As always, when on deck other than in the cockpit, I was wearing my safety harness, but getting back aboard in these seas with all the gear I have on and while the cutter continues to sail at 8 knots would be interesting, to say the least. In addition, I had seen a large shark off the bow as I was putting the jib below. Actually, I only saw a large shark fin, which I suppose could have been on a small shark with an endocrine imbalance. But I would rather theorize than obtain certain knowledge firsthand.

Finally, I was able to come below for a cup of coffee and some biscuits. No prisoner ever took more time or care with his meager rations. I broke each biscuit into three or four parts, even though I could easily eat a whole one in a single bite, and spread jelly on each piece separately. I chewed them slowly, savoring the flavor and texture.

No sooner had I regretfully finished the last bite of the last biscuit, when the boat jibed. Up to that moment, I had kept dry, but I had made the error of removing my foul-weather gear, and there was no time to put it back on. I leaped on deck to turn Egregious downwind. And, of course, by the time I had done so, I was soaked.

I returned to the cabin and, feigning a confidence I certainly did not feel, changed into dry clothes. As I finished dressing, obviously there had to be another jibe. But this time I decided that no matter what happened, I was not going on deck without foul-weather gear.

The jibes were being caused by the wind backing until it blew across rather than with the waves, which would then push the stern around far enough for the main to go over. The solution was to jibe intentionally onto the other reach, but to do so under these conditions is not simple.

The problem is that whenever the storm jib slats, as it must during a jibe, its sheet joins every available line at or near the mast in a knot compared to which that of ancient Gordius was a mere slipknot. Often this creates the interesting dilemma that I cannot get the boat to self-steer until I clear the knots, and I cannot clear the knots until I get the boat to self-steer. On this particular occasion, the knot consisted of both jib sheets, the tail of the jib halyard, part of the main topping lift, the spinnaker-pole topping lift, and the end of a running backstay. All of which had been neatly coiled only moments before.

THE air today is not especially cold, but the rain is numbing; and although I have managed thus far to keep my second set of clothes dry, my face and hands never become warm.

By far the most trying aspect of the voyage so far has not been heavy weather, but the constant tension caused by breakage. In these past twelve hours, the holes around the mast bolts have almost doubled in size, so now the mast moves as much as if there were no bolts at all.

DAY 49 • *January 6*

AT 4:00 A.M. I awoke to the all-too-familiar sound of breaking metal. My first glance was to the mast bolts; my next to the lower shrouds. The upper tang on the starboard lower shroud is broken. This is the same tang that broke before, but on the other side of the mast.

The rain had stopped and the wind returned to the south. With the broken tang, the mast was bent in a great concave arc. As quickly as possible, I jibed so that the intact port rigging would be to windward.

Our present course is a broad reach to the northwest, directly back toward Tahiti. This is the only point of sail off the wind on which I can get the boat to self-steer. In winds of more than 30 knots, the storm jib overpowers any number of shock cords on the lee side of the tiller and pulls the bow off until the jib is blanketed by the main and the cords can bring us back up again. Fortunately, the resulting yawing path is usually a safe course through big waves.

I believe I am truly resigned to whatever happens from now on, and the breakage was certainly not unexpected. Ever since we left Papeete, I have watched the mast move about increasingly despite my efforts to stop it, knowing that when it became loose enough, something would probably break higher up.

Although our course is toward Tahiti, I do not have the least intention of returning there. When conditions moderate, even if we have to sail back into the Thirties, I will go up the mast and try to replace the tang with one of the spares sent to me in Tahiti. I am not yet through trying to get around Cape Horn, although frankly I have little remaining hope.

DUSK. I stand in the companionway, drinking my evening cup of tea, looking aft through the plexiglas at the black waves looming up behind us, and listening to Saint-Saens's Third Symphony, whose grand organ finale struggles against the renewed storm. Two albatross wheel and turn above the breaking crests, down which we sometimes surf at 10 knots, entirely faster than I want to go. But I cannot reduce sail any further and maintain self-steering.

Most sailors tend to exaggerate the force of the wind and the size of the waves in heavy weather, so, with a reverse snobbism, I strive not to do so and perhaps tend to understate conditions. All this afternoon I kept trying to tell myself that the waves were diminishing; only to find, whenever I left the cabin, that they had actually increased. Conditions outside now are those of a standard 40-knot gale: high seas, whitecaps, blowing foam, acute discomfort.

Once, in mid-afternoon, we almost got into serious trouble when an errant wave struck us hard amidships and spun us so far up into the wind the jib could not bring us back. But before I could get on deck, another wave came along, hit us on the opposite beam, and pushed us onto our original course.

I have considered and rejected heaving to as being too hard on the mast. We are simply going to have to run this one out.

DAY 50 • *January 7*

TODAY is miserable. The wind has increased, but the waves have not, and we are being thrown around and about and to and fro. There is no way I can go up the mast, and the sky remains too overcast for any sights. The best that can be said is that at least we are no longer setting a speed record in the wrong direction.

DAY 51 • *January 8*

MID-AFTERNOON. Bright sunshine. Blue sky. A light west wind. I am in considerable pain. And we are sailing at 4 knots toward Cape Horn.

I am amazed to have been able to replace the tang so soon, but when the waves diminished until there was only a 2-foot swell running this morning, I took the chance.

Going up the mast alone at sea is somewhat different than in port, as can be demonstrated by the cuts and abrasions all over my legs. The entire operation required three round trips to the lower spreaders—the first two to run lines around the mast to stabilize it while the lower shrouds were slack, and the last to replace the tang itself—each made by hoisting myself in a bosun's chair with a block and tackle. Even with the relatively small swell, I all too often found myself clinging to the mast one moment, then swinging out over the sea the next. The trip out isn't too bad; but the one back in is. When finally every bolt, nut, and cotter pin was back in place and I was able to lower myself to the deck, I was very close to being seasick and very grateful the tangs break on the lower shrouds and not at the masthead.

None of my wounds is serious, but I look as though I fought a duel with a dwarf. And lost.

DAY 52 • *January 9*

THIS voyage is becoming curiouser and curiouser. The light wind of yesterday has died away, but the swell has increased and we are becalmed amidst 5-foot waves rolling up from the south. Becalmed in the Roaring Forties. Rolling, tossing, turning in circles becalmed. Mast swaying, rigging snapping—which is of course just what it needs—becalmed. Unsteerably, sickeningly becalmed. Grand.

AT sunset, we are sailing east at 2 knots. If the swell were not so disproportionate to the wind, we would be moving twice as fast; but not only have the waves not decreased, we are at present being visited by an occasional 8-foot swell from the west.

Light lingers in the sky long after the sun has dropped below the horizon. As it fades, I wonder what is out there coming toward us.

DAY 53 • *January 10*

THIS is totally beyond understanding. The wind blows at 20 knots from the north, and 10-foot swells come up from the south. As one might imagine, the cross seas are appalling. They hit us from every angle and at practically every instant. Alternately, we find ourselves raised high on a promontory, looking down at the sea around us; or deep in a confused trough, looking up at mountains of water above us. I have tried steering northeast and southeast; but neither is an improvement, so we continue doggedly due east.

DAY 54 • *January 11*

I am going home. Or to be more precise, I am going to attempt to get this boat back to San Diego before the mast falls down. The tang I replaced—what was it, three or four days ago?—broke at noon.

The wind is now blowing at over 30 knots from the south. And, of course, we are sailing back toward the northwest again; and, of course, I will attempt to replace the tang again when conditions improve again.

But this breakage has convinced me that there is no chance—

none at all—that the rig will survive 16,000 more miles in the Forties and Fifties.

The mast ought to be supported at five points: the mast step, at deck level, the lower spreaders, the upper spreaders, and at the masthead. Only the last two of those are intact. The mast step is out of alignment to port, the welds at the flanges on the side supports inside the cabin are cracked on both sides, the bolts running through the mast have eaten huge holes in it, the starboard aluminum support has come adrift from the overhead and moves vertically and horizontally with the mast, and the starboard lower shroud is useless.

I will not rationalize; I will not make excuses. No matter what is wrong with Egregious, I am the one who chose her for this very voyage. In retrospect, I wish I had kept my old boat. I am the victim of my own greed for something a little bigger, a little faster, a little more expensive and prestigious. She has cost too much of my life to have failed so badly.

I wonder if the hours of peace I knew last week are to have been the zenith of my life.

THE schizophrenic wind has swung back to the north, and we have no choice but to reach off toward the southeast again. This storm is rapidly becoming the worst I have ever known, and 15-foot waves sweep the deck. The mast leaps and twists. The wind blasts through the rigging with the high-pitched whine which gives the Roaring Forties their name.

I find myself thinking that this is all pointless now. Why won't the wind let me go? First it breaks my boat, so I cannot go on; then it reverses direction, to prevent me from sailing toward home. What does the wind want of me?

And, of course, the wind wants nothing; the ocean does not know I exist. There is no more vengeance here than mercy. But at the moment I have difficulty in not thinking of the elements as malevolent.

NIGHT. The waves continue to build. I cannot accurately judge their height, but they are greater than those this afternoon. Perhaps more than 20 feet high now. The barometer falls rapidly. Rain drives down. We rush through the darkness on a direct course for Cape Horn at 8-10 knots. A few hours ago, that would have been cause for satisfaction; now it means only that we are being forced ever deeper into the Forties, ever farther away from safety.

. V .

DAY 55 • *January 12*

THE rain smooths the jagged edges from the great waves. The view aft is wild and cold and bleak. One breaking crest after another rushes down upon us. The white panthers of the sea: as graceful, as powerful, as deadly. The wind gusts to 50 knots and creates a medium of absolute change: barren, shifting, flowing, breaking, sliding, foaming, spraying, running, hissing, smashing, whistling, roaring, pounding. We are still being bludgeoned to the southeast. I have no fear for our survival, but I wonder how much more the mast can take. One of the shock cords on the tiller broke this morning, and the mainsail jibed instantly. A few more such incidents, and we will no longer be cutter rigged.

I have ceased to play the would-be saint. After carefully preparing a cup of coffee this morning, I took one step from the galley and a wave hit us broadside, knocking me backward and spilling hot coffee over everything. My curses would have done any sailor proud. One might say my vow of silence has gone to hell.

EVENING. A dismal scene. Icy rain still pours down. Waves bombard us from the port beam. The sky solidly overcast and starless. A damp cold makes my bones ache. However, the wind has decreased to 40 knots.

My response to the most recent breakage surprises me. I find that I do not care. I think I will go back to San Diego and return to work and live a quiet, normal life. I long for the fragile beauty of flowers in bloom and green fields and thickly wooded hillsides and for the soft caress of a woman I love. That my twenty-year dream should die overnight does not seem possible. Yet it seems to be true. And I have no regrets.

DAY 56 • *January 13*

THE storm has passed, leaving swells from the north and a light wind from the south, before which we wallow northeast at 2 knots. The sails collapse and refill an average of fourteen times a minute.

THE numb indifference which protected me yesterday is gone. I feel acutely the pain of failure, but with that pain has come the knowledge that I will again attempt to sail around the world alone. I do not know if I will be able to try again this coming November, or if I will try again in this boat. My own words sustain me: If I truly believe in myself, I have no choice but to persist.

NOW, in mid-afternoon, the sea is glassy; the swells mere lumps of water. We drift west at 1/2 knot. I have no desire whatsoever to go west, but there is nothing I can do to prevent it. First, too much wind driving us southeast; now no wind at all. I cannot go forward; I cannot go back. The ocean has worn me out. I need to rest and would give almost anything to be ashore, to be far from this war of attrition, far from the great gaping wound caused by a thousand tiny abrasions. We spin helplessly in circles; the mast slams against the deck opening. San Diego is 5,000 miles distant, and I doubt we will get away from here before another storm overtakes us.

EVENING. Some wind has returned and enables us to make 5 knots to the northeast. During the calm I got some useful sun sights and found we are at 129°West, 44°South.

* * *

DURING all too much of my life I have played the role of the extraordinary man who would be a hero in a decadent age, the original individual who could find fulfillment only at sea.

Yet I have known and said that I am not only a sailor, but also a writer and a voluptuary and an ascetic. This voyage has brought me some fulfillment, and, if successful, certainly would have brought me more. But it has also brought the understanding that I will not find complete fulfillment at sea anymore than I have found it in women or solitude or writing. I have said that I am a child, but to have thought as I did that my life would be a success after the completion of this voyage, was being too much of a child.

Nothing seems important tonight. Everything has failed.

AS the sky grows dark I am listening for the first time on the voyage to Bach's "Little Fugue in G Minor," which I had planned to save until I was off Cape Horn. Its development from delicate opening notes to a powerful conclusion seemed perfect for that triumphant moment. Now there is no reason to wait.

Johann, you never could have suspected when you wrote your music two hundred years and thousands of miles ago, that one desolate night it would assuage the grief of a peculiar, mutilated man alone among the waves of a southern sea. I would gladly give my life to have written anything as perfect as your "Little Fugue" or the Arioso, or any of a hundred other of the works that fell from your prodigal soul; and I would have been more proud to have been you than any other man who has ever lived.

DAY 57 • *January 14*

I watch the ocean for hours, trying to compare it with my past experience; but there are no analogies, or rather all of the analogies are from the ocean to the land. Now, when I return to the shore and think of gliding grace, it will be of the wandering albatross; of power and majesty, the great waves of this inhuman ocean; of austere beauty, the dying light of evening along the western horizon.

LAST night I deliberately turned Egregious back toward Cape Horn. It is not an act of which I am proud. I had just reread my brave boasts of the past, and they overcame all logic and reason. Unfortunately, they do not make the rig stronger and they will not keep the mast up in a gale. After lying sleepless in my bunk for three hours, I went on deck and changed course to the northeast.

The longer I am at sea, the more I value discipline. In the past two days, mine has collapsed. I have started to talk; I have gone onto the foredeck several times without wearing my safety harness; and I let myself unnecessarily endanger Egregious last night in an act that was not heroic but foolish. Even if the mast stays up, I have thousands of miles and months of sailing before reaching San Diego. I must not allow self-pity to destroy me. I must control my emotions and make the best I can of the remainder of this voyage. I will not throw myself blindly to fate, and I will not succumb to the impatience that almost cost me the boat at Papeete. Cape Horn is not for me this year. I will not waver again.

EVENING. The day continued cold, rainy, grey, and mean. Yet, almost as soon as I wrote this morning's passage, my mood improved.

For the moment, I have quieted the mast by wedging my largest screwdriver between it and the deck opening. I don't expect that will do much good for long, but perhaps I will think of something better.

I am writing this after sunset, while drinking my evening tea and listening to music, this time Mozart. I just came below after setting Egregious on a reach to the northeast, the wind having backed to the west. The sun, which had not been visible all day, broke through the clouds for fifteen minutes while I was on deck, but I was so busy adjusting shock cords and the jib sheet, occasionally glancing back at the gold band of light so sharply defined against black sea and sky, I did not notice until I turned to come below, one end of a rainbow forming off our port bow. Naturally, I lingered on deck; and as we drew closer, the rainbow became a complete arch through which we sailed.

DAY 58 • *January 15*

BY morning, the mast had mangled the screwdriver beyond all recognition, so I gave it an honorable burial at sea and then tried stuffing rags and towels to absorb the shock around the deck opening. They were pathetically ineffective. I finally ran a heavy line around the mast about a foot above the deck and then back to one of my cockpit winches. It does nothing to stop the movement from side to side, but seems to reduce the worst of the fore-and-aft oscillations.

DAY 59 • *January 16*

I dreamed last night that we were sailing into Capetown. Table Mountain vivid against a pure blue sky. White buildings clustered along the shore. Even in the dream I could not recall rounding the Horn, but I knew that because we were approaching Africa, Cape Horn must be safely behind us.

AN eerie night. There is no moon, and the stars are obscured by clouds. We sail through absolute blackness. No phosphorescence outlines wave or wake. Always there has been some light, but tonight not the least glimmer. The light and dark of space have become one and none, as though primordial currents were again flowing blindly toward another unknowing genesis. I peer about, futilely seeking any variation in shade or form, but the cutter ghosts from nothing into nothingness, until I add to the depths of obscurity by falling asleep.

DAY 60 • *January 17*

INDIGO sea, blue sky, scattered fluffy white clouds, gentle breeze. I stand away from myself and observe once again how quickly my mood changes with the wind and sea. There is every reason why it should in this solitary life concerned only with the necessities of keeping alive and sailing.

Yet I do not want to resign my spirit completely to blind forces. I will allow the sea to give me only temporary sorrow, but lasting joy.

BEFORE lunch, I made a new top slat for the companionway from two spare vanes for the self-steering device. Keeping the plexiglas permanently in place was making the cabin too warm and stuffy. But now that the companionway is open, odors to which I have become accustomed are all too pungent. Particularly that emanating from a mountain of wet clothing, some of which has progressed far beyond mere mildew and is, I fear, beginning to ferment.

I am amazed that I almost sense the return of that peace I knew a few weeks ago while sailing south. I do not allow myself to think about Cape Horn. The breakage of the tang six days ago seems much more remote than that. I do not think forward or back. The sea stretches around me for thousands of miles and makes a cocoon in which to enfold my solitude. The nearest men are on islands a thousand miles away. My mind knows that as a fact; yet other people do not actually exist for me now, and I rejoice in being at this moment the most alone man of the billions on earth.

DAY 62 • *January 19*

THERE was a novel of the French Resistance in World War II called *The Silence of the Sea*. I remember it because the title, which was meant to imply the contrast between the surface calm of the ocean and the violent struggles of creatures within its depths, seems a particularly apt description of my passage over the ocean.

I see very little of the life of the sea—a few birds, two pods of whales, two sharks, a few porpoise, flying fish, baby squid—and that is all in more than two months. Often my thoughts try to penetrate beneath the waves, to dive down through a thousand fathoms to the lives and dramas being enacted there.

Obviously I do not know what is happening below me. I look over the side of the hull and see the foam of our wake, a few clouds of bubbles a few feet beneath the surface of the water left briefly by our passage. Whatever life is there is as effectively shielded from me as all life on this planet is shielded from that which lives in the rest of the universe, and seems as obscure and insignificant.

But that is a fallacy. I feel at one with whatever creatures exist beneath me and at one with my friend sailing the seas of the third planet of Antares. I live a primitive life naked between the great cold sky and the great cold sea. They and the rest of the dead universe are nothing. We who live are everything.

WITHOUT believing in the occult, I knew yesterday that Mary has fallen in love with someone else and that they were talking at that very moment about what would happen when I do return.

LONG after sunset, I remained in the cockpit, listening to music and watching the moon through the clouds.

To know true beauty—the great artists, and the sea, and a boat under sail, and a few women—is to be at war with the gratuitous clutter of society. Only a demagogue could find beauty in a crowd.

DAY 64 • *January 21*

MOANS, groans, and squeals from the mast. Blocks banging. Sails snapping. Hull creaking. Egregious rolling so badly that I could hardly stay in my bunk, which really did not matter because I did not get much opportunity to be there anyway.

Last night, in short, is better forgotten. All yesterday forgotten. Our day's run was negative. Repeat negative. We made 14 miles north and 45 miles west. San Diego is farther away than it was twenty-four hours ago.

This morning we were completely becalmed until noon. I lowered the mainsail and restitched a couple of seams. And then, at long last, I hauled myself up and replaced the broken tang. Despite what I consider to be excessive practice, that chore has not become any easier. In fact, the motion at the lower spreaders was incredibly bad. Worse by far than I remembered it being in the Forties, and I would very gladly never go up there at sea again.

These are the horse latitudes, so called because in the days of square-riggers, ships were often stuck here so long that livestock died from lack of water and were thrown overboard. Having no horses, I threw myself overboard instead and had a very pleasant swim, after the initial bite of salt water into my freshly lacerated legs.

The water is very warm, and I stayed in for quite some time. Here, in mid-ocean, I felt no differently than if I had been swimming in a harbor, although I did cheat somewhat and kept a line from the boat tied around my waist.

I noticed that her name has been erased from both bows by the incessant waves, but in no other way does Egregious show sign of having sailed some 8,000 miles in the past two and one-half months. She is like a beautiful woman whose face denies an internal cancer.

AT noon I sensed the least breath of wind coming from the north and managed to turn the boat that way. Gradually we began sailing again. At 1 full knot.

Speed is always relative, but never more so than when you have been becalmed. I would see a patch of darker-ruffled water ahead and steer carefully toward it. In time it would be only a hundred yards away. Then twenty. My anticipation grew. Then the bow was in it and I could feel—if barely—the zephyr against my face and chest. I looked at the knotmeter. 1 knot. 1.1. 1.2. Already a 20 per cent gain. Hosanna! Then 1.1. That is all there is—2/10 of a knot? And I would slowly—so slowly—glide on.

But at 12:30 a real wind of 8 full knots came up from the northwest, and we are at this moment sailing north at 4½. May it last. Oh, may it last.

3:00 P.M. It didn't.

DAY 65 • *January 22*

BY the margin of 11 miles, we are out of the Thirties. I had moments—even hours and days of happiness there—but I cannot say I am sorry to have left them behind. I was beginning to believe we might sail forever between 31°-30°South and 122°-121°West.

IN the early evening I read until 8:30, when I went on deck to watch the gibbous moon appear and disappear behind scattered clouds and the moonlight sparking on the water and the pale sails against the night sky.

I have intentionally not listened to any news on the radio and did not read newspapers while in Tahiti, so I do not know what has happened in the world during the last months. Yet tonight I found myself thinking that beneath this moon, men are killing one another across a geography of insanity. I wonder if any of them look at the moon—my moon—before they kill.

The silent life which I have composed for myself here at sea seems unreal. Yet it is not, only fragile. I am open to the sea and moon; I live by the rhythms of the sun and wind; I gaze for hours at the waves and stars and find serenity in their contemplation. A serenity as real as any terrorist's bomb.

DAY 66 • *January 23*

NOT until I wrote the date did I realize that I left Papeete a month ago today. During that month, I sailed 1,600 miles south,

1,300 miles east, and about 800 miles back north. San Diego is still 3,700 miles away.

FORTUNATELY and unfortunately, I have developed the ability to fall quickly into a deep sleep. Fortunately, because the sleep I do manage rests me well; unfortunately, because when I am suddenly awakened, I must come back through infinite chambers of unconsciousness before stumbling up the companionway steps. At such moments, I am at my most vulnerable; and it would not be inappropriate for me to fall overboard some night, ending a life of trivial accidents with a trivial accident.

The wind which had been so steady; the wind I had come to respect, honor, and cherish; the wind which I trusted to last not only through the night, but for days and weeks to come; the miserable, sneaky wind died away after midnight. So I spent most of the predawn hours on deck, adjusting various lines 1/2 inch here, 1 inch there, in the heavy darkness made for sleep after the moon had set.

Under such conditions, Egregious actually does respond to changes in the helm. Very, very slowly, as though eternities were too brief a span. But she does respond. I fumble for the mainsheet I cannot see a foot away and let it out a fraction; then I make myself as comfortable as possible and watch the compass. For three eons, it remains unchanged; then—oh, joy—it moves. One degree. Then another. She is falling off the wind as she should, but I must wait to see if she goes off too far. The compass needle inexorably crawls past the course I would like to steer, but I am no longer so demanding as once I was. On and on, slow degree after slower degree. Just as I decide it has gone too far, it stops, rests for a millennium, almost as exhausted by its trek as I am; then, with an almost audible sigh, starts back. Now I must wait to see if she will go too far up into the wind. If she does not, if she stops in time and I am tired enough, I go below, knowing full well that in an hour, a breath of wind will touch the sails at precisely the moment to bring the bow about, or a wave will push it too far off, and I will have to go through the entire ritual again.

I do not exaggerate the pace of this enchanting pursuit. If anything I have not described it as tediously as it deserves. I spent a full hour—from 12:30 to 1:30 this morning—trying to get the boat to hold a course, any course at all, and finally met with sufficient success to go back to sleep—until 2:09.

10:15 A.M. Fifteen minutes ago, Egregious shuddered as we were struck by a great gust of wind. Whitecaps and 5-foot waves appeared where none had been for days. Heavy water drove across the deck and into the cockpit, covering me. It was all I could do to loosen the sheets, and it took all my strength to pull the tiller to windward. Long moments passed, with the cutter pressed down, sails slatting, mast throbbing, wave after wave coming on board, before the bow fell off onto a safer course.

Now we are surrounded by giant thunderheads, billowing high up into the sky. Rain falls west, north, and east of us. I am able to write only because I have the jib steering us on a broad reach off to the southwest at 8 to 10 knots. Even if this lasts only another hour, we will have lost more distance than we made all yesterday.

10:40 A.M. My patience is exhausted. Watching those hard and slowly earned miles rush away as we galloped southwest was too much. I decided we must try for at least a northwest course. We are shuddering along on a heading of 330°, burying the bow in wave after wave. If the mast comes down, I will never forget my stupidity; but to have continued as we were was intolerable.

2:05 P.M. The contrast between what is out there now and the calms we have been experiencing is incredible. I endured our pounding and creaking northwest as long as I could—too long, really—then went on deck a few minutes ago and hove to. A 30-knot wind and 5- to 10-foot seas are coming across our port bow; and even with the storm jib backed, we are being driven east at 4 knots.

4:00 P.M. Twice we have been completely underwater. Waves break everywhere, and two of them about five minutes apart covered the entire deck. I felt them strike surprisingly soft, hollow blows, then looked up at the skylight hatch—water, the forward hatch—water, the side ports—water. Certainly the duration of our immersion was only a few seconds each time, but it seemed much longer.

DAY 67 • *January 24*

I strive only to lose as little distance as possible; to try to gain continues to be out of the question. The compass reads east, but we are surely being pushed south as well. If this continues for another day, we will be back in the Thirties.

My hope throughout the night was that by morning we could try to sail again. At 5:30 I got up, looked out, and went back to bed.

Now, at 10:00 A.M., the waves are still a frenzied mob, dashing in every direction, crying for vengeance and power, thrusting up here, collapsing there, rushing on to storm a Bastille in which I am the sole prisoner.

6:00 P.M. We are sailing again, working hard against the seas, but both they and the wind are sufficiently diminished so that it does not feel as though we are being destroyed. When things improve beyond where I can do more than grind my teeth and hang on, there is an entire list of new chores to prevent me from becoming bored.

DAY 68 • *January 25*

AT 5:00 A.M. I was awakened by a nut falling from one of the two bolts that pass through the mast—I will not say "hold the mast," because they have each carved such a considerable tunnel for themselves that they now merely lie there in lethargy and indolence. Naturally, I have become more than sensitive to abrupt metallic sounds—not unexpected, just abrupt—and after my relief that nothing more serious was wrong, I replaced the nut and went on deck.

The wind was only 10 knots and had gone, at last, somewhat

east. I lowered the mainsail, unsnarled the diabolical tangle of halyards and backstays aloft, retied three of the luff slugs which had come undone, threw four flying fish overboard, and tacked. We are now sailing north. North. I may become hysterical. North. What a splendid word. What a splendid direction. North. I may compose an "Ode on the Joy of Tacking to the North."

THE sea is an asexual environment. There are no constant stimuli of advertising, television, movies, pretty women passing on the street; and often one is cold and wet and tired. Hardly erotic. But today my thoughts were ashore, and I was reminded of the first Duchess of Marlborough's entry in her diary on the day after the Duke returned from the continental wars, to the effect, "His Lordship pleasured me three times before removing his boots." I understand, Lady Marlborough. Perfectly.

DAY 70 • *January 27*

LAST night I discovered that the five bolts securing the port bulkhead forward of the mast to a plate fiberglassed to the keel have sheared off. I do not know how long they have been that way; perhaps they broke in our last storm. But the bulkhead is an important structural member. Now that it has broken loose, the flexion in the hull is much worse, and it is not impossible that Egregious will split wide open sometime in the weeks ahead. All I know is that we are going to San Diego or we are going to sink.

THIS is not sailing. It is wading through waist-deep mud. It is riding on a hippopotamus. It is struggle without glory, suffering without reward, battle without victory. We can sail nicely to the west, south, and east. But we cannot point closer than 60° of north.

Every day is the same, and as the boundary of sleep between them continually erodes, they become one immensely long day which began ages ago and may end inconceivable eons hence. I sleep and read and eat, all with countless interruptions to rebalance the helm. Sleep is shallow, and I am always half-asleep and half-awake. Because my mind is dulled and because of the interruptions and the constant nagging thoughts of our lack of progress, I cannot concentrate on books. There is nothing to enjoy, nothing to look forward to except the theoretical wind-shift which ought to come sometime and put an end to the torment of this endless day of days.

BECALMED between rain clouds. If I could end this voyage at this moment, I would gladly do so. I am at my nadir and know my outlook will change. But I know, too, that such moments will come again. I am glad my life is at least half over; living seems an insupportable burden.

We made 75 miles yesterday, but will probably not do so well today.

DAY 71 • *January 28*

I have never been so pleased to admit I was wrong. Last evening at about 9:00 the wind increased and swung west, providing us with our most productive night's sailing in weeks: due north at 6 knots on a port tack. This morning conditions remain unchanged. We are well within the normal boundaries of the southeast trades, but with a west wind. As long as we are able to sail north, I don't care where the wind comes from.

A winter's sea outside. Grey, steep, cresting waves, spray blowing. A day for reading Thomas Hardy in the cabin. We continue north at almost 6 knots. Foul weather but fair progress. The southeast trades are apparently extinct.

THE sea and sky form one somber grey shroud, through which the sun does not quite shine and the moon is not quite filtered. Daylight imperceptibly becomes night with no change of color, for of color there is none; but only the least change of brilliance, grey becoming greyer.

I do not mind. This anomalous west wind has carried us farther north in the past twenty-four hours than we made in the preceding week. The ride is not pleasant; there are no sunsets to admire; dampness pervades the cabin. Gladly would I sail like this all the way home. I can take it if Egregious can—or, more accurately, I can take it and I hope Egregious can.

DAY 72 • *January 29*

THIS morning, individual clouds became distinguishable, and the sun appeared sufficiently long to enable me to be disappointed by our latitude of 23°South. Then, in the afternoon, the sky was divided diagonally from northwest to southeast. Behind us storm and ahead clear blue. At the frontier were seas of hopeless confusion.

SAILING 5,000 miles at 2 and 3 knots is the most difficult task I have faced, much more trying than any storm. I recall not too long ago when I was happy with 7 or more knots, pleased with 6, and satisfied with 5½. Now I am content with 3, pleased with 4, joyous with 5, and apprehensive with 6.

DAY 73 • *January 30*

WHILE visiting the deck about 3:00 A.M., I saw the constellation Scorpio and naturally thought of my friend voyaging on the burnished seas of the third planet of Antares. I imagine those seas literally to be burnished, of copper which cooled and solidified in an instant; forming truly unchanging waves, over and through which he glides in an incredible bark as easily as a thought. I hope your voyage goes well and that you have fair winds.

TOO often it seems that no matter how much or how little one wants of life, he always gets less; and, if in an effort to be free, he allows himself only a few desires, even they will be denied. All I want at present is a fair wind. That is not an unreasonable request in the heart of an alleged trade-wind belt, but apparently it is too much. We continue becalmed and made 37 miles in the day ending at noon.

To look upon whatever happens on this voyage and maintain my vow of silence becomes increasingly important to me. However, maintaining that vow has become a trial of sufficient hardship that I believe I will celebrate this evening with a libation more potent than tea.

Being becalmed is not the greatest disaster in the universe, and I am aware that at this very moment this planet—and no doubt millions of other planets—are filled with beings tormented by hunger, disease, and war. Being becalmed is not even the worst thing that can happen to me. Falling overboard and drowning—which would be quite impossible at the moment unless I had the wisdom not to bother to climb back aboard because Egregious certainly isn't going anywhere—and being dismasted are far worse. More or less in that order. Yet within the limited environment in which I live, being becalmed is bad enough.

In a calm, I realize that the ocean is not much in itself; no more interesting than a block of granite before a sculptor makes something of it. I have had all too extensive an opportunity to survey this particular expanse of water, and can testify that it is blue, smooth, glassy, unmarked by any sign of life—excluding myself, who certainly ought to be excluded because I do not consider this living—reflects clouds nicely, and extends from one horizon to another. That is about all there is to be said for it, yet I so love it here that I am taking up permanent residency.

DAY 75 • *February 1*

AT sunset, I look over the side at the handful of lonely bubbles which constitute our wake. I seem to remember sometime in the distant past when we wore a great rushing white mane there.

Day follows day follows day and we sail nowhere.

January	20	63	miles
	21	minus 31	
	22	45	
	23	36	
	24	46	
	25	50	
	26	80	
	27	44	
	28	121	
	29	123	
	30	37	
	31	20	
February	1	21	

Just think what it would have been if I didn't have a fast boat.

The two great days of 121 and 123 were those of the storm from the west. I remember them as glimpses of heaven.

DAY 76 • *February 2*

THIS morning, clouds began to appear in the north, marring this otherwise unblemished empyrean, this crystal sphere, this perfect orb, this windless waste. They marched down on us like the chorus marching onto an empty stage in a Greek play, no doubt chanting a threnody, and brought with them some light and irregular wind, which has already died away.

I am growing old here.

OUR situation as another sunset nears is that we are beneath the clouds I saw coming over the horizon earlier; clouds I desperately hoped would bring wind. All day we edged toward them or perhaps they edged toward us. Now we reach them and are becalmed.

I cannot remember when our boat speed last exceeded 3 knots, or when I could get Egregious to steer closer than 65° either side of north. I cannot leave the cockpit for more than fifteen minutes and often not even for five. This morning I could not eat a single biscuit without having to stop to move the tiller.

The bow points 055°. I turn and look north as though I could see 3,000 miles to where this ocean ends in surf on Mission Beach and wonder if those I love ever walk beside those waves, gaze south, and think of me. If they do, they will imagine me near Cape Horn. But I am not among the great waves of the Southern Sea. There is no glory in my ordeal. No joy. No sense of accomplishment. Only the disappointing, frustrating days wearing on my soul.

DAY 77 • *February 3*

NOON. Conditions are unchanged, but my mood somewhat improved. I have deliberately turned my thoughts away from the present and picture in detail what I will do the first day back in San Diego; of how I will surprise Mary, who will not be expecting me for three or four more months, of an Italian restaurant where I will eat vast plates of manicotti and finish the dinner with spumoni ice cream. I plan other voyages. Particularly to India and perhaps one day the Northwest Passage.

Briefly my thoughts return to the present when I work the noon sight. Day's run: 48 miles. Did we ever really sail under storm jib and double-reefed main at 10 knots, or under bare poles at 5? Such thoughts only lead to renewed pain. I must think of something else. Perhaps I would rather have Lebanese food than Italian.

DAY 78 • *February 4*

DAY'S run ending noon: 144 miles.

The transition was as abrupt as it was complete. Early yesterday afternoon, we were oozing along, when in a span of five minutes the wind increased and swung east, our course became north, our speed 6 knots.

However, with that increased speed, the mast again awakens, snaps, and growls; and once roused from its slumber, resumes with increased vigor its slamming dance and metallic song. And it has now broken the port aluminum side support free from the overhead. My blessings on you mast. I look up at the universe tonight and find it a worthy adversary. Only yesterday life seemed interminably long; today, all too brief.

DAY 79 • *February 5*

WE took seven days to sail from 22°-20°South, and now we have come from 20°-15°South in two.

A most handsome bird flew with us, this morning, gliding ahead, settling upon the waves, watching us sail by, then flying ahead again. His head and back are a chocolate brown, his breast and the undersides of his wings white. I believe he is a sooty albatross and was looking for garbage from our passage. If so, he chose the wrong vessel; there are no leftovers here. Not a scrap.

I suppose I will not be fully aware of how this voyage has changed me until I am back in port with familiar people and surroundings as benchmarks, but occasionally I see signs of physical change now.

Last night I noticed my hands. The skin is rough and hard; my fingertips are constantly peeling; calluses have formed on the palms; nicks and gouges are always in the process of healing. The hands of a sailor.

Another change is my weight. I am six feet tall and normally weigh about 150 pounds. Without a scale aboard, I do not know my present weight exactly; but from the increased prominence of my ribs, I estimate I have lost 15 pounds.

The constant tension caused by the mast, the hull and being becalmed, can best be measured by my heartbeat. Before I left on the voyage, my pulse at rest was fifty-two per minute. For the past weeks it has steadily increased, and this evening it is sixty-eight. Perhaps it is just as well that I don't know my blood pressure.

DAY 81 • *February 7*

TODAY we completed the seven thousand mile circle and are now again where we were November 21 at 10°South.

I stare beyond the empty western horizon and see a yellow hull slash south at 8 knots through foaming waves; I see myself sitting in the cockpit, one elbow crooked around a winch to hold myself in place. And, even as I watch, I see my attention being caught by a peculiarity in the port lower shroud. I see my eyes follow it up to a broken tang. The boat dashes over three more waves. Then I see myself disengaging the tiller lines from the vane; the bow turns into the wind, jib and mainsail crack and slat. Then they settle down, jib backed. The vessel is hove to. The attempted circumnavigation is over, although I do not know it.

That moment is too real. I could not recall the exact dates the tangs broke the second or third time without checking this log, but I will always remember November 21, 1974.

Conditions are very different now than then, although we are on the same point of sail, a close reach. Headwinds when we went south; headwinds when we go north. But today we have only a 14-knot breeze and 3-foot waves.

I am glad I did not give up in November, that I sailed on, even though the succeeding weeks were replete with frustration and breakage and failure. To have stopped then would have been premature. I would not have been certain that the mast could not stand up to the Forties, and I would not have been alone at sea long enough to find the hours of contentment that came in spite of the abandonment of my hopes to sail around the world alone this year.

DAY 82 • *February 8*

PICTURE a lean, tanned naked body crowned with a battered dark brown felt hat, brim turned down, beneath which is a face largely obscured by sunglasses and moustache and white sunscreen lotion, and you have the lone yachtsman braving the terrors of the deep. Whenever I need to laugh, I have only to find the mirror.

I have felt somewhat ill today, and the reason is overeating. Now that I am back in what ridiculously enough seem to be home waters, I have plundered the stores of my favorite items.

Food was never of much importance to me ashore, but I find at sea that I crave new tastes as never before. This is one of the few new sensations available, and I have no willpower to curb my appetite now that there is no necessity to do so. Consequently, there have been almost no sweets aboard for quite some time, no candy, no cookies, no dried fruit, and I am making great inroads on the canned fruit.

Basically, my provisioning for the voyage was appropriate, and I will take about 90 per cent of the same supplies on future voyages. The only food I have found that I simply cannot eat is canned shrimp, which was intended for shrimp curry. My unvarying breakfasts of biscuits and lunches of wheat germ are dull but acceptable, and I have found a number of ways to prepare the canned beef, chicken, and tuna fish, which constitute most of my dinners.

My present gastric distress is primarily due to the discovery this afternoon of a one-pound canned ham, which I sliced and fried and ate forthwith, followed by two cans of peaches. I am unconscionably bloated and sincerely repent of my sins.

DAY 83 • *February 9*

LAST night I thought it before I climbed into my sleeping bag and I thought it this morning while I was eating my breakfast in the cockpit, and I thought it again just now in the early afternoon: I am very much going to miss this sea life when I am ashore. Miss the total freedom and miss the evenings when I take my cup of tea into the cockpit and watch the night fall, and miss the moment later when I take a last look at the stars through the main hatch and blow out the kerosene lamp and go to sleep to the sounds of the sea.

THE ocean is full of life today. Flying fish are constantly taking flight, both from us and from unknown underwater pursuers. And at about 10:00 A.M. more than twenty porpoises came to frolic around the bow for a few minutes.

Not long afterward I saw a sea serpent—or rather a serrated brown ridge emerge from the crest of a wave 10 yards off our beam. Further observation revealed it to be the shell of a huge sea turtle.

And now, for the past hour, we have been followed by the fins of three sharks.

Surprisingly, with all this life in the water, the only bird present has been a solitary petrel; so small that I fully expect one of the flying fish to leap out and eat him.

DAY 84 • *February 10*

THIS morning I am remembering with some embarrassment the thoughts and conversations I had about my motives before I left on this voyage. Almost all of what I said then seems to me now to have been nonsense. I believe that my motives have become apparent in this log and would add only the following passage from *The Sea and the Ice*, a book I have been reading about Antarctica by the naturalist, Louis Halle:

> One can only speculate on the reason for the penetration of skuas, penguins, and seals into a region so extensive where no life can survive for long. Among crowded or colonial species of birds, the course of evolution has sometimes produced impulses leading to the dispersion that is necessary if inbreeding is to be avoided. The young feel an

impulse, not unknown to the young of our own species, to leave the parental home, to push out into the unknown, to make a new life for themselves beyond the horizon. . . .

Perhaps the impulse that moves skuas and penguins to set out from the rim of the continent . . . is not altogether unrelated to the impulse that impelled Captain Cook and his successors to seek a new world beyond the pack ice. That such voyages of discovery, potentially so rewarding, are hazardous, that they take a high toll of life, is true for skuas, penguins, and for man alike.

I reject all facile labels for myself, and "masochist" even more than "loner" or "suicidal." One does not come out here to suffer or die, but to live. And I have never been more alive. Pain is the price of my obsession; intensity and pride the rewards.

That any explanations are necessary, that adventure is no longer understood instinctively, that people have to ask, 'Why,' is proof of the decline of our civilization.

TONIGHT I am satiated with reading; the food has all been eaten too many times; the classical tape recordings have been heard too often. I crave some kind of new sensation, any new sensation. There is one lone canned cake left. I actually stand in the galley and hold the tin in my hands and gaze longingly at the picture on the label. But I have already promised myself that I will not eat it until I cross the equator, and finally, begrudgingly, I put it back on the shelf. Discipline must be maintained.

Then, for the first time since November, I turn on the radio to normal broadcast bands. Several California stations come in clearly. I get popular music, a commercial for life insurance, a hockey game, and a news broadcast from Los Angeles, with the following headlines:

> President Ford Says Possibility of War in Middle East
> President Ford's Energy Program to Cost Consumers $45 Billion in First Year
> Unemployment at 8.5%
> Inflation Increases at Record Rate

Greatest Manhunt in Los Angeles History for "Skid
Row Slasher"; Kills Nine since December
President of Malagasy Republic Assassinated

At times I have thought I belong everywhere, equally at sea and on land; but at other times, such as now, that I belong nowhere.

THE standard questions psychiatrists ask to determine if one is in touch with reality include "Do you know what year this is?" and "Who is the president of the United States?" and "Where are you at this moment?" I have no occasion to write 1975 for the date, and I had forgotten that Nixon was no longer president. These, combined with my normal vagueness as to our position, would probably result in my being certifiably insane. Many people have thought so for years.

> I want the sea
> for my unmarked grave
> but if I must have an epitaph:
>
>> winds and waves of torment cease
>> to become a poem
>> of this senseless voyage.
>> smile, fool, and sail on

DAY 85 • *February 11*

EARLY this afternoon we startled a school of flying fish whose lookout must have been asleep. They did not take flight until we were among them, and suddenly the air all around Egregious was filled with flashing silver shapes. Several arched completely over the deck; one passed only inches in front of my face, and another fell short and bounced onto my lap. Despite this indignity, I flipped him into the water before he expired.

126   *Storm Passage*

* * *

BACK during the calms of the Twenties, I started using one of my solar stills to make fresh water. There was no necessity; I was merely curious to find if it worked. Surprisingly, it does.

The still looks like a silver plastic beach ball 2½ feet in diameter, with a funnel at the top and a tube connected to a pouch at the bottom. You pour seawater in the funnel, it evaporates inside the ball from the heat of the sun, then condenses, and about 16 ounces of fresh water collect in the pouch each day.

The water tastes of plastic, but is palatable. I use it for washing. Consequently, both the dishes and I are much cleaner than we have been.

DAY 86 • *February 12*

SOMETIME while I am writing this entry, at 1:00 P.M., we are crossing the equator, after almost three months, more than 8,000 miles, one unscheduled stop, two broken tangs, two broken mast bolts, two sprung mast supports, one out-of-alignment mast step, countless snapped rudder bolts, one ripped bulkhead, two broken vane couplings, and assorted and sundry minor breakage.

I believe we will arrive in San Diego sometime in the first half of March, but cannot make a more specific prediction. We have ahead of us a long, wet, cold grind to windward, which will be considerably harder on the mast and hull than has been the sailing since the Forties. After about 1,000 miles of that, I may miss this sea life less than I think.

As I finish writing, it is 1:40 P.M. and we are in the Northern Hemisphere. I will go below and change the chart. Stumble on, Egregious, stumble on.

. VI .

DAY 87 • *February 13*

LAST evening I sustained an injury. It was not serious: just enough to remind me how quickly things can go wrong out here. As though I, of all people, could forget.

I had made a cup of tea, letting the water come to a full boil, and set it down on my berth for a moment while I reached for a book. Suddenly Egregious rolled, spilling the entire cup of scalding water onto my leg. I leaped up, but my trousers acted as a sponge and clung to me. By the time I could pull them off, a circle of skin the size of a half dollar came with them, and my entire thigh was bright red.

NOT long before the accident, I permitted myself to open the long-admired very last can of cake. To maintain my discipline and wait until we had crossed the equator was a great achievement. But once I cut into it, all self-control was lost, and I ate it all, literally wolfing it down.

DAY 90 • *February 16*

WE are sailing through the doldrums again, speed varying from 6-2 knots, but without the spectacular cloud formations or the squalls we had last November. Yesterday evening the wind began backing from the southeast to the northeast. Every quarter-hour after 8:00 P.M., I had to trim the sails flatter, until by 10:00 P.M. we were hard on the wind. Several times during the night, I was awakened by rain, lightning, and changing wind; but we were actually becalmed for only a half hour at about 3:00 A.M.

There is great phosphorescence in the water here, and during one of my spells on deck, three green wakes seemed to form spontaneously and speed directly toward us like torpedoes. At first I thought they might be sharks, but then it became obvious that they were porpoises. I never did see them, but their sinuous paths illuminated the sea around us for several minutes.

DAY 92 • *February 18*

I was able to sit outside and air my moldering flesh for two thirty-minute periods today without getting soaked; but now, after dark, the wind has increased, and water is an element of the sky.

The sailing since the equator has not been any worse than I expected. The fallacy is in expecting anything at sea to be as it "should be." I think I have learned to accept whatever happens wherever it happens whenever it happens. Gales where there should be calms; calms where there should be trade winds; ships where there are no shipping routes; and turtles who look like sea serpents.

DAY 93 • *February 19*

TO write about the mast as often as I think about it would be to fill this log with little else. I mention it again because now that we are going to windward, it has started to emit a cheeping sound, like a hungry baby sparrow. This cry comes from where it rubs continually against the port side of the deck opening. I would have thought the deck would have taken the worst of that chafing, but I would have been wrong. A groove has been worn about halfway through the mast wall. It is going to be a race to see whether we can get to San Diego before the mast shears off. I could change course and try for Acapulco, which we could reach on the other tack; but I will not.

WHILE I am writing about troubles, I should perhaps give some good news, but frankly I hesitate to do so. I would like to consider myself to be a rational man, but this voyage has made me superstitious. The superstition can be stated thus: the opposite of whatever I write will come true. When I write I have never been seasick, I become so; when I write the wind is steady, it dies; or that I am happy, I become discontent. Therefore I have deliberately refrained from writing about the rudder because I have seriously wondered if as soon as I do, it will resume groaning. I have, however, finally mustered sufficient courage to attempt an experiment by stating that the rudder has been perfectly quiet ever since the first week after we left Papeete. . . . Did I just hear something?

DAY 94 • *February 20*

I spend most of the daylight hours reading, huddled in the dry corner of the port transom berth, trying to avoid being dripped on by the black liquid composed of salt water and aluminum dust which runs in rivulets down the mast like blood from an accident victim.

I spend the evenings listening to the radio. This is something I would never do ashore. I seem to be starved to hear anything new and twirl the dial from one station to another.

I sleep on the port quarter berth, which is dry but from which the tripping, spastic motion of the hull is particularly accentuated.

DAY 95 • *February 21*

SAILING to windward for this long is like being in a prizefight. Constant jabs are thrown at your body, fifteen or twenty each minute as Egregious goes over average waves. Then, at intervals, three or four hard rights to the head, when she leaps and pounds against those larger than average. Each blow adds to the cumulative effect. I am stunned, confused. It is difficult to think in complete sentences. But this is not a ten-round fight or even fifteen. And there is no rest between rounds. Rather, it goes on continually, blow after blow, day and night, awake and asleep, hundreds of miles upon hundreds of miles, week upon week.

DAY 96 • *February 22*

TODAY is memorable because I discovered a package of dried figs which had fallen behind a shelf. I will try to make them last at least three days.

DAY 97 • *February 23*

THIS morning we crossed 20°North, which means San Diego is only a little more than 700 miles to the northeast. I know and do not regret that the secure idyllic life I left there last year is a shambles. I am eagerly looking forward to the landfall even though it will not be as I had hoped. For me always the outward voyage and never yet—perhaps never—the triumphant return.

EVENING. I just ate the last fig.

DAY 99 • *February 25*

SAILING is in all ways a reversion to the last century, but particularly so for those few of us who refuse to have engines or radio transmitters. In this age of instant communication, I am returning to the shore just as sailing ships did a hundred years ago. I know that in about a week I will see Mary, but at this moment she is thinking I am halfway around the world ... if she thinks of me at all.

DAY 101 • *February 27*

I am actually beginning to believe that the superstition about what I write has been disproved. The rudder has remained silent. So I will dare to say that I believe we just might get in without being dismasted. Hardly an unequivocal declaration, but the most I will venture until Point Loma is in view—make that astern.

As I noted a few days ago, we have been heading more northwest than north, so that by noon today we were 26°25′ North and 123°45′ West. The direct course to San Diego is 045°, which means that our long starboard tack is over. I brought Egregious about as soon as I had worked the position.

Today is Thursday and I had thought we might be in this weekend. But almost as soon as we changed course, the wind decreased and our present speed varies between 2 and 4 knots.

DAY 102 • *February 28*

THE sun is shining. The sky is clear. The temperature during the day warmer. And we made 5 miles from noon yesterday to noon today. Parmenides was right: motion is not possible. Obviously, there has been and is no useful wind. No, that is not true. To be fair, the normal ocean currents here push us southwest about 12 miles a day, so we have actually sailed about 17 miles in the last day. As I remember all too vividly, we have done worse.

DAY 103 • *March 1*

CALMS are harder for me to endure than gales. And this one—so close to home and safety—could be especially trying. But my adaption to the sea is complete, even if it has taken a hundred days to achieve. I can accept this calm. I would like to believe that I can accept anything, that I could lose Egregious as I almost did at Papeete, but without uttering a single word now. The constants of my life have become silence and self-discipline and openly facing the indifference of wind and sea.

DAY 104 • *March 2*

AT first I thought it was a whale. There was one great splash about a half mile north of us, followed by several smaller splashes. A few minutes later the series was repeated, although much closer and I could see a porpoise leaping up and walking on his tail across the water. He could remain upright for several seconds and continued to perform his stunt intermittently for ten minutes. Doubtless I have been alone too long, because I have the uneasy suspicion he was trying to tell me something.

DAY 105 • *March 3*

FROM Thursday noon until today, Monday noon, we made a less than grand total of 180 miles, most of it in the last twenty hours. San Diego is 320 miles northeast, and the radio reports two storms heading this way: one coming down from the north where there are gale warnings along the Oregon coast, and another coming east from off the Pacific. I am in a state of ever-increasing suspense. Perhaps the storms will help us; perhaps we will all come together in a nautical Götterdämmerung off Point Loma. I do not allow myself to have any particular expectations. We are so close to safety, but the mast is very badly worn and could come down at any instant. We could be in port in a few days, or even yet we could have to turn away under jury rig and run 2,000 miles downwind to Hawaii.

WE again have a passenger. A stormy petrel was shivering in the cockpit when I came on deck this morning. Obviously, he is ill, and I wrapped him in a towel and put him, along with some water and crushed shrimp and tuna fish, in a box in the cabin.

DAY 106 • *March 4*

A storm is definitely approaching from the west. Clouds and wind dash toward us, and we sail fast for San Diego. I am all but crossing my fingers until we get in.

DAY 107 • *March 5*

AT dawn a particularly virulent squall forced our 5,018th accidental jibe. When I went on deck, I was shocked to find us sailing directly for a freighter not more than ¼ mile away. Before I could get back on course, a seam on the mainsail ripped open, but because it was below the first line of reef points, I will not bother with repairs. We will sail the rest of the way reefed.

The ocean almost seems to know that today could be our last full day at sea and is therefore launching a final, frenzied attack. Of course, that is not true. The ocean is not sentient, and I did say "seems."

I thought the petrel had died, but when I lifted his towel, he crawled feebly away from the light. It would probably be merciful to kill him, but thus far I have not been able to bring myself to do so. I feel more helpless about not being able to aid him than I have about the problems with the boat.

A moonless night. Cold rain. Breaking waves. At 10:00 P.M. I undress and go naked onto the deck, deliberately leaving my safety harness below. Mostly there is the terrible cold and the fear that I will slip—I have been afraid twice before on the voyage: in Papeete Pass and the very first instant I thought there was a crack in the hull—but I know what I am doing and make my way forward, past the mast, past the storm jib, then the final few feet until I stand in the very bow, fingers clutching the headstay. Freezing water beats down from the sky and up from the sea against my flesh. I lean forward beyond the bow, far beyond where the guardrail and lifelines would be, and look back at Egregious roaring through the wild sea. For perhaps a full minute I hang there until I feel my numb fingers begin to shake uncontrollably. There is a moment when the headstay is slipping from my grasp, I am about to fall into darkness, and time stops. The white panthers of the sea. An ordeal of grandeur. Mary. The broken tangs. The transcendent hours at 39°South. Porpoises. Raivavae disappearing behind us. The groaning rudder. The overflowing bilge. The spectral sea of Albert Ryder. Bach in the Roaring Forties. The grinding mast. The surge of speed to 11 knots. The white heron. I want the sea for my unmarked grave. Sailing beneath the full moon. Winds and waves of torment cease. Papeete Pass and the palms clustered on the point south of Paea. The voyage has not been the vision I had, but I have lived as intensely as I had hoped. To speak would be unthinkable, and the only possible words unnecessary: I am. My hands drop helplessly open. I twist as I fall and manage to land on the steeply inclining deck, across which I slide until I stop myself with my arms wedged against the deck coaming. I do not believe I have ever been so cold. Each wave washes away more of my meager remaining strength as I crawl slowly aft until at last I fall through the companionway.

DAY 108 • *March 6*

BRUISED and still cold, I was awake long before the grey dawn. We sailed at more than 6 knots all last night, and I have not had a good position fix now for over 200 miles. Visibility varies from a few hundred feet during the heaviest rain to a maximum of a few miles between the squalls. From the radio signals, I know San Diego to be north of us, but I do not know how far. I am concerned about sailing blindly upon the Coronado Islands.

The petrel was dead when I looked in on him this morning.

AT 11:00 I got a rough sun sight through the clouds and now another at 12:00. I plotted them on a local chart of this area and they show us only 3 miles from the Coronados. Nothing is in view, but I have heard the sounds of aircraft, so we must be relatively close to shore.

12:14 P.M. The north Coronado island has just become distinguishable through the rain. We are safe. We really are going to make it.

MID-AFTERNOON. The sky is overcast, but no rain falls. The Coronados have been lost in the clouds behind us and Point Loma is not yet visible ahead, although it cannot be more than 5 or 6 miles away. We are returning as we left, with a south wind. Gulls and pelicans and cormorants rest on the waves, and one of the pelicans opened a startlingly blue eye and watched us sail by.

I have thought of many ways to end this entry. Long before I left San Diego, I wrote, "But even as I approach land, I am already planning other voyages and my return to the monastery of the sea."

Then, not long before my departure last fall, I told some friends that I was no longer as cynical as I had been, that I knew it is better to fulfill your dreams than not, better to succeed than fail. And now, after having been at sea for 109 days and sailed more than 12,000 miles, survived gales and endured calms, but failed to complete the circumnavigation on which I embarked, I believe that more than ever.

I have experienced and learned much; but when I left San Diego last November 2, I had 24,000 miles to sail, and I still have 24,000 miles to sail.

It would be fine to say that as I near land I am looking forward to my next attempt at Cape Horn. It would be fine, but it would not at this moment be true. I am allowing my self-discipline to relax, and I am tired. In a few weeks, I will probably look forward again to sailing as much as at this moment I look forward to being safely tied up to a boatyard dock.

I know that I will attempt another solo circumnavigation, but I will do so more out of a sense of duty than in expectation of joy. I will do it because I said I would, and the honor of my word is perhaps the very last illusion I have.

At times in the past I have thought I could only find fulfillment alone at sea, and at times during this voyage I have thought I could find fulfillment nowhere. Certainly, in the future, I will try to create some balance in my life, to find some way to combine the solitary, silent pleasures of the ascetic with the more human pleasures of love and the shore. But part of me has not come back from the voyage. Perhaps I was a fool to believe that life can be anything but tragic. Or perhaps I was a fool not to have realized that I am meant to struggle and not to be fulfilled.

I am curious to discover what life Mary has created for herself in my absence, and if there is room in that life for me. Having had my chance for happiness, and knowing intimately how fragile life is, I would like to do whatever I can to make her happy. I am curious to learn what can be done to repair Egregious, which I may even keep, and what work of art I can create of this log. I am eager to learn what is to become of the experiment I am.

Point Loma has become visible and is now a silhouette 1/2 mile to the west. Within that dark shape, darker hollows more sensed than seen are filled with the cries of gulls, whose restless forms fall through the somber sky above the cliffs.

POINT Loma cleared at 5:14 P.M.
Ahead the lights of the city come on as I sail up the bay.
Egregious man, boat, voyage, life.
Smile, fool, and sail on.

. VII .

SATURDAY • *March 18*

TO the very landfall and beyond, the voyage refused to conform to my preconceptions. I had intended not to write a single word about whatever happened once I left the sea. But after the past two days, and upon reading that a relatively unknown French solo sailor, Jean Gau, was dying penniless, his ship wrecked, the following poem wrote itself. It is the true end of this part of the voyage.

>Die alone, Jean Gau,
>as you lived,
>the wild cells turning your body to water.
>Any return to the sea,
>even a cancerous death,
>is better than remaining ashore
>where there is no place
>for those of us who voyage alone

Part Two

. I .

DAY 109 • *October 18, 1975*

Resurgam!
Victory or death!

The first—from the cornerstone of St. Paul's Cathedral London—I said to the crowd on the dock. It means "I shall rise again."

The second I kept to myself. It would have been melodramatic and would only frighten those who care for me. But it is the way I feel. I left Point Loma behind at 11:50 A.M. under a pale blue sky, high wispy clouds, heading south yet once more. I vow I will not see San Diego again until the Horn and the world are behind me, even if that means I will never see San Diego again at all.

DAY 110 • *October 19*

ADD to my thoughts yesterday: I was wrong and everything is different.

We had light-to-nonexistent winds during the night under a full moon, and all morning I kept the helm. The tiller extension I installed a few weeks ago has already proven itself. Now, when everything has gone to hell, I can lean back and steer in relative comfort. The best $10 I ever spent. It would be ironic if this time Egregious holds together but we have such adverse weather that we make a slow voyage.

I am not as excited as last year. "Businesslike" some have said of me; "composed" I call myself. Mostly I wonder what lies ahead. I have not yet looked at a chart or plotted a course. I know the way.

DAY 112 • *October 21*

GUADALUPE Island is presently off the starboard beam. Under the influence of a high-pressure system, our progress has been slow—only 220 miles in three days—and we have been forced to stay closer to the Baja peninsula—about 140 miles to the east—than last time.

I have not seen Guadalupe in several years. It was the rounding mark for my first solo offshore passage. At about this time of year, I sailed around it and back to San Diego; 500 miles and five days alone seemed a lot then.

Incredibly, I make the same elementary navigational errors at the beginning of every voyage. How many hundreds of sights have I taken, yet I marked the distances the wrong way on intercepts yesterday and forgot that California is still on Daylight Savings Time, which means that local noon is closer to 1:00 P.M. than 12:00. The navigator says not to worry; it will all get sorted out one of these days. And the captain tells the navigator that we can't afford another Great Leap Sideways, which would put us 8,000 feet above sea level on Baja. At this the navigator retires to the chart table to sulk.

DAY 117 • *October 26*

ON the evening after leaving Guadalupe astern, we finally got some good wind, which increased so that within twenty-four hours I had reduced sail down to storm jib and main. Since then we have continued almost due south at 7 knots under overcast skies, for which I believe the navigator is secretly grateful—if he can't take a sight, he can't make a mistake.

The more expensive of my two chronometers has stopped, and the bilge has some water in it, which I assume comes from the rudder shaft. I bail about 30 gallons every day or so and never give it another thought.

We will have made 1,000 miles by tomorrow.

THIS morning a Korean fishing vessel about 80' long passed close astern. We looked one another over and waved. I'm sure the fishermen were thinking how pleasant it must be to be a rich American with nothing better to do than cruise lazily in his yacht. They are probably right. If I ever find one, I'll ask him.

DAY 121 • *October 30*

THE wind has been light, but so steady that I've broken my own rule and left the spinnaker up continuously now for three days and nights. Even under that lovely yellow and white arch, we make only 5 knots, but considering we are about 11°North and entering the dreaded doldrums, I am satisfied. There is really nothing necessary for me to do, so I might as well take this time to explain why I said earlier that I was wrong and everything is different.

I was wrong to believe that I could find any balance in my life, perhaps ever, but certainly not until this voyage has been successfully completed. Last year I defined the four essential parts of my life: love, writing, sailing, solitude. I know they are not all compatible and it is usually the unmet need which seems the most important. During the years of working toward this voyage, I was loved, but sailing seemed most important; and now that I am free to sail, love does. But there are some goals that will not admit compromise. This voyage is one of them. Until I have rounded the Horn and completed a solo circumnavigation, I can do nothing else. When I almost lost Egregious at Papeete, I thought of all the years I had worked for her. That was wrong. I have realized I must depreciate the value of the boat—and my own life—to nothing. There is some peace in having done that, in knowing with absolute certainty that I will never give up. Now that I know I will pay the price, there is only curiosity to discover what that price will be.

That understanding is one of the things that is different. Another is that part of the price has been Mary.

A month ago I wrote:

> consumed by my voracious dream
> and wanton storms that rage
> without, within
>
> innocent of hope
> surfeit of despair
> I heal myself
>
> for me, for now
> there can be no harbor
> not even you

Once I thought that those who had loved me had treated me better than I them. Now that is no longer true. When I left San Diego this time, all my debts were paid.

Obviously, Egregious is different, or I could not be out here. The first month in San Diego last spring was spent in a boatyard. The mast, the mast step, the side supports, the flanges, the torn bulkhead, were all strengthened at a considerable cost, which— to his credit—the builder paid. A few weeks before my departure, I had new shroud tangs custom made, again at considerable cost. In fact, I earned the money for the tangs by delivering a boat from San Diego to San Francisco. Because of a variety of problems, chief among which was the engine refusing to work halfway up the coast, it took almost a full week to make the delivery. After paying the yard bill for the new tangs, I showed a clear profit of $19 for that twenty-four-hour-a-day labor. Perhaps I should open a boatyard; but then I would probably be my own best customer.

The rudder has been examined and a new tiller cap, which I believe to have been the source of the grinding, fitted. And the breakaway coupling on the self-steering vane has been welded.

In all, I have some belief that even though everything else may fall apart, those things that broke in the first two attempts will not break on this one. At least not immediately.

I have planned my diet somewhat differently. There is no canned shrimp along and no plans for curries. Most of the rest of my basic menu remains about the same, although I do have a simpler biscuit recipe; but I have done whatever possible to provide a greater variety in tastes, particularly in food to snack on. The temptation of that last can of cake as we approached the equator in February is not forgotten. As a result, each two-week bag of supplies now occupies almost as much space as a four-week bag did last time.

And perhaps the most fundamental difference becomes apparent as I glance back at the brevity of the entries of my log these first weeks. The ocean is not the magical place it was a year ago. I have been here and I have been alone before. Perhaps partially because of the easy weather the first few days, but more because of those earlier 109 days at sea, I made the transition from the land without difficulty this time. I am glad to be here; often I still spend hours watching the waves. But the solitude and the beauty are subordinated to one thought: get to the Horn! The ocean is a plain of war. My silence is the calm of a seasoned warrior as he approaches the battlefield. I do not want to die now, but I knew within the first two days in San Diego last March that if it were at all possible, I would try again this year. Nothing in the succeeding months as I waited for the right season to depart changed my mind in the slightest. Other things can be important to me, but I cannot live with the failure to fulfill what began as a dream but has become something much more complicated: an ordeal surely, an unbreakable obligation to myself, an ultimate test, the distilled essence of my life. To make the voyage nonstop is not important to me, although I am prepared to do so if all goes well; but there can be no peace and no harbor—except temporarily, if I am forced in for repairs—until the voyage is complete. Certainly I lose something by such single-mindedness—I have obviously lost love—but I gain much in the knowledge that I have been put to the test and have not quit. Really, it is all sophistry: simply, I have no choice and no thought other than to get to the Horn!

DAY 123 • *November 1*

400 miles north of the equator and we are in a storm with the wind blowing at 30 knots directly from the direction we want to go—south. The waves are not large, but very sharp. We are pounding hard even under reduced sail. The bilge is leaking badly. Perhaps 50-80 gallons a day.

TWO white birds identical to the one who hitched a ride last year are hanging onto the toe rail amidship. Perhaps it should be renamed the claw rail. For about an hour one of them tried to stand on the spinnaker pole, which is aluminum and perfectly smooth. With each wave he lost his balance with a squawk and a frantic flailing of ruffled feathers. When he finally settled into his present secure position and I stopped laughing, it was time for lunch, so I called to the one who had had so much trouble, "You take the watch; I'm going below. I'll be back in an hour to relieve you." But he only glared at me as though to say, "The hell you will," and relieved himself on the spot.

DAY 126 • *November 4*

THE wind continues to blow from the south, making it impossible for us to steer closer than southeast or southwest. We are down to storm jib and double-reefed main and doing only 5 knots, but to go any faster dramatically increases the pounding.

The leak is much worse. I have gone into the lazarette and tightened the bolts around the rudder without achieving the least diminution in the deluge. A steady 5 gallons an hour does not sound like much, but it means lifting 1,000 pounds of water from the bilge with a bucket each day. I had seriously thought of installing a bilge pump before I left, but the tangs cost so much that there was no money for a pump. Perhaps I could do something about the leak if I knew where it was.

Egregious has been out of the water three times in the past year, most recently five days before I left San Diego. Nothing was wrong then; conditions in this storm are unpleasant but not all that rough; there is simply no reason for anything to be wrong now. But there is, and we aren't even as far as last time.

DAY 129 • *November 7*

OUR first day south of the equator is a day of respite, which I am tempted to say came just as I was beginning to resign myself to weeks of battering into head seas; but the fact is that I had long ago resigned myself to such discomfort.

The southeast trades are for the first time in my dismal experience of them gentle 10-knot breezes, and we are making our way effortlessly south across a sparkling sea and under a blue sky at 6 knots with full plain sail set: jib, staysail, main. Wet clothes are drying nicely. I am clean. The leak is reduced to about 50 gallons a day, less than half what it has been.

Although, for the moment, our speed is satisfactory, we are four full days behind our pace of a year ago. By the twentieth day, then, we had been broken and forced toward Tahiti. The difference in our progress is not that I drove the boat harder then, but completely due to the winds. In fact, I have had the spinnaker up more than twice as many hours as on the last run toward the equator. Until today we just have not had good sailing this time.

I loll about in the cockpit, enjoying the sunshine. A tiny voice says, "Enjoy it while you can."

DAY 132 • *November 10*

THE day before my birthday, and the perfect sailing continues. When the ocean gives you an opening, you must take advantage of it. Two days ago we sailed through such an opening at 7 knots on a close reach and have kept right on going. From time to time larger swells come, the tempo of Egregious's motion quickens, whitecaps become more prevalent. The orchestration of the sea rises toward a crescendo, and I think the easy times are over. But then it all slows, the anticipation diminishes, the crescendo is never reached, and we sail happily on.

I could ask for no better conditions. Warm breeze and sun, 7 knots on a course of 160°, 160 to 170 miles a day with no strain on Egregious or myself. These are the trades as advertised, yet only now delivered.

The leak continues to be a mystery, which at least gives me a serious interest in the voyage. So much of the hull cannot be inspected from inside the cabin that I have not really searched too diligently for the crack. One of these days we will be becalmed, and I will go over the side and try to locate it from there. In the meantime I have become an expert at bailing at night. Seven unseen panfuls fill one unseen bucket, which is then returned to its source. Before I left San Diego, I told a friend how easily one can lose muscle tone at sea, leading what is often the most sedentary of lives. Somehow I don't think that is going to be a problem this time.

DAY 136 • *November 14*

THE trades have ended, and with them our best week's run ever: 1,100 miles carrying us from 1° to almost 20°South. Today line squalls are followed by calms, and I am again very watchful and very aware how quickly things can go wrong. Last night I was startled by the first snap of breaking metal. Fortunately, it was only one of the eyes holding a block for a self-steering line and was relatively quickly replaced. But that one sharp crack was enough to bring all the memories rushing back.

DAY 137 • *November 15*

AS we sailed up to 20°South, I was increasingly apprehensive: this was the site of the most frustrating sailing I have known. My concern was unnecessary. During a day of intermittent squalls and a night of too numerous sail changes, we more than covered the distance which took a full week limping north earlier this year.

DAY 139 • *November 17*

TO be almost certain in mid-ocean that your hull is cracked is one thing, but it is another and quite shocking thing actually to see it.

There was too little wind for self-steering last night, and I awoke this morning to find Egregious hove to. After an hour of futile effort at trying to get us sailing again, I decided it was time to go for a swim.

The water was warm and clear, and I found the crack on my second dive. For about 3 inches, the trailing edge of the keel, where it joins the main body of the hull, looks as though someone has carefully sliced it open with a knife.

Back inside the cabin, I cleared the kerosene and water containers from what is designated as the engine compartment and found a hairline crack. When I had scooped all the water from the bilge, the trickle from that crack was obvious.

After mixing some underwater putty, I went back over the side, but it has not really helped. Problems at sea are simple; it's the solutions that are difficult. Even in this calm there is enough motion so that the putty is loosened before it can harden. I applied more from inside the engine compartment, and that seems to have held better, somewhat reducing the inflow but not eliminating it.

The questions are: how much worse will it get how soon; and will it continue to be merely a nuisance or will it kill me? Victory or death, I said. Hmm. (A talent for coining noble phrases becomes dangerous when you try to live up to them.)

Now, in mid-afternoon, the wind has resumed, and we are again on a course for Cape Horn at 5 knots.

DAY 140 • *November 18*

WE have now been a month at sea and at noon were 115°West 27°South, very acceptable progress thanks to that wonderful 1,500-mile sail in the southeast trades, and slightly ahead of schedule for a 191-day nonstop circumnavigation.

That last is as irrelevant as the weather forecast in hell. The hull damage will force us in somewhere; it is merely a question of how soon the storms ahead open the crack farther. Prudence would require that I seek port now, but I am determined to get past the Horn or sink. After the Cape, I will reassess the situation and decide whether to put in somewhere on the east coast of South America or try for Africa.

Last night the warm wind was blowing gently down a great inverted spire of moonlight. It was a lovely evening, and I sat in the companionway and looked out at the sea, to whose beauty I am not entirely indifferent despite my focus on the Horn, thinking of a premonition I had the day before I left San Diego. Beth and Terry were sitting in the cockpit with me, and I would normally have said nothing about my thought except that it came so suddenly I spoke before I realized what I was saying. I told them I did not think I would be coming back from this voyage. The idea retreated to some secluded reserve of my mind until the moment I was underwater looking at the crack.

I am not depressed or even subdued, only eager to sail on to a conclusion. More than death I fear another year lost indecisively. When I think about dying out here, I know that even though that would be an appropriate way for me to die, I am not yet ready. I think of the increasing tension and ultimate despair of those who would wait for me next year. Not until they had failed to hear from me by late June or July could they really know I was dead. I think of the places I will never see, the women I will never know, the poems I will never live or write. I think that I may be writing this to no one but myself.

And I think, despite my premonition, that I do not yet truly believe I will die on this voyage, although I realize my thoughts have nothing to do with the reality of what is very much a survival situation. Living with Egregious is like living with a very beautiful, very sensual, very insane woman. Life is exciting because of the great pleasure and because you know that at any moment without warning she may try to kill you. There is no longer any question in my mind that I chose the wrong boat for this voyage. Wrong, perhaps, in design, but certainly in execution. They did an inadequate job of building her; but she was my choice and I'm stuck.

The coming month is crucial. By December 18 we will either be past Cape Horn or broken. Or both. Sail on, Egregious. Sail on, you beautiful bitch.

DAY 143 • *November 21*

YESTERDAY afternoon was an entr'acte. Clouds and swells, scenery left from the previous performance, were scattered randomly about the stage. Then, from the southwest, came a new line of clouds; the waves built, the wind increased, and a new act began. By nightfall the sky was covered with haze thick enough to obliterate everything but the faintest oval of the full moon and one other pinpoint of light that, I believe, was Jupiter.

During the night, the wind steadily increased, and I as steadily went on deck and lowered headsails. At 6:00 A.M., in cold rain, the self-steering gear was overpowered. My mistake was in attempting to readjust the vane before reefing the main, which before my distressed eyes ripped along the first seam just above the foot. The sail is 11 feet wide there; the rip 10 feet.

Because it is so low, I put in the first reef and will repair the tear when I get a chance. As I look up at the sail, the top batten also seems broken.

And what is particularly disgusting about the whole debacle is that five minutes after the tear, the wind died to less than 10 knots.

DAY 144 • *November 22*

I spent four hours restitching the main and became violently seasick. I have sailed enough to know that the moment I start to wonder if I should reduce sail, I should. And next time I will.

DAY 148 • *November 26*

TODAY would hardly be beautiful except to someone who has been through the past week. Low clouds hang like a smoky haze all about the horizon, but higher the sky is half-clear and blue. The sun is visible, and for the first time in a week, I am getting good sights. We returned to the Forties not long after midnight, and are sailing southeast for the next 1,000 miles before the last sprint to the Cape. Noon today will find us about 113°West and 40°30′ South.

DAY 149 • *November 27*

THANKSGIVING. I just reread about Thanksgiving Day a year ago, when I spent the afternoon raising and lowering and sewing the mainsail north of the Tuamotus. This was the first time I have looked back at what I wrote about that part of the voyage. It was almost like reading about someone else.

I took advantage of some smooth sailing this morning to catch up on maintenance. The tiller lines have been shifted on the self-steering vane; the cabin windows recalked; a boom vang jury-rigged (the other broke last week); and a new piece of leather sewn around the tiller where it constantly rubs against a line.

There are three ways I would know we are again in the Forties even without celestial navigation. Despite being summer, it is very cold. I sleep in my clothes—three shirts, two pair of socks, long pants—in a sleeping bag under two blankets. We are on a new chart, in the very lower right-hand corner of which is Cape Horn itself. And I saw my first wandering albatross of this passage. I had forgotten what an incredible sight they are. No other bird prepares you for them.

OF those primary aspects of my character, the ascetic was more than fulfilled by the solitude I knew earlier this year. On this voyage I have deliberately kept contact with the world by listening to the radio, particularly the BBC. Last night, while I was slowly drinking a cup of tea, an announcer on a science program gratuitously informed me of a recent study which shows tea may cause stomach cancer. I looked down at my cup and thought, "Not you, too." I know the world out there is waiting to kill me, but this betrayal from within I never suspected. Ah, well, I should be so lucky as to live long enough to have to worry about tea-induced stomach cancer. I drank it down with satisfaction.

DAY 152 • *November 30*

A magnificent day. Partially clear blue sky, wild whitecapped ocean, albatrosses and shearwaters swooping and soaring, rigging so taut it hums. We sail at 7 knots directly for the Horn—now less than two weeks away—what pleasure in those words—under double-reefed main and staysail. All would be splendid if I did not know that 8 feet of seam are ripped out between the first and second set of reef points on the main. The wind is abating, and I may take my dose of seasickness this afternoon.

Nights here are only six hours long, which makes the odds 3-1 against problems occurring during darkness. Yet they always manage to. Everything in these latitudes happens so quickly. Highs and lows rush through; the barometer leaps about like a spastic toad, moving not less than a half inch each of the past three days; the weather changes and then changes again; and with every change comes the concern that this time the storm will continue to build and build and build.

So far that has not happened, but last night was bad enough. I had already twice left the haven of my sleeping bag to reduce sail before at 2:20 A.M. the self-steering vane was overpowered by a 45-knot gust and we accidentally jibed. Perhaps 5,000 miles ago the main might not have ripped instantly, but not now. I really have put off repairing it long enough. In these conditions, without that sail set, the motion in the cabin leaves much to be desired. Hello, sailmaker's palm; good-bye, lunch.

DAY 156 • *December 4*

ONE of the regular events of recent days is the 9:00 P.M. gale. Last night I decided by 9:30 P.M. that it was not going to put in an appearance and went to bed, but it was just outwaiting me. At about 10:45—I estimate the time because I lay in my bunk for half an hour hoping it would go away—I was awakened by a series of waves breaking over us, and finally I got up and found Egregious dashing south at 9 knots. In near-total darkness, I reefed and then went back to bed; but by the time I got there, I was so cold that it took another hour to get to sleep.

In other oceans, you can trim for the average conditions and live through the gusts. In these high southern latitudes—49°44′South 91°30′West at noon—you have to trim for the gusts and be content to let the boat sail less than optimally in the average. The gusts are too strong, too dangerous, and too frequent.

DAY 157 • *December 5*

THE sea has never seemed so alive, a symphony of violence. The barometer dropped almost an inch, but is slowly making its way back up. Although the wind is at gale force, we have bright sunshine. Wave crests are being blown off; spindrift everywhere.

While I was on the foredeck this morning lowering the staysail, I happened to find myself staring directly into a 20-foot drop beneath the port bow as a wave passed under us. It is very much a sensation of looking over the falls. A long way down.

THE three biggest waves I have ever seen just came through. Judgments of their size are difficult to make, but I have certainly never seen their equal. The average wave out there now is between 10 and 15 feet, and I would estimate these were over 30. The sight of those immense curling crests speeding toward us was immobilizing. I stood in the companionway—which was hardly a good idea in retrospect, but I didn't think to close it at the time—having just lifted a bucket full of ice water from the bilge and was mesmerized. The crest of the last giant toppled over 10 yards to windward, and I thought we would surely be inundated; but Egregious turned her hip into it and rose gracefully through the foam.

Through years and waves and women and wanton storms that rage without, within, I am coming at you, Cape Horn. And at long last I am very near.

DAY 158 • *December 6*

A seam opened up near the head of the main, which I clawed down to repair. When we continued to make 7 knots under bare poles, I left it down. That seems quite fast enough. The waves are now so high that when we are on a crest, I see albatrosses gliding below me.

DAY 160 • *December 8*

THERE is a real question as to whether we will make Cape Horn before the chart gives out. Every wave that breaks over us—and they are many—manages to find its way onto the chart table. Perhaps the Naval Oceanographic Service should produce heavy-duty charts for such conditions; but then charts carved in granite might be a bit awkward to work with, and even they wouldn't survive more than a single passage round the Horn.

Speaking of charts made me think of pilot charts, one of which I consulted this morning to see what lies it might tell me about the currents here. I have long known that pilot charts have no stastitical relevance to a single voyage. None whatsoever. But I thought I would look anyway. This was just after we had a shower of sleet. Sleet in midsummer! Then I noticed at the foot of the pilot chart a red-dotted line that marks the extreme limit of pack ice. It is only a few hundred miles south of us, so I suppose it can sleet anytime it cares to.

Yesterday I removed the jib from the foredeck after leaving it lashed there for the past week in the vain expectation that I would reraise it when conditions improved. My present thinking is that conditions are never going to improve—or at least not in the foreseeable future—and that when I have the double-reefed main and storm jib set, we are under full canvas.

I have pulled or twisted something in my back, which makes sleeping difficult, as it eliminates one of the few possible positions in which I am comfortable. Also, from the all-too-regular exposure to the water in the bilge, which I believe to be just above freezing temperature, my hands and feet have become swollen. Removing my sea boots is excruciatingly painful.

A flock of petrels follows us, more than a hundred of them darting about in our wake. An albatross comes over at intervals to see what the commotion is about, but apparently he can tell no more than I.

BECAUSE with these west winds the ironbound Chilean coast is a lee shore—the most formidable lee shore in the world—we dare not approach it closely until we are almost as far south as Horn Island itself, which is 56°South 67°West. At noon today, by dead reckoning, we were 55°South and 80°West. Under a solid grey sky, I changed course. We sail east directly for the Horn.

THE significance—momentous significance to me—of that turn to the east a few hours ago just struck me. It is one of the two great turning points of the voyage. So far our course has been basically south. Now it is east. East to the Horn. East, east, east, with the soaring albatrosses and the petrels and the shearwaters and prions. East fleeing before the shrieking gales, running with the foaming waves. East across the South Atlantic, across the Southern Ocean. East past Africa. Past Australia. East past Tasmania and the Tasman Sea. East with the hissing, driving spray. East toward the rising sun. East, east, east past New Zealand. East halfway across the Pacific. East for 12,000 miles. East for days and weeks and months. East until finally at long last we can turn north, we can leave the Forties behind and perhaps be warm again.

DAY 161 • *December 9*

ALTHOUGH I wear gloves, my hands turn blue each time I bail—usually three times daily at present. Even while sleeping I now wear long underwear, wool pants, four shirts, two pairs of socks, and a watch cap, and I am still cold. My hands and feet tingle as they did when I was a child and came inside after playing in the snow. Storms I expected, but never to be this cold in December, when the sun is about as far south as it will ever get. For the third successive day, we had some snow or sleet. Today snow.

LAST night I went to bed at 11:00. I got up at 11:15 and didn't make it back until 2:30 A.M. First we were becalmed, and I went out to see what I could do to reduce the slatting of the sails. I was too late. About 12 inches of a seam had opened up on the main, so I lowered the sail and started restitching it. By the time I had finished, the wind was blowing hard from the east. Because I did not believe it would last, I stayed awake while it backed southeast, until we could settle on an easterly course.

During the night, the wind continued to build, and we were leaping off some fairly big waves. At dawn I went on deck to reduce sail and saw that the seam above the one I repaired last night had opened a few inches. I lowered the sail, but in this wind—almost a gale—it ripped wide before I could get it under control. So I spent the morning resewing it, hoping the wind would go back west before I completed the repairs. It did not. And still hasn't.

AFTERNOON. In some respects, today is quite beautiful. Between the ice and snow-laden squalls, there is bright sunshine on a hard blue sea of wild waves. We sail closehauled on a course of 100°, making 3 knots. I will not drive Egregious harder into these head seas. Yesterday I thought Cape Horn to be three days away, but today it is still at least three days away. We are too close to risk more hull damage now; and even moving as we are, we have taken blows sufficiently hard to make me wonder each time I go to empty the bilge whether the water will go down, and for me to know that yesterday's fanciful song of the east will be interrupted by a stop somewhere for repairs.

I know that there are those ashore who wonder from time to time what I am doing. If they guess either that I am repairing the mainsail or bailing the bilge, they have a 90 per cent chance of being right. The other 10 per cent I sleep or try to get the stove to light.

DAY 162 • *December 10*

DURING the night, the wind swung back to the southwest. I checked the course several times and deliberately let us reach to the southeast, even though that carries us away from the direct course to the Cape. I believe a lone sailor ought to maintain if possible a position which allows a margin of error to either side of his course. Then if the boat takes off 50° or so while he is asleep, it is not an immediate disaster. The rhumb line course to Cape Horn from our position yesterday was 100°, but it carried us too close to the islands west of the Horn.

At present we are still steering south of that direct course, but no longer by choice. We would have to go on a dead run to do so, and an accidental jibe would be inevitable. A front is moving through, which spins us even farther south in gusts. Horn Island is about 200 miles ahead. I doubt very much that we will see it.

While writing this, sitting at the chart table and wearing foul-weather gear, I noticed that the barometer is falling. Several times I have made reference to the action of the barometer, and now that I have spent considerable time in high southern latitudes, I feel competent to lay down some useful rules for interpreting the relationship between the barometer's movements and the weather. This will be particularly useful for those who are tired of spending their vacations doing the same old things and are planning to cruise down here next summer for a couple of weeks or perhaps take a long weekend. The following are Webb's Rules of Weather Forecasting for the Roaring Forties and Screaming Fifties:

  1. If the barometer falls, the weather will turn bad.
  2. Conversely, if the barometer rises, the weather will turn bad.
  3. The speed of the change in the barometer should be noted. The faster the change the faster the weather will turn bad. Unless it is already bad, in which case it will become worse.
  4. Also, the amount of the fall is significant, as there is a direct correlation between the amount of change and how much you worry about it. The greater the change, the greater the worry. However, there is no observable relation-

ship between this change, your worry and the weather; with the single exception, that if everything seems to be going well, the sun shining, the wind fair, the snow flurries infrequent, and the barometer steady, you have real reason to worry because this combination is certain sign the weather will turn bad.

A wave just justified the wearing of foul-weather gear while writing at the chart table.

THE essential characteristic of this wind, as it has been of most of the women in my life, is inconstancy; inconstancy of force and direction. There is no way to establish effective self-steering when the wind blows 15 then 30, 15 then 30, changing perhaps every minute. And there is no precise way to calculate a DR position when with each of these gusts the compass swings from 110° to 175° and then back to 90°, and the desired course is 100°.

Although it has been very cold for several days, today is colder. The cabin ports are fogged on the inside, presumably from what we may laughingly consider as body heat because the stove has not been on. For many days I have been able to amuse myself by watching the steam of my breath here in the cabin, but this morning, when it froze into one solid lump as I exhaled, the joke ceased to be funny.

I spend many hours standing braced in the galley, looking out through the starboard ports, which I must frequently wipe clear of fog, at the oncoming black waves. From that vantage, I can see the compass at the chart table and consider our relationship to those waves and if there is anything I need do to improve our handling the seas.

No sun sights again today and I increasingly doubt that I will see the Cape. We are already south of it, heading toward the Diego Ramirez Islands, a clump of rocks 60 miles southwest of Horn Island. If we get a good position fix tomorrow, or if we sight the Diego Ramirez before nightfall, and if the wind permits, I will change course for Horn Island. But if these conditions are not met, we will have to sail southeast tomorrow night to be safe.

In all the years I have sailed the California coast, I have never seen Point Conception, 40 miles above Santa Barbara, although

I first sailed by it in 1967 and most recently two weeks before I left on the present voyage. Point Conception is called "The Cape Horn of the Pacific Coast." But not by anyone who has been to Cape Horn.

DAY 163 • *December 11*

THIS morning I decided to make biscuit-shaped biscuits instead of dropping lumps of dough onto the pan as I usually do. So I carefully took a cookie cutter and formed six beautiful biscuits. However, no sooner had I put them on to bake, then I realized something extraordinary was occurring outside—the sun was casting shadows.

Without taking the time for foul-weather gear, I grabbed the stopwatch and sextant and dashed on deck, climbing to the stern where I could sometimes see the sun from behind the mainsail and through the clouds. But we were rolling so much, the horizon so irregular, the sun so dim, that I could not manage a useful sight.

After fifteen minutes of futile effort, the fragrance of something on the verge of burning reached me. My perfect biscuits! As I started forward, a wave gave me a freezing bath.

I rescued the biscuits and set them on a countertop, while I tried to dry myself and the sextant. Naturally, another wave struck us abeam, and all but one of my beautiful biscuits gleefully dove into the bilge. At that moment, I found it very difficult to maintain silence.

NOON. Between three snow-sleet storms, I have been able to get good sights. Unless I am completely lost, the Diego Ramirez should be in view in a few hours.

LANDFALL!!! 4:46 P.M. local time. Diego Ramirez Islands directly ahead. The first land since Guadalupe Island more than 6,000 miles ago. You sail without sight of land for weeks, the weather changes, the days grow colder, you plot positions on charts, you tell yourself you are nearing Cape Horn, but you have dreamed and struggled for so long that it does not seem real. Or rather it did not until I saw those desolate rocks ahead. We do not have to go any farther south, and even if the mast falls down, we will be blown past the Horn tomorrow.

From this distance—10 or 15 miles—the islands are grey silhouettes with no sign of foliage. The *Sailing Directions* say they are uninhabited for most of the year. I cannot imagine why they are inhabited at all.

AT 7:00 P.M. we passed south of the southernmost rock of the Diego Ramirez. As we sailed closer, I could distinguish some green on the cliffsides, but no sign of man. I had been wondering why so many birds down here are chocolate-brown and white when this ocean is usually grey. I had forgotten about land. They would blend in well on the Diego Ramirez, and presumably many must nest there because the sky was full of them as night fell.

The wind is only about 25 knots, but the surf against the cliffs was impressive. In storms it must be awesome. One rock reminded me very much of Cypress Rock near Carmel, California.

Just before dark, a seal followed us for almost an hour.

Cape Horn tomorrow. Incredible. I can hardly believe it. But it is true.

DAY 164 • *December 12*

AT 5:00 A.M., we were 70 miles due south of Cape Horn. Those are the finest words I have ever written. How many times my thoughts have sailed here while I stood on Point Loma or walked along Mission Beach and now I have, too.

To say we rounded the Horn would be presumptuous and inaccurate. We merely continued to be blown ahead of a gale, which came up suddenly after midnight.

Ashore, I had imagined I would have a glass of my best brandy and pour one for the sea; but I felt no desire to honor in victory the gods I steadfastly denied in defeat. Now as always, the sea is indifferent to me. And in the event, I did not even want a drink myself. It was a day not for contemplation, but survival.

There was one inescapable debt, though, and that was to Bach. The "Little Fugue" was finally heard, a small but triumphant sound at 57°South.

The Horn has lived up to its reputation, making me glad I gave Horn Island a wide berth. It is an overwhelming storm. By dawn the wind was blowing above 50 knots and, of course, had ripped the mainsail, which I repaired but did not attempt the by-then-impossible task of resetting.

The waves were no higher than others I have known, averaging about 20 feet—which is quite high enough, thank you—but there were two sets of them: one coming from the southwest, driven before the wind; the other from the northwest, rebounding off the land. Both sets were breaking.

For the first time, I tied myself in the cockpit during daylight hours, leaving only sufficient slack in the lines so I could move to steer. Countless waves broke over the cockpit. Without being tied securely, I could have been washed away dozens of times.

Egregious was rolled onto her beam ends regularly, and in those cross seas sometimes she would go over to port, sometimes to starboard. Even though it was not in operation, the servo-rudder for the self-steering remained in the water and as we surfed down some of the larger waves, a rooster tail rose from it, as from a hydroplane. The strain on the tiller was immense, often forcing me to brace myself with my legs and use both hands to keep us on course. There was no time to look back and see on which quarter the next dangerous wave loomed, but after a while I could tell by feel and sound. And though I caught only momentary glimpses of them as they swooped across my field of vision, even in the very strongest wind albatrosses and petrels soared about as usual. At such moments you know that no matter how well you adapt, they belong here and you do not. Determination, skill, and luck give you nothing more than a temporary dispensation to trespass.

Throughout what became a very long, frightening, fatiguing day, I steered. To have left the tiller even momentarily would have been impossible. Finally, at 7:00 P.M., the wind decreased to

30 knots, and stiff and cold and tired and hungry, I stumbled into the cabin.

Since then I have cooked my victory banquet of stew, gone back on deck and set the storm jib, and written this. My hands and feet are frostbitten, and a glance in the mirror just revealed dead skin dangling from my ears in bloody strips.

The first man to sail around the world alone—an American, Joshua Slocum, before the turn of the century—went through the Straits of Magellan. As far as I know, I am the first of my countrymen to pass the Horn alone. But now that I have survived the day, I can believe that even if I were not the first, the struggle would be worthwhile and that the day should have been as it was. A smashed hand, frostbite, piercing cold, fatigue are all made endurable. The water I bailed from the bilge into the Atlantic this morning came from the Pacific last night. Cape Horn, which a year ago seemed so impossibly remote, is behind us.

· II ·

DAY 165 • *December 13*

MY first thought upon awakening this morning was the same as my last last night: we have passed the Horn. But only slowly is it becoming real. Today as I look at the chart and mark a position 130 miles due *east* of Horn Island, satisfaction grows within me.

BEFORE leaving San Diego, I had estimated it would take fifty-five days to the Horn. Yesterday was the fifty-fifth day. I feel like Phileas Fogg striding into the Reform Club precisely at 9:00 P.M.

THE wind and seas abated quickly, so that before I went to sleep last night I reset the main. Today the only evidence the storm was real is an occasional residual wave that breaks over us, and my rough stitching and blood on the mainsail. The blood is from yesterday morning, when I smashed my hand in the companionway hatch while leaping on deck to lower the sail when it ripped. Cold salt water is a good anesthetic.

Despite an overcast grey sky, I got a fairly good sight this morning. Our course is 060° and will continue to be, weather permitting, for the next several days as we try to work our way out of the Fifties. We are well within the limit of icebergs, and the farther north we go, the better the weather but the greater the distance we will have to sail. I could certainly accept being a little warmer and would guess that we will probably not head due east until we get above 45°South.

Today is still cold, but not so cold as the days before we sighted Diego Ramirez. I imagine we were then crossing the Humboldt Current, which flows north from the Antarctic. I don't believe I have commented on how hungry I was at that time. Almost every night when I got up to bail I would drink an entire can of evaporated milk—ice cold from the air temperature. The calories must have been burned up in maintaining body temperature.

My hands and feet tingle constantly with myriad pinprick sensations. I do what I can to restore circulation and keep them dry, although with the bailing this latter is hopeless. My feet are especially painful, often awakening me at night. Each morning my fingers are swollen like sausages, twice their normal size. As the day progresses, the swelling goes down. But it always returns.

THE first black-browed albatross I've seen follows us today. He looks like a prosperous middle-aged financier who has just heard bad news about the stock market.

IN Tahiti last year there was an Englishman about fifty years old, tall, erect, single-handing his 45′ ketch around the world. He was meticulous about his appearance at all times and gave me the impression that even in gales at sea he shaved daily and quite probably dressed for dinner. If so, I admire him, but not to the point of emulation.

I shave usually every third day and bathe in these latitudes once a week. To do so more often is not worth the absurd amount of effort it takes. The days of pouring warm tropical water over myself are only distant memories. Bathing water must be heated to a full boil because it cools almost immediately. I work my way through my rather ineffective cocoon of clothing to bare skin, of which I uncover only a small portion for the briefest possible time. By no reasonable standard could it be considered that I get clean, but then bacteria can't grow at these temperatures anyway.

Similarly, the cabin evinces the effects of almost two months at sea. In the forepeak, my foul-weather gear lies on the unbagged jib. Sea boots rest against the mast in the cabin. Both lower berths are out in their extended positions because they are stuck, and it is too much of a battle to unstick them every time I change course. In the galley as on the chart table, water has flooded everything. Each pan must be cleaned again before being used, and some supplies in the supposedly safe shelves behind the stove have been ruined.

Three dish towels in various stages of decomposition lie about the galley. None is clean or dry. The wooden cover of what would be the engine compartment is broken into two pieces. More soaking-wet clothes and towels lie there, along with my safety harness and the buckets and pans I use to shave and wash in as well as those for bailing. I could do a great commercial for a bucket manufacturer.

Still more damp towels lie on a shelf behind the chart table, next to my brown felt hat, which has become something of a sponge. It looks more than a little woeful, but I am rather fond of it and hope it can be revived someday when we get to better weather.

Various drawers, already once broken and repaired, are broken again. Water runs down the mast and drops from the side supports in a familiar manner, but not as badly as in the past. And the cabin ports leak onto the berths, galley, and chart table, despite a lavish if untidy use of sealant.

On deck, things do not look as bad, except for the unaesthetic bloodstains and wrinkles where I have at various times reshaped the mainsail to my own secret go-fast formula.

One potentially serious problem is cooking. The stove was being subjected to so many inundations that it is beginning to wonder if it has unknowingly and unwillingly become a convert to a religious sect that requires total and repeated immersion. One of its burners has gone into permanent retirement, and the other is giving serious thought to following suit. I have spare parts along, but they, too, have gotten wet. In fact everything from bow to stern, overhead to bilge—especially bilge—is wet. Matches sealed in plastic bags inside plastic containers tucked away in what have always before been dry corners are wet. I have lots of them with me, but I am using them rapidly. Do you suppose the vestal virgins give room service? I didn't mean that the way it sounds. Or did I?

DAY 166 • *December 14*

THERE seems to be a rule that I began each leg of the voyage by being becalmed and then spend the next several thousand miles trying to make up the lost time, only to be becalmed again when I finally do. Obviously, our day's run to noon today was not good. It was, in fact, awful: 30 miles due east. I needed an easy day after the Horn, but not that easy.

On the other hand, this afternoon has been somewhat different. In less than two hours, while I made five sail changes, we went from barely ghosting along at 2 knots to roaring along at 6 under bare poles. At present we are averaging 6½ under storm jib alone. From now on, whenever possible, I will sail in rough weather only with the headsails set in an effort to conserve the main. There is some danger in this because the mainsail, even if reefed, acts as extra support for the mast, but that is a risk we will have to take. The main doesn't do much good when half the time it is inside the cabin providing me with constructive recreation.

I used the peaceful hours this morning for a rare treat: breakfast in the cockpit, and then to oil, clean, coil, and generally sort out everything I could.

* * *

THERE were three unusual incidents yesterday.

In the afternoon an albatross settled on the glassy water about three boat lengths—or one hundred albatross lengths—behind us. For a brief interval, he sat there and watched us drift away; then he swam, doing the albatross version of the duck paddle, after us. To my disgust he rapidly caught up, swam alongside, and then passed us! I half-expected him to kick the hull and demand food. It is bad enough when they flash by in a vulgar display of grace and speed in the air during a storm, but to have one *swim* by was, I thought, excessive.

The second was the sunshine itself. This was the first time in so long that the sun was clearly out that I had to search for my sunglasses. I can't recall when I had them on last.

Then in the evening at about 8:00 the temperature, which had never been warm despite the sunshine, suddenly dropped far below anything I have so far experienced on the voyage. It was literally intolerable, and I lit the galley stove and huddled over the open flame for forty minutes. Not long thereafter the temperature rose again to what has come to seem normal. The most likely explanation is that there was an iceberg nearby. I saw no sign of one despite frequent watches from the companionway, but I did not sleep very soundly.

DAY 167 • *December 15*

THERE has been a conspiracy to which I have been a somewhat reluctant partner to keep us at 56°South. My musings about whether to sail around the world at 40°South or 45°South seemed—as indeed they in fact are—irrelevant when it became obvious we were destined to remain steadfastly at 56°South. I was a partner to this because I was unwilling to sail more north than east, when we need go only about 600 miles north in the next 14,000 miles east.

Now, finally, the wind is letting us go northeast as I wish, and we were 54°30′South at noon, with our first good day's sail since the Horn: 160 miles. The Falkland Islands are north of us.

* * *

THE ocean is different on this side of South America because even 700 miles offshore, we are still to some extent in the lee of the land. In color, the water has been emerald green, then grey-green, turquoise, ice-blue, and grey in the shadows of passing clouds. The waves have generally been smaller—mostly about 5 feet—but steeper and closer together. And the weather less severe, with several isolated squalls passing through adding 10 additional knots to the usual 25-knot wind and dropping ten minutes of hard rain. This has happened four times already today.

TWO albatrosses are silhouetted in flight against the setting sun. They soar and swoop. "Glide" is too gentle and tranquil a word. Not with all the power of this west wind behind them.

THE trouble with any injury at sea, such as my smashed hand, is not the pain at the time but the difficulty in healing. As I've mentioned, the cold kept me from feeling much pain, and it is by no means serious; but I am forever banging and reopening it, particularly when handling the sails.

WHEN I talked earlier about 14,000 miles east, I imply a decision I have made but not discussed. Except in storm conditions, the leak is not much worse than it was back in the tropics. I am definitely not going to put in at South America. We will continue east as long as we can, reassessing the situation as we approach Africa, and if we can continue, Australia or even New Zealand. I do not delude myself that we can make the entire voyage nonstop (well, perhaps a little), but we have sailed more than 4,000 miles with a cracked hull, and we might as well get as much of this Southern Ocean behind us as possible when the weather is as good as it is ever going to be down here. The gamble is, of course, that the crack will not become drastically worse at some point in mid-ocean 2,000 miles from land.

DAY 168 • *December 16*

LAST night when I was emptying the bilge at 1:00 A.M., the sky was clear and I could see the almost full moon, Mars, Sirius, Orion, the Southern Cross. It was like greeting old friends.

SINCE rounding the Horn, I have become somewhat depressed. The Horn had been the goal for so very many years that such a reaction was to have been expected. I reread my log, and it seems so matter-of-fact. For almost two months I sailed south and east and bailed and repaired the sails and it was done. Almost commonplace. Just persist long enough, and if the boat does not fall apart too badly, you round Cape Horn. But with that rounding, I lost the goal on which my life had been focused for almost as long as I can remember. Perhaps I feel more disquiet than depression, and that mood has been further intensified by the low temperature, the prospect of many months and thousands of miles still to be spent in the Southern Ocean, the uncertainty of the cracked hull, and even by the proximity of land.

Although I have seen nothing other than the Diego Ramirez for those few hours, there has been the vaguely unsettling knowledge that not far beyond that ever-empty horizon lay Tierra del Fuego or the Falkland Islands. They have impinged upon my mind, which had become accustomed to being surrounded by vast stretches of open sea. Now the last of that land—East Falkland—is more than a day's sail behind us and I sense a return to the barren wastes which have become my home.

I know that seems inconsistent, that I have said in recent days both that I do not belong here in the way the albatrosses do and yet that these hellish waters have become my home; that the prospect of the thousands of miles before me is disquieting, and yet so is the nearness of land. But the inconsistency seems to me only apparent. Perhaps that is a result of changes wrought by prolonged solitude and stress, or just my present mood. The best cure for such a mood, I have found, is to sail *Egregious* harder, to attack the course before it resumes attacking me. So remembering the captain of the *Alert* in Dana's *Two Years Before the Mast*, saying as they pressed north after their rounding the

Cape, "What she will not carry, she may drag." I, too, did something daring and set the mainsail. But the saying this time is: "What she will not carry, I may restitch."

DAY 169 • *December 17*

I was right. The bloody mainsail ripped last night along the lowest seam, which I had already repaired. The repair had held, but the material shredded around it. Even though the wind was not really strong enough to warrant reefing, I put the first one in and have left the sail set. I realize it is only my foul mood, but I simply will not work on the sail today.

DAY 170 • *December 18*

TWO months out of San Diego. 53°South 49°West by dead reckoning at noon. Rather poor progress since the Horn.

WHAT is so difficult to convey to anyone who is not here is the uncertainty under which I live. That uncertainty was never greater than last night when we began plowing into waves, closehauled against an increasing northeast wind, making 6 to 7 knots on a course of about 100°. Was this the night the sea would break Egregious's back? It began to seem so as waves hissed out of the darkness, the bow leaped into them, heavy water cascaded across the deck, and drained steadily into the cabin from the ports and companionway. The wind shrieked; the hull groaned; water bashed about in the bilge.

I peered from the companionway after I finished bailing at midnight. The sea gave promise of being a cold grave, and the sky a black comfortless shroud. I thought of the biography of the African explorer-missionary, David Livingstone, I had read between voyages, and envied him his unshakable belief that whatever happened was God's will. I climbed into my berth and lay there tense and sleepless, listening to Mozart and wondering very much if we would see the dawn. The crack has opened farther.

OBVIOUSLY we did survive until dawn, if that is what it should be called. Now at noon we struggle eastward through thick fog, dragging a tiny puddle of visibility with us, into which an albatross occasionally stumbles and is startled to find our yellow hull where there is probably no other spot of color within 1,000 miles. We are too far within the ice limit and are being forced farther still. Whenever I dare a glance forward from the companionway, I see vague shapes looming through the fog. Are they ice or only my imagination? I do not know. We have hit nothing yet.

I consider heaving to, but do not. In these latitudes, danger is as much a function of time as distance. The best of the Cape Horn captains always pressed on. We do, too. A voice tells me, "Get out of the Fifties," and another answers, "I would if I could. Show me how." I must keep Egregious's bow to the mark and not flinch. No, that is not accurate. I flinch. My body, already taut with the futile but unavoidable effort to will the wind to the west, tenses still further in those eternities between the instant Egregious leaps into the abyss beyond a wave crest and that when she slams down with a sickening thud. Enough water is coming in so that I must bail six times a day. The thought of having to abandon ship enters my mind briefly, but is as quickly dismissed. With water and air temperature in the 30° Fahrenheit range, I would be dead within minutes on the raft. "Get out of the Fifties." Instead, our course is 100° to 115°. Farther into the Fifties. Farther into the region of ice, but more along the way to Africa. I could turn almost due north, but not yet. I flinch, but I do not ease off. Not yet.

5:00 P.M. As grim a day, as grim a vista, as I ever want to know. The sun made one pusillanimous attempt to burn through the fog and then took the rest of the day off. Visibility is less than 100 yards. Armadas of icebergs could surround us, and I would not know until I felt the crunch. Appropriately enough, I have been reading Dickens's *Bleak House*. His chancery fog has found its way to the extreme South Atlantic, thick, cold, penetrating and cheerless, above a grey sea with only the least hint of a dull green undercoat.

A day when I daydream of sailing naked in the tropics, of being in San Diego again, of an unknown woman I sense I will love who is somewhere in the world ahead of me and toward whom I am inevitably sailing. A day when I wonder if I was ever actually warm or dry or comfortable and doubt I ever will be again. A day when I ironically remember being concerned before I left on the first attempt that nothing eventful would happen, that the voyage would go so smoothly that I would have nothing to write about. A day when I bail and bail and bail. A day when I check the time too frequently, living for nightfall, when I can again try to sleep. A day when I think I would gladly sleep until this is over. An unspeakably grim day.

DAY 171 • *December 19*

I was awakened this morning at 4:00 A.M. by bright sunshine and a clear sky to discover us sailing 030°, the wind at last having backed to the northwest. After getting up to adjust the self-steering vane and trim the sails to a course of 060°, I returned to bed and slept twelve hours with only two brief interruptions. Fatigue builds up quickly during storms from the labor required to perform even the simplest act and from the tension of wondering if you are going to survive.

YESTERDAY I wrote that the sea gave promise of being a cold grave. Perhaps I can be forgiven borrowing from Sir Walter Raleigh, who replied to his friends when they thought him too cheerful the night before he was to be beheaded, "The cutting edge of dawn will find me grave enough." Grave thoughts come easily in the Roaring Forties when your boat has a cracked hull.

DAY 173 • *December 21*

THE weather varies more than I would have thought possible. Each day we have some sunshine, some fog, some rain, some winds of 10 knots, some of 30. At the moment—near noon—visibility is 100 yards and our speed only 5 knots. It is the time each day when I consider setting more sail, but in an hour I will be glad I did not.

Today however is almost as momentous as rounding the Cape. With good sights earlier this morning, I am certain we have left the Fifties at 40°West, having entered them December 4 at 90°West.

THE damage report shows the head bulkhead is sprung, my injured hand infected, and the self-steering vane coming loose from the transom. The infection was inevitable. The gash was impossible to bandage; I have some salve that may help.

But the vane required me to run a line from it to a block on the toe rail then to a winch. Now when I do set the jib again—and perhaps I actually will someday—every time we come about, I will have to shift the vane line opposite the jib sheet. Always complications.

WITH two nights' good sleep, my depression has lifted even though the fog hasn't, and I am reconciled to the great distance before us. The leak has stabilized at a rate of 10 gallons an hour, perhaps half or a third less than it was in the headwinds. We are closer to sinking than we were a week ago, but I no longer have fears of doing so immediately. A few more weeks and we can put into Capetown if we must.

A strange otherworldly sunset. All around the horizon thick fog, not Dickensian but Dantesque; a fog from a frozen hell, to which the sun imparted bilious striations as it sank into a sea of olive glass. I shuddered from more than cold as we fled that sinister display.

DAY 177 • *December 25*

THIS extreme South Atlantic is a miserable place. I can never before remember experiencing such a prolonged unpleasant sail, and it has not been due to great storms. Often I have wished for the wind to be stronger rather than weaker, and always I have wished for it to be more constant. Misery has come from the persistent fog, the daily freezing rain, the featureless grey gloom.

Christmas Day 1975 finds us as nearly in the middle of that gloom as possible—49°South 25°West. Surprisingly, I was able to get a sun sight, before my regular morning bail.

Bailing has become a methodical routine. Dip the bucket into the bilge, one step up the companionway ladder, balance there waiting for the roll of the boat, then up and over the side with the water and back down for another bucketful. A gallon of water weighs about 8½ pounds, and bucketful by bucketful, I lift and return to the sea more than a ton of its contents each day.

My hands continue to be red and raw, but with the somewhat warmer temperature—I would estimate most days are now in the low 40° Fahrenheit range—the painful tingling has gone, as it has from my feet, although I continue to walk in place several hundred steps each day to improve my circulation.

Several people gave me small presents to open: a tin of cookies, a photograph, some books, and a bookmark. I made immediate use of the cookies, one of the books and the bookmark before attempting to prepare my Christmas dinner.

Fashion magazines and Sunday supplements depict dining aboard yachts as an epicurean ritual enacted with elegance and style. Fancy dress, fine crystal and china, polished mahogany tables, and exquisite cuisine, served by a steward wearing an impeccable white uniform. Well, perhaps it is that way for some, but for me it was slightly different.

In the late afternoon, wearing the same clothes that I had worn for more days and nights than I cared to recall—that in fact I could recall, although had someone been with me I suspect they would have gladly recalled for me—I began working on the ever-more-recalcitrant stove. After almost a full hour, it finally condescended to light.

The menu consisted of chicken, rice, almonds, cranberry sauce, carrots, and plum pudding. Naturally, all were served with appropriate flourishes by the doting steward.

"Some vintage port with dinner, sir?"

"Yes. That will be fine, James."

"And afterwards, a liqueur?"

"Well . . ."

"Grand Marnier would seem appropriate; after all, who deserves it more?"

"A taste, perhaps."

Because it is a holiday, I actually did consider trying to eat off a plate. But we were rolling so much that a plate would never have stayed on the table, or food on the plate, so I wedged myself as always in a corner of the galley and ate standing there from the various pots in which the food had been cooked. And I suspect I enjoyed it as much as those too-refined creatures in the posed magazine photographs.

Naturally, my thoughts return to those I have left behind, but they are very distant. Months of solitude, six time zones, and almost 10,000 sea miles separate us. I know they think of me, but they do not even know if I am still alive. I have sailed from the land completely.

And my thoughts reach forward in a continuance of the premonition that there is someone unknown before me. I try to picture her, but I cannot. I do not know if she is in Capetown, or perhaps Australia or New Zealand. What is she doing at this very moment? It is futile. I cannot possibly imagine.

As the day's greyness becomes night's blackness, I go to bed and lie there listening to the radio. A little more than a year ago, I heard "White Christmas" being sung in French in Papeete. Tonight I hear Christmas carols and parts of Handel's *Messiah* from the BBC, Voice of America, Radio South Africa, and various stations in Argentina and Brazil that I cannot identify.

I also catch bits of newscasts, and without repeating the all-too-familiar and all-too-dreary details, it does not seem that the carols, the violence, and my solitary, silent life have anything in common. How odd that truly they are all one.

Christmas never seemed very important to me when I lived ashore. Yet here the day seems very special, perhaps particularly so in this barren ocean. Nothing spectacular happened—for which I am grateful because something spectacular out here usually means something disastrous—yet because of Christmas, I feel closer to those I care for, closer to mankind. I am not lonely or homesick—home has become wherever Egregious is—I am living my dream, the great adventure of my life; but on Christmas Day 1975, as I go to sleep thousands of miles alone at sea, I wish that all men could know the peace that enfolds me as Egregious races east into the night.

DAY 180 • *December 28*

THE wind backed to the south last evening, so I deliberately jibed, and we are on a starboard broad reach for a change.

At about 11:00 P.M. when I opened the companionway to bail, I was surprised to find a clear starry sky, but now in late afternoon the fog has returned.

The sailmaker took advantage of the weather to do some work on the main and both headsails, the latter while sitting on the foredeck as we reached along at 7 knots. He also managed to remove the broken tack pennant from the jib and replaced the jib sheet that had merely been retied when it broke twice yesterday. On a long voyage, the wear on the sails and running rigging is considerable even in moderate weather.

We were 15°West and 47°South at noon. Not quite 10° north of Cape Horn after coming 52°East. In the Northern Hemisphere, we would almost be across the Atlantic, nearing the coast of Ireland or Portugal, but down here we have 35° more before we are south of Cape Agulhas, the true southern tip of Africa.

To put into Capetown for repairs would be easy, and it is even a place I would like to visit before they have their inevitable race war. The leak is certainly worse, but not uncontrollable. I do not want to put in until there is no other choice. We are not yet at the limit and will probably carry on.

DAY 182 • *December 30*

FOR the fifth day in the seventeen since we entered this ocean, we are confronted with an east wind. Thus far the Forties on this side of Cape Horn have been a great disappointment. Instead of the 15 to 25-knot westerlies before which we could dash around the globe, we have had headwinds 30 percent of the time and have been becalmed on four separate occasions, most recently being last night from 7:00 to 11:30, after which this obstructive wind began to blow.

DAY 184 • *January 1*

I started the New Year in a foul mood. There were no big problems, just extreme anger at all the normal little difficulties of sea life—the slopping water in the bilge, cups falling off shelves, the tedious lighting of the stove—to which I am usually accustomed. Probably it was a consequence of four successive nights of poor sleep; the first three were caused by the wind dying, and last night because it was from the wrong direction and the jib kept backing and refilling with a crack. I have not slept two consecutive hours any of these nights.

1976 finds us 4°West 45°30′South with a cracked hull and a disintegrating mainsail, which must be reefed not only in heavy winds, but also in light because it rips instantly when it slats. But life could easily be worse. Another week or so should see us escape from this most miserable of oceans.

DAY 185 • *January 2*

THE game "Let's Keep Webb from Sleeping" was won last night by a new variation: 15-foot swells and 6 knots of wind.

Yesterday we had a gale. Then the barometer raced up, then the barometer raced down, and today we have another gale.

I am today one day longer continuously at sea than I have ever been before, but frankly, after the initial few weeks of adjustment, the length of the voyage is of no importance. It would be no more difficult to be alone for three hundred days than fifty.

Sometime tonight we will cross the Greenwich Meridian. No doubt I will be awake when we do.

DAY 186 • *January 3*

LAST night's variation was the tried-but-still-effective "calm before the storm." Six sail changes between 9:00 P.M. and 2:00 A.M. By then we were down to bare poles, but the storm was violent enough to prevent any further attempts at sleep anyway.

Today, but for the absence of the cross seas, conditions are similar to those off the Horn. Many waves have hit us, but one in particular carried us beam on for several yards before dropping us hard. The hull seems no worse, but I don't know why. It was a shattering blow.

DAY 190 • *January 7*

WE had a very poor day's run and I have only myself to blame. We made 135 miles, but only 90 of that was to the east. I was fooled by a wind shift to the southwest last evening, which I decided was the last of a passing front, so I let us run on under the jib alone to the northeast. Instead, the wind went east and Egregious spent several hours happily churning her way back toward South America.

* * *

ONE of the most troublesome aspects to this part of the voyage is the impossible task of keeping myself clean. I am itching and scratching my way around the world. Perhaps the ability to endure such mundane discomforts for months is the hidden heart of all adventure. Ulysses probably scratched his way around the Mediterranean for ten years, although Homer neglects to tell us so.

DAY 192 • *January 9*

YESTERDAY was a day of transition in more ways than one. We did pass south of Cape Agulhas and therefore from the Atlantic into the Southern Ocean. But we also moved up to 43°South and into the first comfortable weather for two months. Air and water temperatures increase about 5° Fahrenheit for each $2^{1}/_{2}$°—150 nautical miles—of latitude as one sails north from the high southern latitudes. Temperatures should be about 55° here—balmy only in comparison to what we have been experiencing.

Last night I slept without clothing. One cannot appreciate what a pleasure it is to be undressed until he has worn the same clothes day and night for more than a month.

DAY 193 • *January 10*

AND now I face another of the infinite perils of the Roaring Forties—sunburn. Due to a rain squall, I could not have breakfast in the cockpit this morning as I did yesterday, but later the sky cleared and I spent most of the afternoon outside. A rare pleasure.

IN the past I have noted how easy it is to mistake a cloud on the horizon for land. Often clouds look more like land than land itself. But as I lay sunning myself this afternoon, an island appeared about 5 miles directly in front of us. I quickly dismissed it as nothing but a cloud. The tip of Africa is several hundred miles north of us. There are no islands here.

But as we sailed closer, the island did not expose its unsubstantial nature. Instead, it stubbornly persisted in looking like an island. Indeed, it even ventured to look more and more like an island all the time—so much so that I worriedly retired to the chart table to make absolutely certain that there was no possibility of an island being before us. With horrifying memories of the "Great Leap Sideways" returning to my mind, I checked the chart, the calculations of our sights for the past several days, the chronometer and the sextants. All seemed in order. There most definitely was not an island in front of us. If it were anything, it had to be the coast of Africa and that was patently impossible. With renewed confidence, I dared the impostor to have the temerity to be there when I returned to the deck. And I am pleased to report that it did not and was not. But it was the best imitation I have ever seen—a virtuoso performance—and it gave me some bad moments.

DAY 198 • *January 15*

CLAUSEWITZ'S first principle was to have a secure home base, which is for me quite impossible, my first principle is to make acceptable progress in the right direction. "Acceptable" means 6 knots, and although we usually sail faster than that, our average is more on the order of 5½—about 3° of longitude per day at this latitude of 42°South. However, given that, a night's sleep and an absence of freezing cold, I have suddenly found myself to be content.

Only now in this sunshine have I fully come to understand the frozen hell I had adapted to and accepted as normal. Perhaps if I sailed down to 50°South here, it would be as bad. I was prepared to endure three months of such conditions, which make these last few days so welcome. They are not bathing-suit weather, but I can bail the bilge without dreading the contact with icy water, and my hands and feet and ears are healing. I had closed myself in tightly in the South Atlantic, both physically and mentally. I cannot recall a single day of the month we were there that I would want to repeat. Now I am living again, not just enduring.

DAY 199 • *January 16*

OUR new slogan: sails repaired as you sail. Small rips in both the main and jib needed attention, and both could be reached from the deck; so rather than lower the sails, I put on my foul-weather gear and safety harness and had at them.

The main was rather easy, but with the jib I spent half my time dangling over the bow, clutching the headstay as we rolled along at 7 knots and keeping a weather eye and ear for erratic waves. It was no more trouble than lowering them, considerably faster, and certainly more exciting.

DAY 200 • *January 17*

WE have been under a cell of high pressure and spent most of the day sailing at 4 and 5 knots under main and jib. But for the albatross, it could have been a pleasant winter's day off Point Loma. Then, about 5:00 this afternoon, the wind increased; by sunset there was a moment of transcendent beauty, with the setting sun balanced by a rising full moon and Egregious running smoothly east at 7 knots under a half-clear sky. Even knowing we are on a rising swell of wind, which will probably overwhelm the self-steering and force me to get up in the middle of the night to reduce sail, I could not have asked for a better end to the day.

DAY 201 • *January 18*

THREE months at sea. A month ago we were 53°South 49°West. Today we are 42°South 49°East. Those positions define the distance between agony and comfort.

Neither Egregious nor I are in much worse shape than we were a month ago. The leak is not much worse, and the repairs on the mainsail are stronger than they were. My frostbite is cured, and my injured finger is showing some indication that perhaps someday even it may heal. Although we are perhaps five days from the antipodes of San Diego, we have probably already sailed half the distance necessary to circumnavigate because we will not need to go nearly as far south again as we did to the Horn. I almost allow myself to wonder if we just might not be able to make the voyage nonstop.

I am content.

DAY 205 • *January 22*

I don't know how long I'll be able to write. I do not feel well at all. Blood and kerosene are all over the cabin. I have a broken stove, a hopelessly shredded storm jib, and a smashed face—our second capsize in fourteen hours came at 5:15 A.M., bashing me above the right eye with a drawer full of books. This is the most dangerous storm I have been in. The broken stove bothers me as much as anything. Cold food from now on? Perhaps I have a concussion. I'm too dizzy to write more.

• III •

DAY 206 • *January 23*

TODAY I have a black eye—more precisely a vivid magenta eye—from which I cannot see clearly, a severe headache, continued dizziness, a desperate need for a storm jib, and as desperate a longing to be in port with the voyage successfully completed.

The barometer rose rapidly last evening and as rapidly fell, with 50-knot winds returning near dawn. I lowered the jib, and we drifted ahull for five hours. Then, although the barometer continued to fall, so did the wind, and we resumed sailing. Now, at 3:00 P.M. we run at 8 knots before a near-gale.

I will try to go back and make some sense of these past few days, but they are very jumbled in my mind. From now on any errors in judgment or navigation can be blamed on brain damage.

THE afternoon of January 20 was so sunny and warm that I thoroughly washed myself and then sunbathed in the cockpit; but the increasing wind in the evening led me to lower the main about 7:00 P.M.

As soon as it was down, I almost reraised it because our speed dropped momentarily to a fraction below 6 knots. However, I decided to leave the sail down and make another evaluation later. By the time I went to sleep at midnight, there was no doubt that the jib alone was enough. We were doing a solid 7 knots under a cloudy night sky.

At 2:00 A.M., I was awakened to feel Egregious heeling over farther and ever farther. There was no special noise; we were rushing smoothly through the water, pressed over on our beam. I waited for the boat to rise back onto a more even keel, but she did not. We simply stayed there. No fuss. The sail was not flogging. We were not pounding. There was no particular sound of the wind, only the hissing of water outside the hull. And still we did not come up.

I pulled myself from my bunk, donned clothes, foul-weather gear, safety harness, and climbed on deck. All this time we continued steadily on, sailing heeled 80°.

On deck, the sensation of speed and the force of the wind were awesome. Everything had seemed quiet inside the cabin because a 50-knot wind had come up so quickly that there were no seas.

I crawled forward on the inclined deck as one would crawl along the face of a wall. It was a solid wind, a wind to lean against—indeed, a wind that must be leaned against.

Because it is easier to lower the jib when it is partially blanketed by the storm jib, I attempted to raise that sail first, but had difficulty in freeing one of its lashings. I wedged my feet onto the toe rail, held onto the forestay with one hand, and fumbled with the knot with the other; all the time in a standing position, face to the deck, feet only inches above the water.

Finally the storm jib was free, and I raised it and lowered the jib. Egregious rose from her lethargy into something resembling a normal sailing angle, and that was all for the night.

THE leak in the hull is never more irritating than in the morning after a night of heavy weather. The water splashing about makes the cabin sound like the inside of a washing machine during the *agitate* cycle. When I got up to bring some order to that chaos, the barometer was low and steady. But, in the early afternoon, conditions deteriorated.

I had fallen asleep sitting in my berth reading and was again suddenly awakened, this time by successive waves breaking over us. The compass by the chart table revealed we had been spun 90° off course and were sailing directly south. I thought I had better steer.

For the fourth time on this passage, the wind was gusting to 60 knots, and the waves averaging 20 feet. But these waves were steeper, more concave, and more vicious than any I had seen.

During most of the afternoon, the sun continued to shine between fluffy low clouds, and the temperature was not uncomfortable. I was able to keep us headed east, and our speed averaged about 7 knots under the storm jib alone, although often we exceeded ten while surfing down crests. At 3:30 I thought it would be safe for me to go below for something to eat. I was only too wrong.

About a minute after I got into the cabin, just as I was opening the cabinet in the galley, we were turned upside-down by a wave, mast perhaps seventy degrees below the water. I felt that wave coming, but did not expect it to be any worse than many that had playfully thrown us about the ocean earlier; and reached out to brace myself against the companionway ladder. Wasted effort. I flew, or more accurately dropped, down through the cabin against what is designated as the overhead but which was peculiarly below me, finally coming to rest in a corner near the chart table, accompanied by pans, plastic canisters, packages of food, eating utensils, water containers, cups, books, and four guaranteed unbreakable plates, one of which however was *not* and fragmented into hundreds of tiny slivers. The lid came off a jar of sugar, which liberally coated everything with a sticky saltwater syrup.

Further forward in the main part of the cabin, a hundred books were thrown above the restraining rail on the starboard bookshelf across to the upper berth on the opposite side of the cabin. As were various articles of clothing, a compass, and my Zenith radio. These, too, ended on the upper port berth, having seconds before been on the upper starboard one. Nothing fell into the center of the cabin or the lower port berth. We were so far over, their trajectories followed mine, ricocheting against the overhead before fetching up to port as Egregious's 8,000-pound keel quickly pulled us back upright without our doing a full 360°. 160° is quite enough. Once the boat is that far over, it does not make much difference which side she comes back up just so long as she does.

Fortunately, I had closed the companionway behind me, but considerable ocean still managed to find its way into the cabin. I opened the hatch and looked out. The cockpit was full of water, and the wooden vane on the self-steering gear had sheered off flush with its mounting bracket. With no control on the helm, we were pointing up into the wind. The storm jib was slatting horribly, shaking the mast and rig as if to tear Egregious apart. I did not seem to be injured, although later my left wrist began to swell, and I knew that before I could do anything in the cabin, I had to do something about the steering.

Not having removed my foul-weather gear, I was able to go immediately on deck and take the tiller. A stray line was blocking one of the drains; so the water subsided only very slowly from Egregious's large cockpit. Sometimes I had looked at it and thought it might be too large, that it might hold so much water if we were swamped, she would have difficulty in subsequent waves. Now I found out. Even with all that additional weight aft, Egregious had adequate reserve buoyancy and rose easily to the continuing confused seas; a boat to be loved as well as hated.

Although I needed to be several places at once, I had no choice but to remain at the helm until the cockpit finally emptied. Then I managed to find and fit a spare vane and went below to attempt to bail out the cabin.

But as I bailed, wave after wave broke over us, sending more and more water cascading in. I would stop, close the companionway, and wait for a lull. Then I would try to throw another bucketful into the cockpit—there was no time to send it over the side—and another wave would come aboard and below.

For more than an hour I was clearly losing and began to wonder if my luck had run out. In my insistence to sail Egregious to the limit, I knew there lay the danger that the limit would not be merely reached but suddenly exceeded far from port. Now it seemed to have happened. Water covered the cabin sole several inches deep, and I could not determine if it was due to water coming down the companionway or up from an enlarged crack in the hull.

An old saying declares that there is no bilge pump as effective as a bucket in the hands of a frightened man. Being probably the most experienced bailer in the world today, I can attest that one can move as much water with a bucket as with a pump, even though he spills as much on himself as he throws outside. The secret is not to go at it frantically, but to maintain as steady a pace as bracing yourself while your vessel sporadically careens out of control down two-story high wave crests will allow, a pace you can maintain indefinitely, a pace that by 5:00 P.M. enabled me to lift one last bucket from an almost-empty bilge, and then turn to restowing all the debris that had come loose and picking up all the slivers of glass I could find.

During all of this, the sun was shining merrily and the barometer while low was not exceptionally so and remained steady, as it did for the remainder of that evening. When I got up to bail at 3:00 A.M., we were sailing southeast at 7 knots, the wind and waves were still powerful but definitely not so strong as earlier and the barometer was rising rapidly. The bilge seemed fuller than it had become in the past during a similar length of time, but I would have to wait for more normal weather to know if the leak actually was worse. All the indications were that the storm was passing. I went back to bed and fell into my first real sleep for nights.

Two hours later, I was awakened from that sleep by a violent blow in the face as we were again capsized. It seemed to take Egregious longer to right herself than before. I knew instantly what had happened, but was trapped in the tangle of my sleeping bag; pinned not in my berth, but between the railing on the upper berth and the aluminum side support to the mast. As the keel swung back into the sea, I slid down the piece of wood I normally lean against when sitting on the berth. A drawer of books went with me and landed on the cabin sole. Everything else—books, the radio, galley equipment, supplies, the whole mess—that had come adrift before was scattered about again.

Blood ran into my mouth and onto the sleeping bag. I noticed that my pillow was gone, and for a moment it seemed important that I find it; but without my glasses I could not do so (much later I discovered it beneath a sail bag in the forepeak). I touched my nose and forehead hesitantly with my fingers, which came away coated with blood. As I looked at them, I thought, "Of course they're bloody. What did you expect?" and with that I struggled from the sleeping bag.

My reflection in a shard of mirror showed a skinned nose and a 2-inch gash diagonally across my right eyebrow. But even as I was inspecting these wounds, it was obvious that something more urgent was wrong outside.

That we should be thrown off course was to be expected and the compass by the chart table showed us heading northwest. I thought the self-steering vane had broken again, but a glance aft found it intact. But we did not come back on course and the storm jib continued to flail about. Naturally it would when it had been torn in two and the corner to which the sheets were still attached trailed 20 feet behind us, and the larger piece of the sail still hanked onto the forestay had split into two more pieces. The sail is so badly damaged that I don't believe even a sailmaker ashore could save it.

Without a storm jib there was no choice but to lie ahull, which we did throughout the morning, while I repeated the drill of cleaning up and then tried to repair the stove, which would not work. The main fuel tank has a leak and will not hold pressure. Whether the capsizes had anything to do with this or it is just a coincidence of timing, I do not know. Of the spare stove parts aboard, none is a fuel tank. I cannot bring myself to joke about it. To have to face this fierce weather without any hot food—not even a cup of coffee—is extremely disheartening. I worked on it for hours, spreading soot and kerosene everywhere and accomplishing nothing more than making myself vomit. I don't even know if that was due to the smell of kerosene combined with Egregious's spastic motion or a symptom of a concussion. The stove is definitely useless for the duration. Much of my food cannot be eaten uncooked, such as biscuits and spaghetti, and more is unpalatable. Cold hash would be like eating dog food. I can find enough to stay alive, but what a misery. I've even tried heating water over the kerosene cabin lights. After a twenty minutes' balancing act, it might be called lukewarm.

WHILE I have written this the wind has continued to build. Without a storm jib, my choices are to carry on under the jib, even though it is at present too much sail, or lie ahull. With any further increase in wind, I will lie ahull.

The sun was briefly visible late this morning and I have a line which puts us at 43°44′ South, but have to guess at the longitude. Dead reckoning is too dignified a designation for my estimates of our position these last three days. However I believe we are near 63°East, the antipodes of San Diego. Africa is almost 2,000 miles behind; Australia more than 2,000 ahead. Being halfway around the world should be cause for celebration, but somehow I don't feel up to it. As little as two days ago I thought we were not doing too badly; these last forty-eight hours have seen too much trouble. At this moment I would gladly be tied to a dock in Perth.

DAY 207 • *January 24*

DARKNESS. Darkness of the alien nights in harbor. Darkness of the eerie sail in zero visibility in the South Atlantic. The terrible darkness of the spirit when I had to turn away from the Horn on my first attempts. And now a new darkness: the silent darkness of fear as I lie in my bunk and wait.

I do not know the time, but it could not yet be midnight. I came to bed about 9:00, and the water in the bilge is not yet too noisy.

Egregious is lying ahull under bare poles. Outside the storm is in a fierce ecstasy, an exultant rampage, a climax of violence; but my main impression from inside the cabin is of quiet. I hate lying ahull, but there is no other choice unless I want to steer. On another boat I once kept the helm for thirty-three out of thirty-six hours and was good for nothing for three days afterward. I cannot afford that exhaustion yet. And I cannot get any sail on her; it is physically impossible. I have tried.

Several times this storm has paused, deceiving me into believing it to be abating. Until tonight, despite the capsizes, it had not been any worse than weather we have known three or four times before. The capsizes were not caused by exceptionally big waves, but by especially steep and concave ones. Now the storm is fulfilling its destiny. I do not know what force the wind is. More than 60 knots, but I do not know how much more.

From the beginning I have felt this storm was going to get me. I will not fall into the pathetic fallacy. I know the wind is no more sentient than the sea, but this storm has carried an aura of almost-determined destruction. No doubt it is only my perfervid imagination; but then the storm has gotten me, hasn't it? And it came close to finishing the task earlier this evening. Perhaps it was only toying with me, preferring to wait until later tonight.

After writing this afternoon and eating a dinner of cold ham and beans, I went on deck to decide if I should lower the jib. For almost an hour I sat in the cockpit, until something urgently told me to get the sail down. No sooner had I let the halyard run than Egregious was knocked down by a blast from the south. I consider the boat knocked down when the mast approaches the surface of the water; capsized when it goes below it. For the duration of the knockdown, I clung to the mast; then, when she came back up, made my way to the bow to lash the jib. While I was there, I had another presentiment of danger and grabbed the headstay with both hands just as a wave crashed over us. Egregious was again knocked down and I washed overboard, suspended in space and water until she struggled once again to her feet and I swung back aboard. My safety harness was on, but I am grateful not to have put it to the test.

In rereading the above paragraphs, I see that several times I have talked about feelings and presentiments that could be considered superstitious. I do not believe they are that at all, but rather the natural consequence of having been at sea so long that I am so sensitive to it I can form judgments from observations and subtle impressions of which I may not even be consciously aware. My religious friends no doubt are certain that an angel watches over me at such moments, but if so, it had better have the wings of an albatross.

We are heeled 15°-20° from the force of the wind against the mast. The howling wind seems distant. The main impression is of quiet. Then a wave hits us, sometimes with a crack like a rifle shot, sometimes with a hollow thud as though we were a bass drum, sometimes with a warning roar of foam, sometimes with no warning at all. We heel farther and farther over; the hull groans and crackles; we are pushed and driven and slammed down against the stone-hard sea. I really do not know how much more Egregious can take; I really do not know why one of these killer waves has not already found her wound and split us wide open. Not since Papeete Pass do I remember being this afraid at sea. I know I am projecting that fear into the elements, but this storm seems too relentless, too sinister, too vindictive. Rain pounds against the deck. Three huge waves hit us in rapid succession. Somehow Egregious lurches back from each. Then there is a lull, and I drift into an uneasy sleep.

I have been reading a biography of Clarence Darrow—or rather, I was ages ago before all this started, in the good old days when I had time to read—and as I sleep I dream I am a lawyer in a courtroom. I intend to address the jury and I stand and say "Your Honor" and at these words the courtroom lurches and I am thrown back into my chair. I stand again. "Your Honor." The room lurches and I fall. That is all there is to the dream: the endless repetition of my standing, the words "Your Honor," a lurch, and I fall.

I am awakened by another onslaught of waves. The sky is still dark, so it cannot be 4:00 A.M. yet. The water in the bilge is wild, obscuring even the breaking waves and the roar of the wind. I have grown accustomed to the leak and usually it does not bother me too much any longer; but now I hate it, hate having to pull myself from my berth, dress and bail it out in the middle of the night, hate listening intently in an effort to determine if it has grown worse, hate wondering if it will kill me.

I look at the watch I use as a chronometer. 11:00 GMT. 3:00 A.M. here. The barometer which rose 1/2 inch and then dropped 1 inch has risen 1/10 inch. Wonderful.

I open the hatch and am met by an undiminished blast of wind and rain. Slowly, mechanically, I began to bail. My left arm, injured in my flight through the cabin in the first capsize, has stiffened during the night, and I cannot lift a full bucket.

Taking half-buckets obviously means I take at least twice as long, probably more, because there is more time for waves and rain to come below.

Before I am finished the sky is becoming lighter. I glance at the watch before I stumble back to bed. 3:55. I don't know if there was that much water or if I was just that slow.

I lie there and try to sleep. The onslaught of the waves continues, but at least we have survived the dark night.

THE wind decreased in the morning. I raised the jib and thought yet once again that the storm was ending. But the barometer has now in late afternoon lost the 1/10 inch it had gained and the wind is again increasing and the clouds again re-forming in the west.

DAY 208 • *January 25*

THE most trying storm of my experience is over, but not before it gave me one last bad night, during which fierce squalls alternated with periods of moderate wind.

At 9:30 P.M. the bolt holding the tiller to the rudder head broke, and I replaced it while we continued on our way. Replacing it every 14,000 miles is somewhat better than on the previous voyages, when it broke once a week.

Often during the night I lie sleepless in the squalls, feeling us bashing through the ocean much too fast under the jib, heeled over much too far, seeming at times to skip from wave to wave like a flat stone skimming across a pond. I continue to believe that in these latitudes one must trim for the gusts, but I can no longer do so without a storm jib. So I lie there knowing conditions are too severe, yet unwilling to lie ahull, my mind calling silently to the wind, "Relent, relent," knowing that all the bits and pieces of Egregious are being tested to the utmost, hoping they will hold.

Today conditions are still rough, but the worst of the storm has definitely passed. I may even have a night without fear of imminent destruction.

DAY 210 • *January 27*

A storm is not over merely with the passing of the great wind and waves. Not until the normal winds resume behind it, not until I have one good night's sleep, not until I reorganize the boat again, is the storm over; not until I am ready to face another. So, today, with beautiful sailing under main and jib, the storm that began a week ago is over.

At sea as on land, long periods of routine alternate with episodes of intense excitement. The difference is that at sea I prefer the periods of routine. Ample—even excessive—excitement comes without my seeking it.

DAY 211 • *January 28*

I have discovered that I can cook after a fashion over the open flame of the kerosene cabin heater, which I have never used at sea because it seemed too dangerous. However the prospect of another month or two of cold food has made me more than willing to take risks.

As is always the case, there is an unfortunate consequence in using the heater for cooking. When it is used as intended, the flame can be adjusted to burn cleanly; but for cooking it must be partially disassembled to get the pot close enough to the flame and a considerable—even enormous—amount of oily black, sooty smoke fills the cabin. I sit with my head to one side, trying not to inhale the fumes, but sometimes feel after a session in my improvised galley as though I were in Los Angeles during a smog alert. Poor Egregious's interior is beginning to look like a coal mine.

While I can again look forward to hot coffee and hash, baking is impossible and so I tried, with something less than total success, to fry biscuits this morning. The externally charred, inwardly raw end product tasted more like fritters than biscuits. Well, not exactly like fritters either. More like bark from a tree recently struck by lightning. A petrified tree.

DAY 212 • *January 29*

AN uneventful day; what a relief.

DAY 213 • *January 30*

ANOTHER beautiful day of mostly blue sky and sea, with Egregious making good progress toward Australia 1,400 miles ahead. But two successive good days have resulted in my being certain that the leak is 30 percent worse than before the capsizes and my deciding that unless it becomes still worse, we are not going to stop at Perth. I know we cannot make the entire voyage nonstop. Egregious could not stand up to the final beat against the northeast trades even if we were lucky enough to get that far. But we might as well put as much as we can of this Southern Ocean behind us during the austral summer. And Egregious is not yet to the limit. I think we can get to Sydney or Auckland, New Zealand.

DAY 216 • *February 2*

WITH very light winds and sufficient swell to collapse the sails, the main ripped again this morning. I spent the rest of the day sewing. On the lowest panels immediately above the foot there are now patches on patches on patches. New tears develop along the outer perimeter of stitching, so the repairs spread ever on and ever out like a malignant cancer.

THE contentment I knew before the storm has returned, and so long as we have reasonable sailing and Egregious does not disintegrate further, it would be easier to sail on endlessly than go into port. Perhaps this is more true for me now than in the past because I have no sense that anyone—except the woman of my premonition—is waiting for me ashore.

DAY 218 • *February 4*

CONDITIONS continue light and variable, and Egregious continues to try to sail due north each night. I continue to bail five or six times a day, and I regularly look at the shattered fragments of the storm jib and as regularly conclude I cannot salvage it. So I will instead use this time to mention some of the qualities essential for a solo sailor which have not been given sufficient attention by other writers on the subject.

Primarily, he must be literate. If I did not read, it would be impossible for me to be alone for hundreds of days at sea—but then I could not survive ashore without reading either, and many people do in some incomprehensible fashion; so perhaps literacy is only a personal whim of mine. Next, he must have an immense tolerance for inconvenience. The level of comfort and cleanliness aboard a small sailboat on a long voyage is not quite equal to that of the average cave dweller of Paleolithic days. One adapts to conditions which would be unacceptable to the poorest of the poor ashore and lives in what is actually the world's most expensive slum. And last on this short list, he must heal well. Scrapes, gouges, bruises, cuts, sprains, strains, and occasionally burns appear as if miraculously, often without my knowing their cause; a kind of stigmata of the sea.

The two most recent lesions are the direct responsibility of my friend, Terry Russell, whom I would sue upon my return to civilization, were he not himself an attorney who would undoubtedly get the better of any litigation.

On the evening before I left San Diego in 1974, he gave me a rigging knife with a blade of such fine steel that it holds an exquisitely sharp edge—as I once again established by carving my thumb like a Thanksgiving turkey while playing sailmaker yesterday. The knife should be required by statute to have engraved on its handle: "Warning. This knife may be hazardous to your health. Exercise extreme caution when cutting sailcloth with a following sea." Particularly when blood-red sails look so garish above a yellow hull.

ONE is not aware of the process of adaption that occurs on a long voyage except retrospectively as it is illuminated by small incidents: where once I thought of a few hundred miles as a long sail, now 10,000 is not daunting; where two weeks ago the loss of the stove seemed tragic, I now routinely live off what can be rendered partially palatable over the cabin heater.

During the first few weeks at sea, there is a restructuring of my personality. Initially, sexual desire is heightened by deprivation and dreams are usually lascivious; often with girls years distant abruptly recalled as vividly as those I knew immediately before leaving land. Gradually, that need becomes less intense, although the need for this voyage—literally in Milton's words in his sonnet on his blindness, "death to hide lodged in me useless"—never became dormant or even quiescent in all those long years when it was unfulfilled. Is my desire for grandeur stronger than that for love? I often think that those men who compromise or abandon their dreams do so from a pathetic inability to imagine their own deaths. They live as though death were optional. I know that I could not contentedly face my death after a life in which I was no more than a lover of women.

I continue to keep in closer touch with the affairs of the world on this voyage than in the past. The radio receiver is the only evidence other than my navigation that the continents we sail past are real. South America, Africa, and now approaching Australia: all have seemed insubstantial phantoms drifting on the edge of consciousness but for the radio signals that reach me after sunset. Yet world events do not really touch me, and I have often gazed up into the night sky and known that if Egregious were able to rise from the sea and I voyage alone through space never to return to earth, I would set my course that instant not for the nearest but the farthest star.

I deliberately resist the role of the great loner, but people cannot be alone for as long as I have and not be affected by that austere solitude. Last year I defined myself as a sailor, writer, voluptuary, ascetic. Two hundred eighteen days alone have made me more adventurer and ascetic than lover. The most passionate of men is also the most celibate. Presumably, when I return to shore, I will become gregarious again; but at the moment it seems as though what I will gain in gratification of one pleasure will be lost in the denial of another.

DAY 219 • *February 5*

FULL gale. A wall of wind fell on us yesterday at 5:00 P.M., increasing in an instant from 18 knots to over 50. I arrived on deck in time to watch the jib split full across. There was no sharp crack, only a steady inexorable overload of pressure. The cloth separated for 14 feet in almost slow motion. Only the 2-inch luff tape joined the top and lower halves of the sail and while I was clawing it to the deck, the top half was swept overboard and almost lost.

From 6:00 P.M. until midnight, and then again for two hours today, I sewed on it, all the time on the verge of seasickness as we lay ahull. Egregious is drifting southwest at 2 knots. We are no longer strong enough to be down here.

DAY 220 • *February 6*

AFTER breakfast this morning I reset the jib, which looks fairly good. I hope it holds. I have run out of the thread I prefer to use for repairs, having exhausted four complete rolls, and had to finish up with some less strong. The barometer is high, but the sky cloudy and air temperature colder than it has been since we were in the South Atlantic.

DAY 221 • *February 7*

AT intervals we seem to get stuck in one spot. That happened right after leaving San Diego, and in the Twenties beyond the southeast trades, in the South Atlantic, and now here a few hundred miles south and west of Australia. For several days the crosses marking our position on the chart have clung together in a dense little group for comfort; where at other, better, times they march boldly across the meridians.

THE last damage to the jib caused me to examine the storm jib once again. It still looks hopeless, but I'm going to try to reassemble it.

DAY 222 • *February 8*

COMPLETELY overcast. We have now gone a full week without a position fix, but I believe we have just completed our first respectable day's run this month, making a steady 7 knots under jib alone.

When we are on a relatively even keel, water spills out onto the cabin sole every four or five hours, and I am again moving well over a ton of water a day from the bilge.

FOR five hours last evening, I worked on the storm jib and made some progress, although two or three more such evenings will be necessary before the sail can be used and even then it may disintegrate in the first strong wind.

Repairing a sail in a sailmaker's loft ashore, where one has ample room to spread it out smoothly on a stationary surface, is a bit different from working in a confined, bouncing cabin. Merely fitting the pieces back together into some semblance of a sail is difficult. I was particularly intimidated by the remnants of the storm jib being in three pieces, with one split running across—rather than with—the seams. From one of those pieces an area shaped similar to the country of Austria—and almost as large—has vanished. My evening's entertainment is assured for quite a while.

THE new chart differs from those we have been on since December. Not only does it have land—Australia—stretching most of the way across the top, but the scale is such that a good day's run—which has been perhaps 1½ inches long—is now 3 to 4 inches. The illusion of rapid progress is magnificent.

I have been rereading Samuel Eliot Morison's great biography of Columbus. He, too, had firm religious faith to sustain him. Even in moments of contentment, sea life is hard. For me there is only the image of myself I must try to live up to.

AT the sound of something breaking the surface of the water for the first time in 10,000 miles, I glanced aft to see an apparently endless procession of dolphins and what looked like small whales gamboling toward us. They all swam together in one great pod. The dolphins were about 3 feet long, with grey backs and tan bellies. The other species—much the more numerous—averaged 8 to 10 feet in length, although some were more than 14. They had high-domed foreheads, a white stripe near the eye and a white patch aft of their dorsal fin. Hundreds of them swam very near, seeming to pass to windward by choice, and when a series of breaking waves approached, a dozen or so hurried over to surf down the crests. It took more than forty minutes before the procession was gone and I again had the ocean to myself. I could not help but wonder what they feed upon. Whatever it is, the amount necessary to sustain so many creatures living together must be enormous, and their effect, as they pass, devastating.

DAY 224 • *February 10*

THE best sailing days in the Forties are the equal of the best days anywhere, and the worst the worst. Unfortunately, the latter are far more common than the former.

I was about to declare today one of those best days, but the wind has gone too light now in late afternoon, and I am tired of our overall slow progress this month, which has seen an average of only 4¾ knots made good. Nevertheless we did have sunshine, smooth water, decent winds most of the day, and were visited by the first albatross in a week. But so far February could be forgotten. Not only have we gone slowly, the month has swindled me out of the moon. Thinking that perhaps we were experiencing a prolonged eclipse, I checked the nautical almanac, which swears the moon is half-full. Not around here it isn't.

I can remember a time when I was very particular about sail trim, never satisfied unless each sail was at optimum efficiency. Now such fine concerns have been subordinated by the ogre of chafe. Sheets, halyards, and the mainsheet traveler are set so as to provide only as much speed as is consistent with keeping wear to a minimum. I am somewhat surprised that even with such compromise and a mainsail whose leech is scalloped and overall shape laughable, we continue to sail as well as we ever did, even in light air. Surely it isn't possible the sailmakers have been putting one over on us all these years.

I do not inspect the crack in the hull: what could I discover? If it is too gaping, I would only become frightened; and if it is not, what is the point of looking?

TO close this random entry of a random day: sometimes I think I will not survive, but that is merely a passing thought. (Fortunately none of my friends are close enough to groan. Puns, again, in the Roaring Forties.)

DAY 225 • *February 11*

THE storm jib—rechristened Lazarus—has been resurrected after surgery lasting twenty hours over the past four nights, and probably just in time. The barometer is dropping steadily, although so far the increase in wind to 25 knots has only given us our first good sailing in many days.

Early this morning I set the rebuilt sail, as anxious as any artist at an important unveiling. It is something less than a thing of beauty, but I am proud of my effort. With it, the jib and the mainsail all set and all extensively patched and repaired, we look like an advertisement for a dealer in used sails—in very used sails.

Encouraged by my success at what had for so long seemed an impossible task with the storm jib, I steeled myself this afternoon for another attempt at that other seemingly impossible task: cooking biscuits over the cabin heater. And although I did somewhat better than last time (to have done worse would have been a true achievement), the results proved conclusively that I am a better sailmaker than cook. I cannot bring myself to describe the taste of the final product, which I ate but do not care to remember.

FOR much of the day, I was able to sit in the cockpit, and I noticed this evening that the strip of new skin formed where the bridge of my nose was attacked by the drawer during the second capsize is badly sunburned. There has been so little sun for so long, that I had forgotten the possibility of sunburn.

While I was in the cockpit in early afternoon, the first good wind reached us. Egregious came alive and began singing through the sea at 7 knots. She lifted over one low swell and dove through another and suddenly we had a bow wave again. No matter how often experienced, that transformation from plodding to real sailing is a thrill. I say that with the knowledge that soon I will probably be moaning about too much wind. If only there were some way I could arrange a permanent 15-knot warm, steady beam wind. But if I could, I suppose I would become bored.

* * *

EGREGIOUS has long had her own way of doing things and consequently has forced me to devise various unique bits of running rigging. There are at this moment thirteen lines in the cockpit. The standard ones are two jib sheets, two staysail sheets, the mainsheet, a running backstay. There are also two control lines for the steering vane and two tiller lines from its servo-rudder. Then there is the line running across the cockpit to keep the tiller from being raised too high by the vane. And then the line to keep the vane from wobbling that I call the vane vang. And finally today the newest was installed, which is a renewal of the mast guy from previous voyages.

While I was asphyxiating myself over the biscuits, I could not help noticing the mast moving fore and aft considerably more than it should. In San Diego between voyages the side supports were bolted through the deck to a new aluminum collar. Examination revealed that those bolts had enlarged the holes through the supports, which once again have demonstrated that they were poorly engineered and constructed of too soft a material.

The problem is not yet serious, but I wasted no time in getting the old line from the lazarette and tying it around the mast, then taking it back to a cockpit winch. The simple life becomes ever more complex. When both jib and staysail are set, I now have more lines than winches; and even with only the jib set, in order to tack or jibe, I must cast off the mast guy and the vane vang, then the jib sheet, then trim the opposite sheet, then move the guys to the opposite side of the cockpit and resecure them, unless I also have a running backstay in use in which case I . . . etc. etc.

Before I left on this passage, an expert looking over the strengthening of Egregious said, "You have backup systems for your backup systems." Which was quite true. Why, then, I wonder in fatuous moments, do I seem to spend most of my time, energy, and ingenuity, holding this voyage together with string and bailing with an old pot?

DAY 226 • *February 12*

I am standing in the galley writing this at 6:00 P.M. For thirty-six hours the barometer has been dropping steadily and is now much lower than in the gale which capsized us. But so far we have not had any equivalent wind. I've been keeping close watch for the past three hours because in mid-afternoon a squall went through that caused me to lower the jib and raise the storm jib. But after it was gone, there was not enough breeze to give us more than 5 knots under the smaller sail, so I reluctantly re-raised the jib. Reluctantly, because I have heard the sound of sails ripping all too often. The difference in boat speed is 2 full knots, which is too much to sacrifice. We must keep sailing while we can. I do wish the barometer would rise and the weather clear. We could afford to miss a gale every now and then.

There is a nacreous glow to the west through the solid overcast which must be sunset. These last nights have been extremely dark, and I have yet to see any sign of the moon. Egregious is flying east at 7 knots, but I don't expect to sleep well tonight.

NOT long after I wrote the above, the sun broke through on the western horizon, and a completely arched rainbow formed against the still clouds before us. Then, at 10:00 P.M., I looked out to find the sky half clear, the almost full moon and myriad stars. Wind and seas were moderate. It was the clearing after a storm. But we have not had a storm, and the barometer continues to fall.

DAY 227 • *February 13*

BETWEEN when I bailed at 2:00 A.M. and when I bailed at 4:30 A.M., the barometer which I had hoped and expected to rise, began a steep decline—a decline which carried it into virgin territory far below any previous reading in my experience. This was to be a day, though, far beyond my previous experience.

With that precipitous drop, still there came no increase in wind. Egregious continued boisterously but safely east, while I searched the dawn sky in vain for signs of the apocalypse. I returned to my berth but did not undress or try to sleep.

Every half hour I got up. The barometer quickened its downward acceleration; Egregious continued her fine sail; I continued to be ever more anxious. Something incredible and probably terrible was happening, but the only warning was the barometer.

There was no point in lying down any longer. I donned my foul-weather gear and stood in the galley, drinking coffee and looking out at the sea and waiting. When at 7:30 A.M. conditions began to change, they changed rapidly. Within a few minutes, the wind increased to 40 knots, and I replaced the jib with the storm jib. A few more minutes, and I lowered the storm jib. And then the wind went off the scale.

Just before it struck, I finished tying myself in the cockpit. At one moment, everything was under control, Egregious moving safely along at 5 knots under bare poles; then the tiller was wrenched unexpectedly from my hands and slammed over against the starboard cockpit seat. I remember being glad I had lowered the storm jib in time. No sail could have stood to such a blast. Egregious careened to port, broadside to a wind far beyond any I had imagined, a wind that leveled everything before it, a wind that pressed us down into the sea until I began to think we would be forced under.

There were no great waves. That wind flattened the sea. Using all my strength, I fought Egregious's bow back on course: 9 to 10 knots under bare poles. Not surfing, just being inexorably forced ahead of the wind. It was like sailing through fog. I could not see the compass 2 feet before my eyes. Yet there was no fog. The wind had torn the surface from the sea and flailed it about my eyes. I had to breathe cautiously, trying to inhale more air than salt water. I would like to believe I am inner-directed, but I thought, "This is too much, simply too much. It is too bad no one will know I got this far, that I rounded the Horn before I was killed."

When it struck, I did not know how long it would last, but I knew that I was at the tiller for the duration. This was the time to steer beyond exhaustion; there could be no other choice. But fortunately that prodigious wind passed within an hour, leaving us to lie ahull gratefully to a 50- to 60-knot gale, which by comparison is a relief.

For the superstitious, today is Friday the thirteenth.

DAY 228 • *February 14*

AT 3:30 this morning I successfully raised the storm jib, only to discover that the self-steering gear has been broken—more than broken—dismembered. The shaft holding the servo-rudder snapped above the coupling, the arc on which the vane pivots is bent forward, and the gears between the two wrenched apart. I do not blame the vane this time. Nothing in so exposed a position could have endured that wind. Frankly, the vane has taken more punishment and lasted longer than I expected. R.I.P.

That storm was incredibly tight, dense, and, thankfully, small. A barograph for these past days would be an almost perfectly symmetrical funnel: the long, gradual decline, the precipitous drop, a minute base, followed by a rapid climb, then a continued gradual rise. Had the center of the storm been any larger, had it lasted for ten or twenty hours, survival for any small boat would have been unlikely.

If I had written this earlier today, instead of at sunset, I would have said how tired I was of the constant battle, tired of shackles that won't open, tired of halyards that foul aloft, tired of being constantly wet and often cold, tired of lying ahull, tired of being in pain every time I put on my sea boots, tired of the terrible weather. We have been unfortunate enough to encounter an exceptionally bad summer here, with Australia having devastating storms and floods and New Zealand record rainfall and we many, many more days of gales than to be expected on average; including, according to the pilot chart, a zero probability of gales where we just experienced that incomparable wind; tired of knots that jam, and most of all tired of the leak, or rather the sound of the leak; tired of awakening to thrashing water in the middle of the night and pulling on wet clothing and dragging myself from my bunk to bail it out only to awaken to it again every morning; tired of having to live with that sound all day if the weather keeps me cabin bound, tired of the worry as the leak becomes ever worse.

As I said, that is what I would have written this morning and it is all true; but today was so fine with blue sky and sea and a steady if cold wind, that it revived me. I am pleased just to be alive today and know that I have subjected myself of my own free will to all those things of which I am tired. Nevertheless, for a hot shower and an uninterrupted night's sleep, I would gladly mortgage my somewhat-tarnished soul. The Devil never seems to be around when you really need him.

DAY 229 • *February 15*

UNDER storm jib and double-reefed main—now that the vane is useless, we must have both set to achieve self-steering—we continue sailing east. For the first time since approaching the Horn, we must change course because of an obstacle before us. Tasmania is about a week away, and we have to go down to 44°South to clear it.

In three days we will have been at sea four months and covered about 16,000 rhumb-line miles. We cannot remain at sea much longer. These last two days of moderate weather have verified that again the leak is worse. An average of 30 gallons of water enters Egregious's weakened hull each hour, and after bailing, the respite from that demoralizing sound of splashing water is now only thirty minutes where not long ago as many as three whole hours of peace ensued before it resumed. The sails, too, are nearing destruction and will be subject to greater strain and wear since the loss of the self-steering vane. I have already decided not to go to Melbourne and to go south of Tasmania. It is possible to pass north of that island, but the space is too confined, too frequented by shipping, and too likely a spot for headwinds, which, in our condition, we want to avoid if at all possible. But we are going to have to choose a port soon. It will be either Hobart, Sydney, or Auckland. Beyond Auckland, as I know all too well, there are no good repair facilities until the United States. I will have to decide soon.

* * *

I have a recurring nightmare. In it I am lying on my bunk paralyzed. Something has broken in my back so that although I cannot move, my mind is clear. Being unable to bail, water is filling the hull. From the corner of my eye, I watch it rise toward me. I know I am going to drown, but no matter how hard I try, I cannot move. The water splashes against my face, and I awaken.

DAY 230 • *February 16*

AT dinnertime we are making 6 knots under a low grey sky, but it is only a minor rain front. We've moved along smoothly now for two days, and it is fine. To hell with grandeur; I'll take tranquillity. For now, anyway.

DAY 231 • *February 17*

FROM time to time, boats seem to develop a will of their own. Just as Egregious once seemed reluctant to leave Tahiti, now she apparently has determined to throw herself on the west coast of Tasmania. In the light winds since last night, no matter how often I turn her south-southeast, within a few minutes she always manages to resume a course due east. The coast in question is still 500 miles distant, which seems ample to make the 70 more miles south we need to be clear. At our present desultory pace, we will reach there at an inauspicious time—the Ides of March.

THERE were two special moments today: not spectacular, but an essential part of my solitary life that is too easily forgotten in what is becoming a succession of horror stories.
   The first came in mid-afternoon, when, despite the overcast, I was sitting in the cockpit, half-reading, half-gazing out at the sea, thinking that I had seen no birds for quite some time. Then I noticed a single stormy petrel skim past, and then another, and suddenly I became aware that the sea was alive with them

richocheting from wave to wave. Within a few boat lengths, there must have been hundreds; so much the color of the slate sea that they had passed unnoticed until that first one caught my eye.

Then, a few minutes ago at dusk, a wind shift made me readjust the storm jib sheet tied to the tiller. On the western horizon there was a pencil-thin orange line as though the ocean had caught fire and as I watched, the flames swept toward me. Too soon the steady rain snuffed them out, and I was once again sailing alone in a cold and remote universe.

DAY 232 • *February 18*

TO maintain the tradition of comparing our position and status at monthly intervals: a month ago, we were 42°South 49°East; today, four months out of San Diego, we are 43°South 137°East. But this month the significant difference cannot be measured in degrees. That difference is the two great storms which turned a 10-gallon-an-hour leak into a 30-gallon-an-hour one, that tore the sails time and time again, that broke the self-steering vane. The true difference is that a month ago Egregious, though damaged, could still face these seas. Now she can't; now she no longer belongs in the Forties. The difference is that a month ago, the end was not in sight.

DAY 234 • *February 20*

IN some respects I could not have asked for a better day before a possible landfall. There were some clouds, but the sun has been visible, the sea smooth, and the boat steady; all enabling me to get a series of perfect sights which establish our position 100 miles west of Southwest Cape, Tasmania. However, the high pressure which caused these fine conditions has also taken our wind, and we are becalmed as evening nears.

Yesterday at noon we were exactly where I wanted us to be—already south of Tasmania and its outlying obstacles—but during the night Egregious snuck back 45 miles, and what little wind there has been today has forced us even farther that way. If my navigation is at all accurate, we could not run into anything tonight (and at our present speed there is no chance whatsoever); still it is interesting to watch Egregious seem to maneuver surreptitiously toward the coast.

DAY 235 • *February 21*

EIGHT days ago saw the lowest barometer reading of the voyage, and today sees the highest. What a rotten, rotten month.

In the twenty-four hours ending noon, we drifted 45 miles, of which a little more than 20 were east.

I was up every hour all night in a vain effort to get us sailing. I saw the deformed moon rise at 11:00 P.M., looking as though some Cyclops on the far side of the earth had plucked it like a ripe fruit, taken a single bite, then negligently thrown the remainder over his shoulder; I saw a lovely, vivid orange sunrise; and I too frequently saw a sky full of stars in between. But my only success was finally to get Egregious to maintain a heading due south at 1 knot.

About 10:00 P.M., the lights of a freighter became visible to the west, the first sign of the planet being populated by man other than myself since the fishing vessel off Mexico four months ago. The darkness was complete, we were becalmed, and the ship was steaming at us. My only method of indicating our presence would have been to shine my last operative flashlight on the sails. There was no possibility of our moving from his course.

I went below for the flashlight, but when I returned to the cockpit, he had vanished. For a few moments, I wondered if I had imagined the ship, but then I discovered his stern light to the east. He had been much closer than I thought and had probably passed without ever knowing I was there. As always, on those rare occasions when I sight another ship, I was somewhat indignant at his cluttering up what I have come to consider to be my private ocean and glad when his lights disappeared over the horizon.

Mentioning that fishing vessel seen off Mexico made me wonder how often those fishermen had been back in port, seen their wives and children, been clean and slept soundly, while the "rich American cruising lazily" has been continuously tossed and driven on the cold, cold sea.

DOLPHINS have been around the boat for much of the past day. A number were near at noon yesterday; then several followed at sunset and could be heard swimming alongside during the night. They seemed unusually curious about us. Perhaps they thought the becalmed Egregious had died; I know I did.

WE finally started sailing—back toward Tasmania, of course—on a heading of 070° at 11:00 A.M., averaging only 4 knots. Now, at sunset, what little wind there has been is decreasing.

According to the radio, Hobart had a temperature of 24°C. today, which I convert to about 75°F., and I assume the temperature where we are is about the same; so in many ways the day has been fine. But when we are making so little progress, nothing else matters.

It will be good when we move on from here if for no other reason than I have taken so many sights during the past two days that the chart is almost black with position lines. This is so literally true, that I have lost track of the lines for the last two sights while plotting them and had to remeasure the assumed position and start again.

DAY 236 • *February 22*

LANDFALL at dawn. Southwest Cape directly ahead, with the Maatsuyker Islands visible off the starboard bow and Port Davey off the port, all purple against a pale rose sky moments before the sun emerged dripping from the sea. Quite a beautiful scene, and yet I don't feel any of the excitement I did at sighting the far less impressive Diego Ramirez 10,000 miles ago.

With the assistance of a stealthly wind shift in the night, if left to herself, Egregious would have fulfilled her pernicious plan and gone ashore for a rest. And from the looks of that shore, at a distance of about 5 miles, it would have been a rather permanent rest.

The single good consequence of having to bail so often is that I soon become aware of any change in conditions. At 2:30 A.M., I got up and stayed awake for more than an hour because I thought I saw a flashing light ahead. Finally, as the light climbed higher in the sky, much too high and much too fast to be on land, I realized it was actually a star which had "flashed" due to atmospheric distortion when it was near the horizon.

6:00 P.M. A hot, sunshiny, glassy, becalmed day spent spinning uncontrollably in slow circles a mile or so south of an offlying rock called the Mewstone. Tasmania is known for rough weather. Even the names on the chart mocked me as we sat there futilely in sight of "Storm Bay."

Given reasonable sailing, we could be in Hobart in a few hours; but because we are not going to Hobart, it doesn't really matter. I have decided to cross the Tasman to Auckland. The recurring mental process has become obvious even to me: a storm makes the leak and sails worse; I think we cannot take much more; the storm ends; I repair the sails, increase my bailing, and adapt to our new circumstances; I decide we can try to go just a bit farther. Now I have done it once again. Auckland is about 1,500 sea miles ahead. Less than two more weeks, with any luck at all.

I do not know why I keep sailing onward in a vessel which is so badly damaged. Before the Horn, I knew why. Even before passing Africa, which held the first convenient ports where I was certain of finding repair facilities, I knew. But since nearing Australia, I have passed Perth, Melbourne, now Hobart, and soon Sydney. I have told myself that I want to get as much as possible of these southern waters behind us before the austral fall, but that reason does not fully satisfy. Perhaps it is partially resistance to change; perhaps I still harbor a vestige of hope that somehow miraculously—and it would be—we can complete the voyage nonstop; but mostly I think I keep on because I know we have not yet quite reached the limit. I cannot say how I will know short of Egregious' sinking when that limit is reached. But I know we have not done so yet. Sometimes I wonder what I will do if we have not reached it when we clear the North Cape of New Zealand and must change course to put in at Auckland. It is perhaps the nature of commitments that they are endless; when one is fulfilled, there must be another. And last November's "reach the Horn or die" has become February's "sail to the limit."

. IV .

DAY 237 • *February 23*

7:00 P.M. We sail smoothly east closehauled at 6 knots. Our course across the Tasman will be northeast, but I want 100 miles or so of offing from the east coast of Tasmania first. There must be a pun about the mania of sea room and Tasmania, but it eludes me. Perhaps that is for the best.

I spent the first half of last night in a probably unnecessary and certainly useless watch for the last offshore danger, a cluster of rocks—the largest of which is called Eddystone—on which Egregious could impale herself. Probably an unnecessary watch, because I was fairly confident our course would take us safely south of them; and certainly futile, because the low clouds which obliterated the sky and made visibility nil.

DAY 238 • *February 24*

I am a reasonably patient man, but you can tell yourself that one more day really does not matter only so often before you are talking about one more week, two more weeks, then perhaps another month; which matters very much when you are trying to keep a wreck afloat in the Forties.

This morning, after tacking Egregious a dozen times in a hopeless effort to steer a course better than due north on a starboard tack or due south on port, my frustration, which has brought the dark depths of my soul to the surface—the last two nights my dreams have been of murder: night before last I was murdered, and last night I murdered someone else; progress of a sort, I suppose—overwhelmed me and I became a minor Vesuvius, leaping about the cockpit, erupting invective like lava. I cursed the wind, the sea, the weather, the boat, several spirits in which I do not believe, and life in general. When I was through, I felt a little better, a little abashed, and very hoarse. The universe responded to my outburst with Olympian detachment, so I did the only reasonable thing: left Egregious heading north and went back to bed. We may end up in Sydney yet.

HORRIBLE day. Rain. Calm. Tack heading due north, come about, and head due south. Time and again. Patience exhausted. Never want to see ocean or sail again. Know this is edge of two weather patterns, if only I can survive the transition. Be lucky if we don't have gale. Two parallel squall lines similar to those off Mexico on first voyage, but then everything was new. Now just ordeal. I am so tense I can hardly write.

WE had our third successive beautiful sunset. Rose and peach and purple shadows melting and fusing together across the sky. I felt like a child being compensated with a piece of candy for a dose of bad medicine. I will not be appeased by sunsets: give me a fair wind!

DAY 240 • *February 26*

I am an animal at bay. Every way I turn, I am headed. For the past two days, I have been giving serious thought to heading for Sydney. We can make nothing toward New Zealand, unless I am willing to go down to 47°South around the South Island. I even considered that briefly, but it would be a deadly delusion to try. Egregious no longer belongs at sea, much less deeper into the Forties.

Under blue skies, a steady, high barometer, we are presently pounding badly, course 005°, into steep head seas, even though I have eased Egregious's path through the waves as much as possible and reduced sail.

DAY 241 • *February 27*

WE lie ahull against a rising gale. It might be possible to sail with it, but not against it. For us it is a headwind. For us that elusive limit is being reached. Those few hours' pounding yesterday opened the hull further. Water floods in at more than 50 gallons an hour. I am so tired I can't multiply, but that is more than 1,000 gallons a day, isn't it? I don't keep track of how often I bail. It seems always, but is really not more than ten or twelve times in twenty-four hours.

Although we are still about 41°South, the days and nights are warm. Last night I fell asleep at 7:00 P.M., and when I got up a couple of hours later to bail, I heard a thumping on deck. A flying fish had come aboard. The first in 15,000 miles. I was as surprised as he as I flipped him back into the ocean and hope he suffered no harm from his excursion.

Sometimes I almost think we should try to sail against this wind rather than lie here and sink; then a gust comes, a wave breaks over us, and I know we must wait it out. If the wind were from any other direction, the risk might be worthwhile. I have calculated that for every day of pounding at 6 knots against this, we would gain only 20 miles toward North Cape. More and more I think of Sydney, which is so much closer. We can't sail there either, at present, so it doesn't make much difference what I pretend our objective to be.

DAY 242 • *February 28*

THE gale ended abruptly at 6:00 P.M. yesterday. By 6:30 the wind was under 10 knots. It has continued light and the sea choppy ever since, but we have made something good toward New Zealand.

Our single sun sight today proved that we have left the Forties three months and one day and 270° of longitude after entering them. I had saved a tinned cake for that event; as usual, it does not seem a time for celebration.

DAY 243 • *February 29*

5:00 A.M. I cannot sleep so I might as well write. Strong headwinds are rapidly again building to gale force. The sea and wind seem to know we are nearing the end. We are not quite there yet, but nothing will lead me to try to go beyond Auckland. Sydney is only 400 miles to the northwest. I do not know how much longer I can keep Egregious afloat. I have nothing against Sydney. But even if we could start sailing again I would not go there. Turning back would be wrong. If Egregious sinks, I will get into the inflatable dinghy. In these warmer-water temperatures, I could survive.

DURING the years I lived in San Diego, February came to be one of my favorite months. The contrast was greatest then between the mild weather there and the harsh winter back in the Midwest where I grew up, and there was always at least one weekend so pleasant that I could go sailing comfortably in a bathing suit. If I live, February will ever more be tainted by the memory of this February. My days in the South Atlantic were more uncomfortable, but for pure poor sailing and obstructive and destructive weather, this month is unmatched. We have had only two 150-mile days; the rest have been mediocre to disastrous. The barometer has been at its highest and lowest. We have had four gales and seem on the verge of a fifth. We have had the strongest wind I have known, where there should be none; we have had dead calm, where there should be none; and we have not had a fair wind for eleven days, ever since I was—or so I thought—perfectly placed southwest of Tasmania. If it is to be victory or death, I would give odds at this moment on death.

12:00 noon. The dinghy is partially inflated, and I have made a list and collected the supplies to take with me: food, water, solar stills, navigation gear, clothing, hat, can openers, buckets, vitamin pills, sunburn lotion, passport, money, rigging knife, utensils, foul-weather gear. If Egregious is to sink, here would be as good as place as any, although I could wish to be a few hundred miles farther north and more to one side or the other of the Tasman Sea rather than near the middle as I now am. Nevertheless, one can hardly expect to pick one's spot; and from here, by drifting with the putative currents and rowing, we should be able to make 20 miles a day to the east where we would be bound to come upon New Zealand. My chances of survival in the dinghy are better than they have been for months.

LONG ago I gave up trying to keep shoes and socks dry and now walk about the cabin barefoot and with my pants rolled up to the knees as though I were wading in a tide pool. Which I am. A new routine is established: I read a chapter and then I bail; I read a chapter and then I bail. A slow reader would drown that way. Finishing *Brideshead Revisited* yesterday, I am finding an ironic pleasure in rereading Cecil Woodham-Smith's account of another vain dream of vain glory, *The Charge of the Light Brigade*.

I continue to reserve judgment on Egregious. There is only one test: that she survive. I always knew there would be no problem recognizing when it arrived: we are at the limit.

5:00 P.M. Halyards clang against the mast like fire alarms; banshees wail through the rigging; and outside every evil, frightful spirit from the nightmares of childhood screams and shrieks and cackles. I sit with too-practiced stoicism, ignoring the water rushing over my feet and silently sew stitch after even stitch into the seam of the mainsail that blew out early this afternoon. Hearing the familiar rip, I looked out and remained completely calm at the sight of a seam torn all the way across. There was no reason to rush, so I put on my foul-weather gear before wrestling the shreds of the sail down the mast, off the boom and into the cabin. Rain rattled down all the while.

When I first looked at the flailing cloth, I thought perhaps I would not bother to repair it; but then I told myself if I did not, we would surely survive and I would only have to do so later, when it would cost us time. Perhaps I can be forgiven this touch of superstition. Egregious is a rock half-awash.

DAY 244 • *March 1*

FEBRUARY ended with us lying helplessly ahull against a gale-force headwind while great solemn waves considered how best to destroy us. Add a steady rain and today is the same.

Sometimes I count the buckets when I bail. Water is coming in at between 60 and 75 gallons an hour. More than 1,500 gallons or 12,000 pounds a day lifted from the bilge and thrown into the cockpit. Eight hours out of every twenty-four are spent bailing; fifteen minutes an hour during the day, and at night I sleep never more than ninety minutes before having to bail. There is no problem about awaking in time: water splashes up onto my face when it is deep enough over the cabin sole. I am nearing physical exhaustion. There is no respite from the sound of the water, not even for a minute. When I finish bailing, water comes back in so quickly that it is sloshing around before I can get to my berth. The rare sleep I do manage is filled with nightmares in which that sound is transformed into women crying, bombs exploding, locomotives thundering over me.

During the past eleven days, we have averaged only $3^{1}/_{2}$ knots. I am more than a little uncertain about our position, having had no good sights for five days and only one in the past seven; but I believe we are about 160°East. The middle of the Tasman Sea, the middle of a killing ground.

DAY 245 • *March 2*

WITH a final blast of wind and torrent of rain, the center of the storm passed last evening and the barometer began a rapid rise. By 10:00 the confused conditions had been resolved by a fierce southwest wind, and we sailed through the night at 6 knots. A fair wind at last.

But sometime in the darkness the main ripped and the wind increased again. We are lying ahull.

DAY 246 • *March 3*

BECALMED all night. Resumed headwind this morning. Sailed briefly under jib and double-reefed main. Hard on the wind, the storm jib does not need to be sheeted to the tiller. At 5:00 P.M. the jib ripped. I lowered it, repaired it, raised it, and the wind became so strong that we had to lie ahull.

All this in addition to bailing as usual.

DAY 247 • *March 4*

I don't understand what is happening. Perhaps I am so exhausted I can't see what is obvious. The weather doesn't make any sense, unless there is a cyclone wandering about nearby. The wind decreased again to about 20 knots, and we tried to sail again. Both jib and main ripped all the way across. I am running low on repair materials. Headwind. Bailing. The waves are about 20 feet and as steep as those that capsized us.

DAY 248 • *March 5*

"NINETY-EIGHT. Ninety-nine. One hundred," I counted to myself and then stopped to rest. The numbers were buckets of water bailed at 3:00 A.M. With a few more, the bilge was as empty as it would be. Outside, the wind was hideous. The waves ever steeper. It *is* a cyclone.

The capsize I had been fearing came moments after I returned to bed. Three huge waves struck us in rapid succession, the first two knocking us down, the third rolling Egregious over to port. For a moment I hope it will be no more than a knockdown, but then the mast goes beneath the water and all the objects which seem impossible to dislodge fall through the cabin, even though in preparation for just such an eventuality I had carefully restowed everything only hours before. I am beginning to think Egregious is more watertight upside-down than right side up. Then the keel pulls us back, and I struggle from the mess that tries to bury me in my berth.

My first step is to the bilge. With every blow from every wave, I have been fearing Egregious would split open. Now, as I stare down into a bilge overflowing again with water, I think it has happened. The Tasman is a sea too far. We are finally going down.

Hope and heroism do not enter into my actions at such a moment: I struggle out of habit and because there is nothing else to do. I could never abandon ship in these 60-knot winds. The dinghy would be blown away the instant I got it on deck. So I begin to bail, using that same methodical pace as when I bailed after the last capsize. I do not think as I bend and dip the bucket into the depths of the hull or as I brace myself against the onslaught of subsequent waves or as I throw the water out into the cockpit. There are no visions of the pleasures of life I will not know. There is not even any regret. There is no fear. Perhaps I am too near exhaustion, but I do not feel tired. Truly I am resigned. Bucket after bucket, gallon after gallon make no appreciable difference. I know I have made a mistake; beyond Egregious's every weakness, these moments are of my own making. Bend, dip, lift, throw. Bend, dip, lift, throw. I could have made many ports. But then, if I had not persisted, I would never have kept going for the Horn. The ancient Greek concept of the tragic flaw is proven once again: my strength has become the instrument of my destruction. Bend, dip, lift, throw.

I do not think I can keep us afloat, only that I will try to do so as long as possible; that I must continue to total exhaustion, that I must go to my limit as well as Egregious's. Bend, dip, lift, throw. Part of me is detached, aloof, watching as I work mutely. Often I have wondered what my last word would be if I were lost during the voyage; now I know there will be none. My silence and myself are inseparable. Bend, dip, lift, throw. I have been bailing a long time; I have no idea how long, but the sky seems less dark; and oddly, the longer I bail, the less tired I become. Dawn reveals a leaden sky, 20-to 30-foot seething waves, and that I am gaining on the leak. I am actually disappointed. This must be carefully explained. I adamantly do not want to die, but thinking—no, knowing—I soon would had the unexpected effect of filling me with life. I was bursting with it. I was euphoric. I could bail forever. Everything was so simple: I bail. That was all. There was absolutely nothing else. Nothing at all. I was very happy. Bend, dip, lift, throw. I would have bailed as the water rose above my knees. I would have climbed the companionway steps and bailed when it reached my waist. Absurdly I would have bailed as Egregious lay awash an instant before she sank, and I would have known it to be absurd, but I would have bailed anyway. And now I would not have to. Life drains from me as I drain the sea from the bilge and is replaced by an unutterable fatigue.

DAY 249 • *March 6*

WE are no longer a sailing vessel but a derelict heading for the nearest port: Auckland, if we can make it, but I will sail Egregious onto a beach on the west coast of New Zealand's North Island if I must. Because the wind continues from the northeast, a headwind for New Zealand, even now I consider turning back for Sydney.

The storm jib and double-reefed main are set. The wind is too strong, the sails too weak. I eye them dubiously, expecting them to blow out at any time. But we must sail if we can.

DAY 250 • *March 7*

BY exposing myself and the sextant to repeated soakings, I managed to get some sights today. We are 400 miles southwest of Cape Maria Van Diemen, the northwest corner of New Zealand. These are the first sights and this the first accurate position for eleven days. During the cyclone our DR positions formed an equilateral triangle, with us being 50 miles farther from New Zealand on the third day of the storm than we were on the first.

I have been trying to get weather forecasts, but when I finally do, wish I hadn't. Australian radio says another cyclone is wandering about the Tasman after battering the Queensland coast. New Zealand radio ignores it completely. And so we pitiful souls at sea continue to worry about every fluctuation of the barometer. Certainly we could not survive another storm or the slightest additional hull damage. Egregious is balanced precariously on the very edge of survival now. We need some luck. We have not had any for a while. It is time. I continue to bail eight to ten hours a day. One or more of the sails requires repair every day. And we continue to have headwinds.

DAY 251 • *March 8*

STILL a headwind, but less strong and less obstructive, allowing us to sail only 10° from the rhumb line to Cape Maria Van Diemen.

In sunshine and 3-foot seas, I hove to and went over the side. Egregious was being thrown about so much that two dives convinced me I could do nothing from in the sea.

We sail under jib and double-reefed main. I did not think she would balance under that combination, but we were not moving well with the storm jib so I gave it a try. The main has ripped and been repaired and reripped so often that it can now only be set double-reefed.

Land is 300 miles away. Three days? Four? Five? I do not permit myself to guess. It all depends on the weather. I do think of what I will do if I have to beach Egregious and she is wrecked:

salvage what I can and buy another boat—I could probably not afford more than a 20-footer—then sail back until I crossed our course and resume the circumnavigation.

Before that can become a problem, I must keep us afloat a few more days. Everything in the cabin is wet. My body is covered with saltwater boils. Bailing as usual.

DAY 252 • *March 9*

THE first relatively uneventful day in a long, long time. We are under a high-pressure trough 200 miles from Maria Van Diemen, with overcast skies and a very light wind. Our speed varies from 1 to 3 knots, but often we can sail the rhumb line for the cape. With these light winds, the sails did not need restitching this morning, and all I have to do is bail. One plastic bucket broke. I am down to my last three.

Some places take on specific aspects of light or darkness in one's mind. For me when I was leaving the Forties I was sailing up from darkness—Stygian darkness—darkness cold and wet. The Tasman Sea, then, is the antechamber to hell; yet the antechamber has rivaled hell itself: two calms, two gales, a cyclone, and constant headwinds. With each slow mile I tell myself: one more mile I will not have to sail again. I will be overjoyed when Egregious is finally hauled from the water. The sea has become her unnatural element.

DAY 253 • *March 10*

THE past day has been a standoff: the sails are a little more worn, I have bailed six more tons of water, the leak is no worse, and we have made no progress. A sun sight this morning put us 15 miles east of yesterday's position, and I believe we are about that much farther north.

The flat calm gave way, of course, to a light northeast wind, against which we can sail 350° or 120°. The desired course is 050°.

Out of curiosity I searched through the log for the first reference to the leak. It was last November 1 when I wrote, "The bilge is leaking badly. Perhaps 50 to 80 gallons a day." Without doubt the funniest thing I ever said. "Fifty to eighty gallons a day." What an innocent I was to consider that a bad leak.

DAY 254 • *March 11*

ALL day yesterday we moved slowly north in the hope we could round Maria Van Diemen after coming about; but shortly after we changed course, the wind did, too, veering east-southeast to continue to head us. I am very tired of headwinds, of . . . but it has all been said. I am just very tired.

DAY 255 • *March 12*

WE should come on Cape Maria Van Diemen around 10:00 P.M. For two hours this afternoon we had sunshine and a beam reach. Pleasant sailing. Then the headwind returned.

A squall yesterday tore the storm jib, but surprisingly not along my repairs. This time the luff split.

The leak is greater than a gallon a minute. Until these last few weeks, I had not lost weight; but now the combination of never sleeping longer than eighty or ninety successive minutes and performing hard labor eight to ten hours out of every twenty-four has pared me down; and although I eat abundantly, I am always hungry.

The thought came while bailing last night, that if Egregious's designer and builder were here, I would tear them apart with my bare hands—and thanks to them, I could do it, too. But if they were here, I would do no such thing. Pure foolishness. I would make them bail.

* * *

OUR first sign of land was a bee sitting in the cockpit this afternoon while we were 30 miles offshore.

Then, at sunset, with the sky overcast and a light rain falling, I got a bearing with the radio direction finder on Cape Reinga, a few miles east of Cape Maria Van Diemen, and not long afterward saw the beacon light.

Had I not gotten a fix on something, I would have had to heave to for the night, which would have been a shame because we were sailing smoothly and well for a change; almost as though in the last few miles, the Tasman wanted to say, "Well played, old chap. No hard feelings now; just a game, you know." Perhaps; but I think I'm going to hold a grudge anyway. We were treated all too badly by the Tasman. In fact, the only good moment I can recall in the last two months was the sight of the craggy silhouette of Tasmania purple against the dawn. A conscious effort is necessary to avoid feeling as though I am being unjustly punished; but if I could laugh at anything these days it would be the image of me as a modern Job.

So we sail back into the Pacific: a year ago a prison from which I could not escape, now I hope a refuge for the derelict we have become. We are close enough to land so I know I will survive, but there is no immediate relief in that knowledge. Egregious must, too.

DAY 256 • *March 13*

A peninsula reaches for 180 miles northwest of Auckland, never more than about 45 miles wide, and terminating with a 20-mile shore bounded by Cape Maria Van Diemen on the west, North Cape on the east, with Cape Reinga in between. So our course, which in the Tasman had been northeast, became during the night east, and southeast this morning. I kept telling myself that soon we would no longer be hard on the wind; but again as we turned, it did too. There were very choppy seas, due to the strong tidal currents around the capes, and gusty winds. The jib ripped on the seam above the one I restitched west of Australia. Then the entire luff of the storm jib blew out. Were we in the middle of an ocean, I would probably spend the next week repairing them, but there is not enough time now. The jib would take at least twelve hours, and the storm jib another fifteen or twenty.

With the genoa staysail and double-reefed main set, we are steering south against a headwind. Of course. I can smell the earth and clover. A smudge of land is visible ahead, but not identifiable at 11:00 A.M.

DAY 257 • *March 14*

IN the last twenty-four hours we made 60 miles east and almost nothing south. Sunshine today. Continued southeast wind.

Yesterday afternoon an incident occurred about which I hesitate to write. It is not the way I want to be remembered.

At about 3:00 P.M. it became obvious that we could not weather North Cape. I brought Egregious about and put us on the other tack, course 070°, when, without warning, I began to cry. For what seemed to be a long time I could not stop and sat in the cockpit, eyes tightly shut, tears running down my face. The single word "no" kept repeating itself inside my brain. "No. No. No. No. No." I may have spoken it aloud. Finally I stopped and after a while opened my eyes and looked and saw a seam opening near the head of the mainsail and heard the seething water inside the cabin. I repaired the sail first.

DAY 258 • *March 15*

LAND was never more of a mixed blessing than this morning. Obstacles litter the sea between us and Auckland, particularly the last 35 miles or so, where I count references in the *Sailing Directions* to more than forty islands and rocks. The approach is being made as was the one into Papeete with no chart other than that showing an entire third of the South Pacific, but there was less to run into off Tahiti. On the present chart, those last 30 miles occupy ½ square inch. We need a break from the wind, but I expect none.

Not long after dawn, we nearly had the final disaster when the main ripped full across above the second reef, while we were less than 2 miles to windward of a stark uninhabited mile-long rock called the South Poor Knight's Island. The wind was blowing from the southeast—where was this wind when we were in the Tasman and would have welcomed it?—and Egregious would not come about under the genoa staysail alone. To change course I had to jibe. But whether her bow pointed northeast or southwest it made no difference. Without the mainsail, we were rapidly being driven onto the cliffs to leeward.

Ignoring the water which rapidly rose above the cabin sole and splashed across my feet, I stitched the sail as quickly as possible, pausing to dart a glance at the ever-nearer cliffs only when I had to stop to rethread the needle. Then I stitched faster. Still, it took three hours before the sail could be reset.

Waves were smashing against rocks only a few hundred yards away. I rereeved the reef lines and carefully hoisted the main. The rip was in a particularly bad location, an area of great strain at the leech. As soon as it was up, it ripped again. Instantly, before the tear could extend across the sail, which would have been fatal—there was not enough time for so extensive a repair again—I let the halyard run. Then I cut two very rough patches and stitched them on with giant stitches. A poor job, but my only hope.

In ten minutes I raised the sail again for what I knew would be the last time. I thought, "We have not come all this way to be wrecked here 90 miles from safety. Hold. Hold for just thirty minutes. Perhaps even just twenty minutes. And then I can do more. But hold!"

It did.

DAY 259 • *March 16*

AFTER easing away from that treacherous lee shore and applying two more patches to the main while it remained set, we spent the afternoon threading our way between islands that loomed through a low mist and seemed to bear no resemblance to any descriptions in the *Sailing Directions*. But at sunset we had some good luck. The wind lightened and backed to the northeast, giving us an easy beam reach beneath a full moon down the sheltered waters of the Hauraki Gulf. And I became certain of our position as unmistakable Little Barrier Island appeared off our port bow. A gentle sail at last. I should have known better. That very tranquillity was still almost to destroy us.

Often I seem to suffer for no reason, yet be saved at other times from the just consequences of my mistakes. We would surely be in Auckland not long after daylight, but the land was very near. Ahead of us the loom of the city lights touched the night sky, and to the west I could distinguish headlights on individual cars driving along the shore. All I had to do was remain awake and keep us off the land one last night.

But as Egregious sailed softly on, I became more and more tired. At about 2:00 A.M., a very bright navigation light was abeam, which I correctly concluded was TiriTiri. With the full moon, visibility was good and I could see that although there were some islands ahead of us, we would not come upon them for well over an hour. Fatigue overcame me. *I can safely sleep for an hour,* I told myself as I went below and lay on my berth still fully dressed. And I was right: I could have safely slept for one hour. But I did sleep for two.

I was dreaming. I cannot now recall what that dream was about, but I do remember that it was a very deep sleep one instant and the next some part of my mind brought me wide awake with complete knowledge of exactly what had happened. I leapt to the companionway and looming over us was a great shadow. The jib sheet tied to the tiller for self-steering tangled. I ripped it free and slowly—so slowly—Egregious's bow swung back into the wind, back the way we had come.

Later I learned that rock was one of a group called The Noises. Judging distances in unfamiliar waters at night is difficult, but The Noises are not very big and I was quite definitely looking up at the crest of that shadow. It was a long way above me. But our speed was only about 3 knots. Perhaps we would have bounced off.

At dawn I turned us back toward Auckland and we slowly limped past Rangitoto Island and into the harbor on a bright, warm day.

My first impression was how quiet it was for a commercial port on a working day. From a man aboard a yacht powering by I learned where to go to clear customs. He was the first person I had spoken to in one hundred fifty days.

At 2:00 P.M. I sailed Egregious up to King's Wharf. A city and a nation in which I knew no one. Within three hours, fate began to bring me to her.

. V .

I swarmed up the wharf pilings and stood on land. The transition from five months of sea and solitude was that quick and that easy. No cultural shock. No earth moving beneath my feet, as some people claim after voyages but I have myself never experienced.

But the transition was not truly complete for two more days, not until I arranged for Egregious to be hauled out for repairs. I had gone for so long sleeping only a single hour that I continued to awaken often while tied to the wharf, and for that matter, even motionless, Egregious still had to be bailed four times a day and twice during the 10-mile tow to Half Moon Bay Marina. Only when she was finally in her cradle, a stream of water flowing for a change from rather than into a deceptively innocent-appearing hairline crack, could I relax. And then I slept for fourteen hours.

I liked Auckland from the beginning, and that liking has lasted, though later tempered by inclement weather and the reaction of some people under stress that was too insular even for islanders. People were helpful, friendly, boat mad, and hospitable, this last to a point where ultimately I could not accept all the invitations which were offered and still get on with my preparations to make Egregious seaworthy again—if in truth she ever had been.

THE return to the land is a return to lists. When I made my first list of necessary repairs, it was only six items long: hull damage; sails; stove; navigation equipment—the sextant, radio direction finder, and fathometer all needed attention; rewedge mast; self-steering vane. All but the vane, for which parts were not available and would take too long to import, were soon in the process of repair or replacement. But by then the list, as is its pernicious character, had grown longer, soon extending over both sides of a large piece of paper.

I said "repaired or replaced" because, as I had expected, the sailmaker took one look at my storm jib and said it was the most battered sail he had ever seen. That was before he looked at the main, on which we counted twenty-one seams I had repaired. It was obvious I had to have a new main, storm jib, and jib made; but several times in New Zealand, I enjoyed the experience, unparalleled in ten years of boat ownership, of being quoted prices which were less than I expected. The new sails did not cost much more than I had planned to pay to repair the old ones.

The most important repairs, of course, were to the hull. It was fiberglassed on the outside and the bilge filled with three pieces of wood and two wooden knees, all heavily glassed in place to close the leak and prevent that area from flexing excessively while under sail. To my skeptical eye it seemed a professional job, but the only relevant test would be at sea.

Sometime during my very first few days in Auckland I decided to complete the circumnavigation at Tahiti. Partially I wanted to give paradise another chance; partially I looked forward to a few months of rest after what I had been through.

Remembering prices in Tahiti all too painfully, there were an increasing number of items that I might need which could be purchased more cheaply in Auckland. The list soon became lists, and our departure seemed increasingly remote.

OTHER people's reactions to an important part of one's life are interesting and even mildly instructive. When Americans heard I had sailed 18,000 miles alone nonstop around the Horn, they invariably asked why. New Zealanders are not that decadent; they never asked why; but some did wonder why I continued on after first learning the hull was cracked. I tried to explain, but they could not understand. It was simply that they had never wanted anything as much as I wanted the Horn and a solo circumnavigation.

And most surprisingly my friends back in the United States all wrote how disappointed I must be to have been forced to stop. I was amazed. Disappointed to have stopped? Hardly. I was thrilled to be in port. But then I realized that they had just learned what I had known for months, and that even now they could not conceive how long I had been at the limit in the Tasman. To have put in any earlier would have been wrong. But I was at peace with myself. As I read their letters, I knew that if I were not at that moment reading letters on the hard stone steps of an Auckland post office, I would be dead.

I have mentioned how difficult it is to judge wind strength and wave height during storm conditions at sea. I make a deliberate effort not to exaggerate and to check my subjective estimates whenever possible; so on one of my expeditions through the quaint arcades of Auckland in search of elusive boat parts, I took time to visit the government meteorological office where a most helpful gentleman pulled the charts for the date of March 5 and explained to me what they meant.

At the time of the capsize, the center of Cyclone Colin—woman's lib has progressed so far some tropical storms are now named for men—was about 50 miles south of us, with 60- to 70-knot winds radiating out 150 miles. In the comfort of his office I could take satisfaction that my impressions of the wind force had been accurate. But I became retrospectively frightened as I recalled similar wind six other times during the voyage and particularly that one hour of much stronger wind south of Australia. How much stronger was it? I will never know with any certainty. At least 20 to 30 knots more than in the cyclone, so at least 90 to 100 knots. It may have been much more. But whatever its true force, as I thought at the time, it was too much—simply too much.

* * *

ONE day while I was riding into the city on the bus, I heard two bits of nonsense which in themselves would have endeared New Zealand to me. The first was a popular song being played on a transistor radio, which formed a rhyme of the words "fear" and "Maria." "Fear" being stretched to "feeaaa." And the other was a joke told by another passenger; a joke so bad it must be preserved.

A man went into the city where he unexpectedly won a goose at a raffle. He put the goose under his arm and prepared to convey it home on a commuter train, but had the misfortune to sit down next to a drunk.

After several moments of careful observation, the drunk said, "That certainly is a fat, ugly, greasy pig you've got there."

The man replied, "You're mistaken; it's a goose."

To which the drunk snapped, "Quiet you, I was talking to the goose."

A world of such rhymes and jokes, I thought, cannot despite the newscasts be all bad.

AUCKLAND soon came to mean to me one person: Suzanne. That I should meet a woman—even that I should fall in love—is not so surprising; but there was an inevitability about my meeting and falling in love with her—even an ease, although that is an odd word to describe something which later began to seem so complicated and painful. Naturally, I was reminded of my premonitions at sea.

We had so little time together, yet there are so many good memories. We walk hand in hand through a graveyard at the end of the street where her grandmother lived and where she sometimes played when a child. It is on a hill overlooking the harbor, very quiet, and mostly filled with dead priests and bishops. We look at the inscriptions, but the dead remain dead to us. We walk hand in hand on Eastern Beach, not far from the boatyard where Egregious is being repaired. We lie in the grass on Mount Wellington where Maoris once fought.

In the past two years, I have come to feel very old. I have lived lifetimes, and before I left San Diego last October, I said that one of the ways in which I felt old was that friendship had come to mean more to me than love. But it was not true. Forced to choose between them in Auckland, I did not hesitate to betray some of the friendship offered me there.

AT the end of six weeks, the new sails—the last essential item to be crossed from the by then utterly vanquished and abject lists— are delivered. I remain in port one more week for love.

. VI .

DAY 260 • *May 7*

AT 2:30 in the afternoon I slipped our mooring and Egregious swirled down the Tamaki River on the outgoing tide and before a 25-knot wind from the south. I was very glad to have had the use of the mooring, but I was also very glad to see the last of the Tamaki, where the tidal currents swept in and out at 3 to 5 knots and the wind blew more boisterously than I like in such confined quarters. Once for three days I was stormbound 100 yards from shore, thinking that those of us who live on boats rather than in comfort ashore are insane, while gusts were measured at 55 knots on a friend's boat nearby; and another time it took me an hour and forty-five minutes to row the half mile from the marina back out to Egregious against wind and tide.

As I sail around Rangitoto Island and into the Hauraki Gulf, I look back one last time at the white city sprawling about its hills and bays, a city where I am loved and hated. Good-bye, Tamaki. Good-bye, Auckland. Good-bye, Suzanne. Good-bye until you come to me, as I hope, in Tahiti.

The wind continues from the southwest. The new sails look good. Egregious seems eager to return to the sea. So am I.

DAY 261 • *May 8*

UNDER a half moon, we sailed past Little Barrier at about 11:00 P.M. last night, ghosting through the edge of her wind shadow. The way out of the Hauraki was much easier than the way in. I even had a detailed chart for a change: it seemed like cheating.

I very much enjoyed that night sail. In cities I lose the sky and seldom look at the stars, which are mostly obscured by the city lights. That is, perhaps, the primary function of cities: to block the vision of an overwhelmingly uncaring universe from those who have not the strength to face it.

By 1:00 A.M., the last dangers were abeam and I went to bed.

For much of this morning we were becalmed, but at noon are making 5 knots over a smooth sea. The sun is bright and warmer than it had been for my last few weeks in Auckland. Egregious is pointed directly east. Headwinds are to be expected for the first 1,500 miles, so we will continue east as long as we can or until about 160°West before turning northeast for Tahiti.

After being in port for seven weeks, I thought I might have to readjust to sea life, but the transition back has been as easy as was the one from sea to shore in March.

I do not make the mistake of taking the ocean lightly, but there is a unique feeling at the beginning of this passage. Tahiti is about 2,600 miles from Auckland, although we will have to sail 3,000 to get there; and I estimate the voyage will take three to four weeks. The 3,000 miles seems negligible. I departed as casually—no, more casually—than I would have a few years ago to sail from San Diego to Santa Barbara. I will not have to ration water. I carry fresh food which should last most of the way. The sails do not have to be restitched daily. Egregious does not have to be bailed. The wind is from astern. In only a few weeks the dream will be fulfilled; we will have completed a true antipodean two-stop circumnavigation. The worst must be behind us. Ah, indolence. Ah, easeful, luxurious life. But a voice inside admonishes, "He whom the gods would destroy, they first make . . ."

DAY 262 • *May 9*

EXHILARATING sailing at 6 to 8 knots under grey skies and intermittent showers. It is good to have the bad weather coming from astern and to listen last night before I went to sleep to the music of water rushing past *outside* the hull. It is time sailing became fun again.

There is some water in the bilge—only a few gallons—I believe it is coming in around the guaranteed leakproof hawse pipe I installed in Auckland for the anchor chain. "Never leaked a drop on my boat," the man said.

I saw an albatross this morning. I am truly back at sea.

May 9 (The Second)

BY my dead reckoning, we have crossed the 180° meridian and will have to do Sunday over again. Instead of being twelve hours ahead of Greenwich, we are now twelve hours behind.

During one of the squalls last night, a line securing one of the blocks leading the staysail sheet to the tiller broke. One moment we were sailing at 8 knots, and the next reduced to familiar chaos. Staysail sheets knotted themselves together, sails shook and thundered, two accidental jibes: in short, the complete fiasco. Now, even more than after seeing the albatross, I feel as though the voyage has begun.

DAY 263 • *May 10*

I am glad Sunday is finally over. There is something disquieting—almost depressing—about having to live a day twice. One loses the essential illusion of progress, and it seems like killing time in the most basic sense. Besides that, given a forty-eight-hour day, the sea began to beat up on me.

A reef cringle on the main ripped—and I thought I wouldn't have to use my sailmaker's palm on this passage—and a berserk winch handle bashed my left wrist and right elbow. The wrist is merely stiff, but the elbow is quite painful. I would not be surprised to find I had a chipped bone. I don't know what to do for a chipped bone, so I am eating an orange. Isn't vitamin C a universal panacea?

Despite these minor mishaps, I could not have asked for more favorable winds. They continue from the southwest, and we continue to sail quickly east.

DAY 264 • *May 11*

THE wind is cold, reminding me that we are only 250 miles north of the Forties and winter is near, but we are making fine if not comfortable progress across a deep blue sea at day and a black moonlit sea at night.

At regular intervals a rogue wave roars up from the south and smashes over us. They are so unexpected that each startles me more than it would during a storm.

Suzanne is very much on my mind. I know that if I had stayed in New Zealand longer, she would have been mine, and I hope she will not be the final sacrifice to the great god Voyage.

DAY 266 • *May 13*

BECAUSE of the Dateline, we have been at sea a week today, although we left on a Friday and today is a Thursday. By my noon DR position of 35°South 167°West, we have come over 900 miles, all reaching before westerly winds where we could have expected headwinds.

DAY 267 • *May 14*

AT 6:00 P.M. last night, fear returned to me as I sat huddled in the darkness by the chart table while lightning flamed all about us. The mast is allegedly grounded, but the corner by the chart table seemed safest. My complacence about this passage was shattered by the first bolt that split the sky nearby. I have come to expect Egregious to survive great winds, but suddenly I knew we could again be destroyed at any instant. I could envision myself spending a month or two in the dinghy before reaching some island, then buying or building a small boat, retracing the voyage, and trying to reach Tahiti, which might be months or even years away instead of only two weeks.

In a few hours, the lightning diminished, but the storm has continued. It is not up to the high standards set by the Roaring Forties, but is quite strong enough for my jaded tastes and has managed to rip the new mainsail and give me two sleepless nights.

The main took three hours to repair, but when I was finished at 9:15 this morning, the gusts were too strong to reset it; so I raised the storm jib and steered until 1:00 P.M., when I could get the main up and achieve self-steering again.

DAY 268 • *May 15*

SEVERAL accidental jibes when gusts overpowered five shock cords on the lee side of the tiller yesterday afternoon forced me back to the helm and then trapped me there for four hours. Trapped because the wind was so strong we should have been lying ahull, but I could not leave the tiller long enough to lower the sails without the certainty of an accidental jibe, which was unthinkable because the main topping lift was tangled about the upper starboard spreader. An accidental jibe would have snapped the spreader, and with it we would probably have lost the mast.

Squall after squall blasted over us as I sat there steering with utmost care down, over, and under breaking waves, waiting for the least pause in the wind; only thirty or forty seconds would be enough in which to free the topping lift and let go the main halyard. But hour after hour passed, and that pause did not come.

I must confess to enjoying that wild ride, during which on two occasions as we surfed down waves the boat speed indicator hit 12 knots, the highest reading on the scale, and held there for several seconds as our bow wave rose high above the deck. Never before had we gone quite so fast, but never before had I set so much sail in those conditions. In reality, it was too much sail, but I was not in charge of such matters just then.

With the coming of nightfall, it became cooler and my enthusiasm waned and my desire not to remain at the helm increased. At the last light from the west, I decided to make a move while I could still see the twisted topping lift aloft. After tying the tiller amidships, I leaped onto the deck and tugged at the topping lift. It obstinately refused to come free. In seconds a wave would catch the stern and spin us either up into the wind where the slatting would only make the tangle worse or off into a jibe. I left the topping lift and let go the halyard. As the sail came down, the boom swung across; but the force was so reduced that no damage was done. I lowered the storm jib, lashed both sails in place, and left Egregious to lie ahull.

2:00 P.M. I have had no accurate idea of our position for three days. Squalls continue to sweep over us every ten to fifteen minutes. Although the barometer is back to normal, we continue to lie ahull. I had hoped to make a quick, uneventful passage to Tahiti. I am sure such voyages must happen for others, but apparently not for me.

The time I give for these entries is as always local time, but I am keeping track in my mind of local time; time in Tahiti: one hour ahead; in California: three hours ahead; Greenwich Mean Time: eleven hours ahead; and Auckland: twenty-three hours ahead or one hour earlier tomorrow. If all that seems confusing . . .

* * *

NIGHT. We are sailing again, but three nights without sleep have had their effect: Auckland does not seem real; Suzanne is merely a lovely invention of my imagination; Tahiti unreachable. It is always night; it always has been night; it always will be night; and I am always alone, standing braced against the chart table, looking ever aft through the companionway at great dark clouds gathering astern; Egregious is always rushing through crashing seas, always yawing wildly, always almost out of control.

A few days ago I read Tolstoy quoting Lermontov:

> He in his madness prays for storms
> And dreams that storms will bring him peace.

Once that might have been said of me. Certainly I came seeking to measure myself against stormy oceans, but I am satiated with storms. They are all beginning to seem alike; all seem one. One great unending storm in which I lower sail and we lie ahull, waves break and toss us about, wind shrieks, I am cold, wet, tired, often frightened, and never at peace. There is no reason to measure myself further. We will probably survive, and if we don't it will be because of blind chance. I am no longer testing myself or even Egregious. Now the test is only of my luck. Great storms are reduced to an inconvenience. Four months of wet feet have done substantial harm to my romantic notions of battling the elements.

DAY 270 • *May 17*

EARLY yesterday the storm diminished, and we turned northeast directly toward Tahiti. Today we continue to hold that course, 040°, with fine sailing, still before a west wind.

Not long after working our noon position, we startled a school of flying fish, two of which landed on deck, the first since that lone lost creature in the Tasman.

I feel Suzanne's love reaching out across the ocean to me. But at the same time, and even more strongly, I feel someone's else's hate. I know at certain moments that he is wishing for me to disappear at sea. And I am made that much more cautious.

DAY 273 • *May 20*

DAYS of golden sails and silver horizons; seas of indigo and pewter; skies of white and azure. We are on the edge of the tropics.

It is a curious fact, however, that during these last successful passages, no poetry has written itself. Perhaps I have been out here too long and suffered too much, and poetry requires a breathing space beyond the edge of survival in which to flourish; or perhaps defeat is more poetic than victory.

For whatever reason, no poetry comes, and I find it pleasant enough to do nothing more than replace minor breakage and chaff—a staysail sheet and the block for the topping lift today—and read a hundred more pages of *Dombey and Son*.

We roll down generally small waves, but two or three times a day a series of immense swells advance upon us majestically from the south. Four or five great hills of water—perhaps 20 feet from trough to crest and with a flat plateau 10 yards across on top, suddenly loom sinisterly on the horizon. But they slope so gradually, that they cause no trouble except to my overwrought imagination.

With each wave, we come closer to the end of the voyage. It does not seem possible that it is so near.

DAY 274 • *May 21*

I had hoped to reach Papeete without more bad weather, but it does not look as though that is to be. The barometer is falling, and we are closehauled on port tack against a north wind.

Last night, as every night of the past several, the wind decreased at sunset and was fluky until dawn. By awakening every hour or so, I kept Egregious moving; but our course was too much eastward, and we are still 600 miles from port.

DAY 275 • *May 22*

I do not know that there is any advantage in hearing weather forecasts; but because foul weather is obviously near, last night I decided to find out the nature of the beast.

To my enlightenment but hardly pleasure, the radio informed me that there is only one bit of bad weather in the entire South Pacific, and it is a band of severe thunderstorms 100 miles wide and 2,000 miles long, sitting directly between us and Tahiti. Yesterday it was 300 miles north of our position; today, 100.

So now I know; but what do I do with this precious knowledge—nothing other than worry. I cannot go around the front; the radio did not deign to mention which way it is moving. So I sail on, beset with images of Egregious being struck by lightning three days from Papeete and forlorn hopes that the whole 2,000 bloody miles of clouds will somehow dissipate before tomorrow.

At noon today we were 480 miles from Papeete. Tomorrow we should pass through the chain of the Austral Islands, of which Raivavae, some 250 miles eastward, is one. Thoughts of the voyage's end are lost in my concern about the storm, already present in the form of moderate squalls and increasing winds. Apparently there is to be no rest for me until Papeete and no trade winds at all.

DAY 276 • *May 23*

THE radio giveth, and the radio taketh away, blessed be the . . . The thunderstorms have obligingly moved east from our path, or so I was informed by the oracle last night. It was a conclusion I had already drawn myself from the rising barometer and moderating seas. Probably I will continue to listen to weather forecasts from time to time, but it is like reading pilot charts and signifies a defect in my character of which I am not proud.

THE wedges fell out from around the mast, thus enabling us to maintain our perfect record of never entering a port without the indispensable main guy in place.

SOMETIME today we passed between Rimatora to the west and Rurutu to the east without seeing either. The Australs are behind us. Nothing but open ocean to Tahiti.

DAY 278 • *May 25*

A dreary day. Low clouds through which there has been not even the faintest outline of the sun. Rain every hour, accompanied by gusty wind.

If I could establish our position, we could probably be in Papeete by noon tomorrow; but since I cannot and my DR position shows us likely to come upon the island tonight, I will probably heave to after dark.

DAY 279 • *May 26*

A constant dismal slow rain yesterday was broken only by squalls of harder rain. At 8:00 P.M. I hove to, letting us head on a course of about 110° until 4:00 A.M. It was one of the most unpleasant nights I have spent at sea, with the sails rattling and Egregious being thrown about by the waves. Although there was almost no visibility and I told myself our course was a safe one, I got up every thirty minutes and peered into the oblivion of rain, always half-expecting Tahiti to be looming over us.

At 4:00 A.M., I donned my foul-weather gear and resolutely turned us north. Sunrise would not be until 6:30, but I did not think there was any possibility we could hit anything before then. I remained in the cockpit anyway.

Not long before dawn, the sky cleared partially, and a few diluted stars were visible; an omen that during the day I might be able to get some sun sights. At that point, after 300 miles of dead reckoning, which included a night of drifting becalmed in circles, several deliberate course changes, and several hours of the boat's yawing 80° to 90° in squalls, I felt as much lost as I ever have at sea; much more lost than found.

When daylight came—an euphemism if ever there was one, because the insipid pallid cast that turned the rethickening clouds one infinitesimal shade of grey lighter than they had been bore only the most remote family resemblance to true daylight—something of a sister's neighbor's mother's brother-in-law's dog to daylight, if even that is not indeed too close a relationship. Anyway, when daylight came, I sat poised in the companionway, sextant in one hand, stopwatch in another, awaiting any brief shadow of a silhouette of the sun. At 9:10 I was rewarded by a three-second glimpse of my prey, but it was gone before I could lift the sextant to my eye.

The steady rain had ceased, but heavy squalls still passed once or twice an hour. That I welcomed this as a considerable improvement is an apt commentary on the relativity of value systems.

Egregious swooped north at a minimum of 7 knots and often more; too much more for my liking, as I kept a close eye on the leech of the mainsail, where the leech cord had broken during the night. Before my next circumnavigation, I may replace or repair the self-steering vane, but I will definitely experiment with twin headsails for self-steering on a run, a concept that before this voyage I ignorantly disdained. The saving in stress on the mainsail, the rigging, and my nerves, would be well worth whatever disadvantages such a system might entail.

As the morning wore on I occasionally saw off the port bow an outline with a sharpness of edge and constancy of position that made me think it might be land rather than cloud; but I was far from certain. Then, at 10:30, the sun was dimly visible through several layers of overcast for two intervals of not more than fifteen seconds each, and I grabbed two of the quickest sights ever taken.

I worked them out eagerly at the chart table. Both resulted in a position line that put Tahiti only 10 miles away. I returned to the deck and looked for my questionable land. The horizon cleared to the northwest, and there was no question any longer: it was land and we were found.

The location of the island off the port bow, when I had expected it to appear to starboard, was somewhat puzzling, until after another hour the solution appeared in the form of the high mountains of Tahiti only 3 miles to starboard. Visibility had been so limited to the northeast that we had been sailing along the Tahitian coast for 15 miles without the least sign of those 7,000-foot heights, and my first sight of land had been Moorea, although it was smaller and farther away.

By noon, long after our position had definitely been established, the sky cleared to the north and the sun shone brightly. And the wind died to the lightest of zephyrs. More and more of Tahiti became visible; a dim jade jewel shrouded in mist and clouds, with mysterious valleys and a line of waves crashing on the reef offshore, as we ghosted up the passage between the islands.

Self-steering was not possible, so I held the helm while the sky darkened again. A great black line formed behind us and marched slowly up our desultory wake: 5 miles, I think, 5 more miserable miles—less than one hour of average sailing—and we would be in. Then the squall swallowed us. Our speed leaped from 1 knot to 8, almost wrenching the tiller from my grasp. It was just such a squall which struck us when we left Papeete on December 23, 1974. I have learned something in circumnavigating: this time I have my foul-weather gear on.

Fortunately, it passed over us in ten minutes; unfortunately, it took all the wind with it.

By 3:30 P.M. we were a quarter-mile off the pass at Papeete, having slowly glided by the unnecessary warning of a wrecked ship on the reef at the northwest corner of the island. I could feel no wind; there was no sign of wind on the horizon, not a single cat's-paw anywhere; the boat speed registered zero. Only by dropping a piece of paper over the side and watching it drift aft inch by inch could I tell we were moving.

For more than an hour we sit there, bow deliberately kept offshore because I think we might have to spend another night at sea. With only five minutes of wind, we would be in the harbor. But another hour passes, and we drift another 100 yards offshore; the sky remains still, the sea flat and leaden. Not only are we to have one more night at sea, it is to be spent in such dangerous proximity to the land that I must not sleep. I gaze enviously at the yachts at anchor along the quay and at the automobiles driving along the shore.

Smoke rises lazily straight up from a hillside above the town. Low clouds sit motionless on the high slopes of Tahiti and Moorea. To the east, limp sails are lowered on a ketch, and an engine is started. I am tempted to ask for a tow but cannot bring myself to do it. We are only a few hundred yards short of a circumnavigation completely under sail. Egregious has been towed only twice, and then only inside harbors to boatyards. We will wait. Fish leap, breaking the glassy surface of the sea, and one of them catches my attention and directs it west, where a faint outline of wind darkens the water on the horizon.

Steadily that line of darker water moves east and as it finally reaches us I bring Egregious about, trim her sails, and square off for the pass. I am not yet certain I will actually attempt to go in, but I want to see how well we can sail on that course. The boat speed hovers around 4 knots, and I decide to continue on; then it drops to 3 and I weaken. Then back to 4, up to 5. The buoys are coming nearer as are the waves breaking on the reef. If we are to sheer away, we must do so now.

I have no time to consider the voyage, which has now covered more than 33,000 miles and 279 days and which will come to total 38,000 miles and 312 days when I return to San Diego in October, completing the circumnavigation San Diego—Auckland—Papeete—San Diego in 203 sailing days, not far off my original estimates and a world record for a solo circumnavigation in a monohull; no time to remember the disappointments of the early damage when I thought Cape Horn would remain ever elusive; no time to recall the beauty of moonlight on the sea, or the power of the albatross, or the freezing cold of the Horn, or the great storms of the Forties, the capsizes, the leak, the ever-increasing exhaustion of bailing, the struggle to survive and the moments when I did not think I would, the coast of Tasmania at dawn, or Cyclone Colin, the near-wrecks on the approach to

Auckland. I did not think, then, of my friend on Antares, whom I had often felt during these past months has been back in his home, his voyage successfully completed, hoping mine would be, too. I did not think that later that night I would row out on the black waters of Papeete harbor and look back at Egregious as I had a year and a half before; that from inside the cabin the trees seen through the companionway and the mad crowing rooster on shore would be the same. I did not think that for the first time I was entering a harbor without having immediately to look for a boatyard. I did not have time to understand that the voyage really was only moments from being over.

I did think of Suzanne. Even for me, it is odd not to know if I am going to marry a woman or never see her again. And I think of Mary. And of Bach. The "Little Fugue" plays merrily in my mind as the breakers are abeam.

Then we are through. We are inside the harbor. The circle is closed. The dream fulfilled. The vow to myself kept. I have sailed around the world alone.

I have reserved my final judgment on Egregious. Even now I am uncertain whether to be angry I had as much trouble with her as I did, or grateful I did not have more. Few boats have ever been sailed harder and she did not kill me. Quite. I have come to expect her always to be broken and always to survive. She is a boat to love and a boat to hate. The words uttered first in anger remain true in tranquillity: she *is* a beautiful bitch.

Briefly I consider the future and wonder what an obsessed man does when he has fulfilled his obsession.

When he was a young man, St. Augustine prayed, "God, make me pure—but not yet." There will be other commitments and other voyages for me, including another solo rounding of Cape Horn—after all, who, having visited hell, would not, given the opportunity, return to see if it really was as bad as he remembered. But, like St. Augustine, I say "Not yet." For the moment, I have no ambition beyond lying in the sun like a lizard and swimming tomorrow in the warm sea off Maeva Beach. I know I will tire of indolence, that having lived on the edge of life, I can never return for long to something less. The intensity is too intoxicating. But not yet.

I do not delude myself that I have conquered the sea; it is enough to have faced it. And I am more proud that I continued to struggle against defeat than of my ultimate victory. To struggle was in my control; victory in that of chance.

Resurgam, I said, and now I must learn the Latin for "I have risen." "Time and chance and Cape Horn: I am still coming at you," I said, and I kept coming until Cape Horn was mine; and for one brief moment in my life, time and chance subdued. "Victory or death," I said, and though death often seemed the more likely, finally it is victory. Wind and waves of torment cease, and for a while they have. Sail to the limit, and I sailed beyond. "An ordeal of grandeur," I said, and it was. It truly was.

In Auckland, Suzanne and I attended an exhibit of Chinese art. One of the objects was a figure holding aloft thirty-two concentric spheres, only the outer half dozen of which were visible, all carved from a single piece of ivory. The satisfaction of the artist upon completing carving all thirty-two spheres and knowing that each—even the innermost which would never be seen—was perfect, is the same as that of a man who completes a solo circumnavigation, who fulfills any dream, even though no one else knows.

I smile to myself as Egregious sails slowly across the dusky harbor; and behind the sea-etched face of the man, a small boy grins because he has made his dream come true.

Egregious man, boat, voyage, life.

The fool smiles and sails on.

THE VOYAGES OF EGREGIOUS

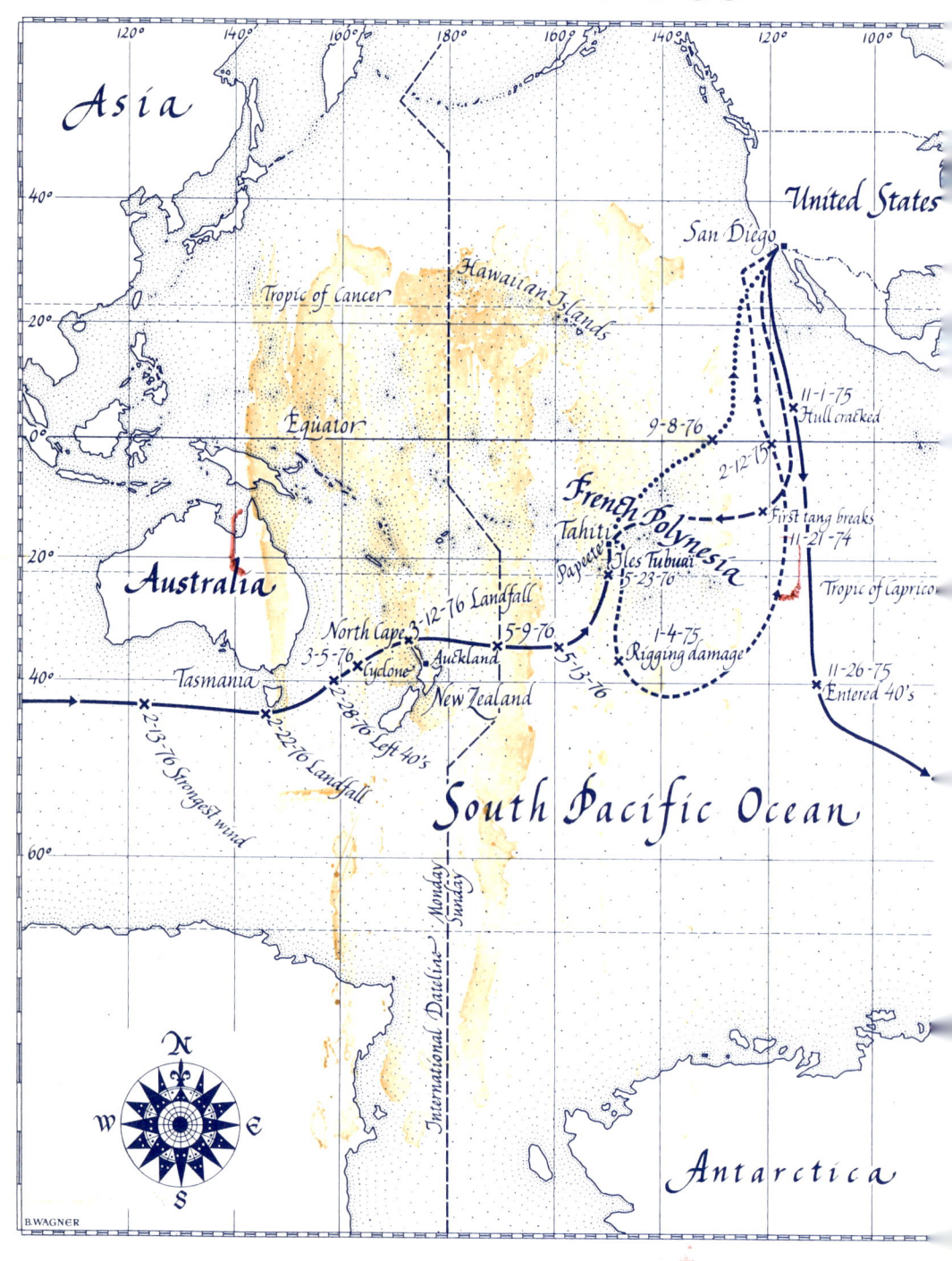